Building a Value Portfolio

Building a Value Portfolio

Learn to Uncover the *Hidden Value* of Shares

Ken Langdon and
Alan Bonham

FT
PITMAN
PUBLISHING

London · Hong Kong · Johannesburg · Melbourne · Singapore · Washington DC

PITMAN PUBLISHING
128 Long Acre, London WC2E 9AN
Tel: +44 (0)171 447 2000
Fax: +44 (0)171 240 5771

A Division of Pearson Professional Limited

First published in Great Britain in 1997

ISBN 0 273 63029 6

British Library Cataloguing in Publication Data
A CIP catalogue record for this book can be obtained from the British Library.

10 9 8 7 6 5 4 3 2 1

Typeset by Northern Phototypesetting Co, Ltd.
Printed and bound in Great Britain by Bell & Bain Ltd, Glasgow

The Publishers' policy is to use paper manufactured from sustainable forests.

About the Authors

Ken Langdon

After a career in a large computer company, Ken Langdon has been an independent trainer and management consultant since 1986. One of his specialisms has been teaching financial matters to non-financial people.

His seminars on 'How to read the Financial Times' and other topics have been enthusiastically received by people who expected to find the topic uninteresting.

He runs his own pension fund and is the Treasurer of an investment club with 20 members. He is the author of books on business strategy and contributed to *The FT Guide to Reading the Financial Pages* and *The FT Handbook of Management*.

Alan Bonham

Alan is a Chartered Accountant. Most of his time since qualifying has been spent teaching others about accountancy. For qualified accountants, Alan provides updates on new developments either on public or in-house courses.

Alan's strength in teaching accounting and finance to non-accountants is his ability to explain complex issues in layman's terms. A subject which can be dull is brought to life by his illustrations and anecdotes.

He was the founding Chairman of the investment club mentioned above.

Feedback and further information

If you have any comments on the book, the authors would be delighted to receive them. If you need help in doing any of the calculations, please telephone the number below. If you would like information on the courses which the authors run, or on the software which supports the ideas in this book please contact them at:

KPL Associates
24 St Marks Road, Maidenhead
Telephone: 01628 782193   Fax: 01628 771035

For Judith Bonham, and in memory of Arthur Ward, Ken's colleague, mentor and friend, who taught him, in the most enjoyable way, much of what he knows about business and life. He is sadly missed.

Contents

Scenario: The Dog and Duck, Darnley Village xi

Introduction: What is in this book, and who it is for 1

The starting point 3
What should I be looking for? 4
How is the book structured? 5
The secret handbook 5
A guide to what is in each chapter 5

1 *The case for buying individual shares* 13

The monstrous power of inflation 15
Whether you like it or not, some of financial life is a gamble 17
How the financial markets tell us about risk 19
Is it best to do it yourself or give your savings to the professionals? 25
Conclusion 31
Exercises 32

2 *Setting the investment strategy* 33

The seven-step process towards identifying the right shares for your portfolio 35
Setting personal objectives 35
Establishing a strategy for risk 39
Exercises 51

3 *The financial starting point: an introduction* 53

Introduction 55
The key financial ratios 56
Forty years in the life of a growth stock 62
Conclusion 71
Exercises 72

4 *Designing the portfolio and choosing sectors*   75

Introduction   77
Choosing sectors for investment   77
Designing the portfolio   84
Exercises   88

5 *What makes companies thrive?*   89

Annual reports   91
Conclusion   122
Exercises   123

6 *Getting to the right numbers*   125

Introduction   127
The bookshop 128
Identifying the information   137
Conclusion   148
Exercises   148

7 *The key business ratios: an introduction*   149

Introduction   151
Profitability ratios   158
Liquidity ratios   161
Asset utility   163
Gearing   166
The employee ratios   169
Growth ratios   171
Calculating the ratios for Sherwood Industries   173
Conclusion   180
Exercises   181

8 *Some advanced ratios and the rest of the annual report*   183

Industry averages   185
Some advanced financial ratios   188
Some other ratios and measures   191
The annual report   193
Conclusion   201
Exercises   201

9 *Keeping score* 203

The documents you need to keep score 205
Conclusion 226
Exercises 226

10 *Of PEPs and investment clubs: an introduction* 229

Introduction 231
Personal equity plans (PEPs) 231
Investment clubs 235

Appendix 1: The annual report of Sherwood Industries 241

**Appendix 2: Corporate governance statements in an annual
report** 267

Index 271

The Dog and Duck, Darnley Village

The atmosphere during Sunday lunchtime at the village pub was different that week. The regulars were seated round their usual table, but were less noisy and more thoughtful than they normally were. The group was, as always, very diverse in age, occupation and interests, linked only by their residence in the same small village and their liking of a pre-prandial drink, pub wit and conversation. They came from the tennis court, the church, the long country walk and some came straight from bed.

The dampener had come from Bill, a local shepherd for longer than anyone could remember. He was about to retire, and had just found out what his pension – occupational and State – would add up to, and it wasn't very much. 'The worst thing is that I didn't know,' said Bill. 'I suppose if I had worked it out I might have done something about it, but it's too late now.'

'Yes,' said Iain, 'The days when you could live on what the State provides have gone, and in say 20 years the situation will be even tighter. It's difficult to know what to do. I've been putting money into a private pension scheme for some time now, and they've just sent me a statement. Last year it managed growth of about 8 per cent. That's terrific when you remember that the stock market went up by 16 per cent in the same year. It hardly grew at all the year before. It isn't going to be worth as much as I thought, even given the tax relief. How are you supposed to know which of the thousands of funds available is going to do well?'

'Well, I've tried the building society way,' said Emily, a career woman famous for her workaholicism, 'and even with the tax free scheme it only turned £9,000 into about £11,600 in 5 years. Take off inflation of about a thousand, and it's hardly worth doing. It certainly won't cope with my old age.'

'And,' said Diana, 'look at the sums of money the fund managers make if you put your money into unit trusts. That man who was fired from a million-pound a year job simply walked into another one. It seems to me that if the managers are being paid silly money, it's the punters who are saving with unit trusts who have to foot the silly bill.

'The only thing you can really believe in an advert for financial products is that investments do go down as well as up, and that past performance is no guide to the future. Quite honestly, I think we have got to take more interest and do our own savings, even if it means getting into buying shares.'

Keith wasn't sure, 'But how do you know what to buy, how do you know how many shares to buy, how do you tell a company with a good future from one that is *comme ci comme ça*? The annual report of some of my customers comes on to my desk and frankly, I can't make head nor tail of it. How, finally, can you be sure you are not buying into the next Polly Peck or BCCI, and losing all your money in the process?

'You can never be a 100 per cent sure, but there are some simple rules that reduce the risk of making bad mistakes, and there are some interesting ways of finding out what is really going on in a company. I'm going to find out about it and think about investing for myself.'

Graham added, 'You're probably right, Iain, generally speaking if you buy direct, rather than through a middle man, you normally get better value. Here's another thing. I've been looking at investment clubs, and they might just suit our little group.'

What is in this book and who it is for

How private investors can use this book to understand the real value of companies and build a portfolio

- The starting point
- What should I be looking for?
- How is the book structured?
- The secret handbook
- A guide to what is in each chapter

It is quite possible for a private investor to do as well, if not better, than professional advisers and fund managers in selecting and tracking shares in public companies. Rather than being a 'Get rich quick' scheme, this book shows you how to set about making money, gives you exercises you can do and actions you can take to make sure you have understood the principles. In short, it helps you to make your own investment decisions by understanding the real value of a company.

The starting point

Most people are now paying much more attention to their long-term finances, given that the increase in the number of old people is causing governments all over the world to encourage everyone to plan for their own old age. People are also thinking about medium-term savings, aimed at meeting many different objectives, such as the deposit for a house, paying for a wedding, school fees or even a round-the-world holiday.

For many in this situation, the only thing that inhibits them from becoming investors in equities is that the art of picking the right shares seems like alchemy or like the reading of a thriller except that your failure to detect the right solution will cause real, as opposed to fictional, financial pain.

BACKGROUND FACTS

1 In the five-year period since October 1991, if you had followed the performance of the Financial Times All-Share Index of Total Returns (that is dividends and capital growth) accurately you could have made £1,000 into £1,960.

2 If you had deposited £1,000 in a building society for the same period, it would now be worth about £1,276.

This lack of capital growth and protection from inflation was described by a canny Scot only slightly inaccurately as '*Wonderful things building societies, you give them the price of an overcoat and five years later they give you back the price of a shirt.*'

The other side of the coin is, of course, the risk that the shares investors actually buy may be the ones that do badly and investors could lose some or even all of their original capital.

These risks can be summarised in part as:

- *market risk*, which is the risk all shares are subject to – the risk of their value rising or falling for economic, political or other reasons that are little or nothing to do with the fundamental ability of individual companies to produce profits and dividends (everybody remembers the crash of 1987)

- *company risk*, which is the risk of the actual performance and potential of the company being reflected in the rise and fall of its share price.

This book is about this latter kind of risk, and how to use simple analysis tools to understand the *real* value of companies. It is also about how to select those that are likely to perform well against a strategy that controls the amount of risk required to attempt to produce a planned objective.

> For many, the only thing that inhibits them from becoming investors in equities is that the art of picking the right shares seems like alchemy or like the reading of a thriller except that your failure to detect the right solution will cause real, as opposed to fictional, financial pain.

Some 11 years ago, one of the authors of this book became self-employed and started to run his own pension fund. He was thus forced to become a regular purchaser of shares in public companies or equities. This is the book he wishes he had found at that time.

What should I be looking for?

A book that enables you to:

- decide on personal investment objectives and investment strategies in equities

- take apart the annual report of a company so you can understand properly the company's actual strategy, financial position and performance against comparable companies

- read between the lines of other published materials and know where to go for information

- apply the tools quickly – it must be possible to invest logically and still have time for full-time jobs or other things in life

- understand the practicality of the processes from real-life illustrations.

How is the book structured?

Some 11 years ago, one of the authors of this book became self-employed and started to run his own pension fund. He was thus forced to become a regular purchaser of shares in public companies or equities. This is the book he wishes he had found at that time.

The book follows a logical path, progressing your understanding of the fundamentals behind the performance of businesses, and giving you opportunities to test the success of your learning and carry out exercises to determine what you are going to do in the investment field.

The secret handbook

Financial information held in materials like company reports is like a detective story; all the facts are there for the reader to find to come to the correct conclusions. This book is the private investor's secret handbook that will help in spotting the clues and getting results.

A guide to what is in each chapter

Chapter 1 *The case for buying individual shares*

Earlier we mentioned the obvious fact that investing in shares carries more risk than putting savings into a bank or lending it to the

Financial information held in materials like company reports is like a detective story; all the facts are there for the reader to find to come to the correct conclusions.

government by buying their bonds. In Chapter 1 we set out the reasons it is important for anyone trying to save for the long term to have at least some of their money in equities. We look at inflation, gambling and risk. We compare picking your own shares with trusting your money to the professionals in unit trusts, for example.

There are guidelines for how to act as a contrarian, which is someone who deliberately goes against the current thinking of the market, and we also introduce the art of searching for clues to investing that lie in the financial pages of the newspapers. This guide to reading the financial pages emerges steadily, with more details being given in each chapter.

Also included in this chapter is an introduction to the two main shareholder ratios – yield and price/earnings. The chapter ends by introducing the topic of portfolio planning, in terms of when to buy and when to sell, including the benefits of regular investing.

▶ **Action points**

This chapter involves evaluating the effect of inflation on yourself and calculating your future needs accordingly.

You will also move towards becoming familiar with some of the ratios in the business pages, and thinking about the potential benefits of periodic investment.

Chapter 2   Setting the investment strategy

If you regard the singling out of a particular share as similar to detective work, then there are an awful lot of suspects to begin with. In fact, there are some 2,000 companies on the London Stock Exchange to choose from. It makes sense, therefore, to narrow down the choice by setting an investment strategy. All this means is that, before you go to the trouble of getting hold of company reports and analysing them, you will have a good idea which industry sector you want to buy into next, and at what level of risk. This helps you to build a balanced basket of shares, or 'portfolio'.

Chapter 2 explains the seven-step strategy, which is aimed at identifying the right share for your portfolio and objective. It shows how the investigation is started and introduces the trail of clues that needs to be looked at in order to come to the correct conclusion.

You first need to be sure what your purpose is in going into equities. In Chapter 2, you will be asked to set your savings objective and decide what level of risk is necessary to have a good chance of achieving it.

As a simple illustration of risk, compare investment in ICI, with its huge income streams and track record of performing, with investment in a new pharmaceutical company. The pharmaceutical company has, say, a good idea and a drug that is going through the long process of gaining the acceptance of the authorities for marketing the product. This

> If you regard the singling out of a particular share as similar to detective work, then there are an awful lot of suspects to begin with. In fact, there are some 2,000 companies on the London Stock Exchange to choose from.

company could be valued at many millions of pounds, even though it has not yet made a penny. Not all companies of this type will prosper, and investment in them must be regarded as very high-risk, particularly compared to investment in a company such as ICI.

A portfolio, if it is to achieve a stretching objective, needs to have a mix of risk appropriate to the investor and their objective. A suggestion for different types of risk is made and the chapter covers the main shareholders' indices.

The chapter ends with a number of examples of appropriate objectives and strategies.

▶ Action points

This chapter will take you through a series of questions aimed at agreeing an appropriate objective and strategy.

Chapter 3   The financial starting point: an introduction

Here we give readers an overview of how to interpret the main shareholder and corporate ratios. The chapter shows how a company develops over a long period of time and tracks these ratios at each stage of the business's development. From this we can produce a benchmark guide, which gives us the ability to understand quickly the type of enterprise we are looking at.

> A portfolio, if it is to achieve a stretching objective, needs to have a mix of risk appropriate to the investor and their objective.

This benchmark will stand us in good stead as we go through the more detailed investigation and prove itself over and over again by example and, unfortunately, by exception.

While all ratios are unique to the business and the time of measurement, we need some guidelines as to what is a promising ratio, given the circumstances, and what is a threatening one.

Chapter 2 also introduces the concept of the company's strategy. We discover that the numerical analysis is only really useful if it is compared with what the company is trying to achieve. Looking at the figures on their own will lead us to the wrong suspects and, potentially, the wrong conclusions.

▶ **Action points**

You will be asked in this chapter to try the key ratios out with real companies and take your portfolio plan a step further.

Chapter 4 *Designing the portfolio and choosing sectors*

Now we have to align industry sectors to our investment strategy. To do this we need to understand the basic characteristics of businesses and, in particular, at what stage of the business cycle they tend to prosper and at what stage they tend to mark time.

Moving to the financial side, Chapter 4 explains the availability of industry averages, which are figures that allow the investor to make relevant or meaningful comparisons between one company and another. For example, we must not measure the performance of a bank in the same way as we measure the performance of a department store – their characteristics are very different.

▶ **Action points**

Chapter 4 gives you the opportunity to determine the sectors you will study to find your first investments. It is also an opportunity to decide how much time you will put into the process. Some people want to spand all their time on the investigations, others want a faster track. Both are possible.

Chapter 5 *What makes companies thrive?*

Careful investors are well aware that the likely future performance of a company is revealed by two different types of information. We shall describe them as 'hard' and 'soft' data. Hard data typically describe past performance in terms of figures. These figure not only describe issues such as profitability, but also productivity and so on. You measure, for example, the performance of a hotel by its percentages for room occupancy as well as by its profitability. Such hard data are published in various ways, including, of course, the company's annual report.

The report also contains much soft data. Soft data are, by their nature, less precise and objective than are the facts and figures. They concern the future strategy and position of the business. How good is the management, for example, or how likely is the product to remain popular? It is the marriage of the hard data with the soft that reveals the culprits and good guys.

> Some people want to spend all their time on the investigations, others want a faster track. Both are possible.

Chapter 5 details the contents of an annual report, and comments on how each section has some use for the investing sleuth.

Reading the Chairman's report or the report of the directors is very much a detective story as we have to tease out the real position lying within the 'spin' of the PR people. We do not read a company report, we take it apart.

▶ Action points

This chapter is a testing exercise as we read an actual report and you try to detect the business strategy of the company it is about using a simple technique. By this time you will have narrowed down your search to a number of possible 'buys'.

Chapter 6 Getting to the right numbers

Having detected the company's strategy, we move on to a consideration of the hard data and, particularly, the numbers found in the main financial documents in an annual report: the profit and loss account, the balance sheet and the cash flow statement. The first skill to acquire is the ability to recognise the appropriate numbers and extract them from the report.

Chapter 6 starts with a simple explanation of the fundamentals of financial statements, and moves to a refresher on the terms that are used in them.

▶ **Action points**

In this chapter, after having worked on a case study, you will extract the financial data from the report of a company and record it in a form that makes the calculation of the key business ratios straightforward.

Chapter 7 *The key business ratios: an introduction*

This chapter gives advice on how to turn the raw data into useful ratios. The example introduced in Chapter 5 forms the basis for this interpretation. The detective story is in full swing by now and you will use the ratios to compare the company's performance this year to that of last year. You can go back further and trace the history of the company over a number of years as it changed strategy and developed more or less successful parts of the business.

We have to deal here also with the question of acquisitions and disposals as companies manage new situations in their marketplace. This complicated area gives the enquirer real problems in making an accurate assessment. The detective needs help to cut through the jargon to reach the truth, and to develop further their ability to read the financial papers.

▶ **Action points**

Remembering always that different people want to put differing amounts of time into the exercise, the summary in this chapter will make sure that everyone is familiar with the main comparative ratios and comfortable with the principles behind profitability, gearing, liquidity and asset usage.

There is an option to do a full analysis of a real report, comparing the strategy with the ratios. You will be nearly ready to make a decision to buy or not to buy.

Chapter 8 *Some advanced ratios and the rest of the annual report*

A vast amount of material on the comparative performance of companies and sectors is available to the investor. For completeness, we take one of the well-used publications and show the additional ratios which it uses.

We then complete our look at the contents of the annual report.

▶ **Action points**

There is an opportunity in the chapter to take the company you are favouring and compare it with one of the industry average publications.

Chapter 9   Keeping score

Earlier, we boldly stated that investing in shares is, for a number of reasons, likely to prove more lucrative than putting the money in dead safe savings schemes. However, you need to be able to prove that this is actually happening. This chapter tells you how – using more or less sophisticated means – you can monitor your portfolio and see how you are doing.

Chapter 9 also describes the paperwork involved in buying and selling transactions and portfolio valuation.

▶ **Action points**

In this chapter, you will develop a statement of your personal assets, including your share portfolios and know how to measure whether or not you are achieving the objective set in Chapter 2.

Chapter 10   Of PEPs and investment clubs: an introduction

PEPs are a tax-efficient vehicle for holding a portfolio. Chapter 10 describes how they work.

> For remarkably little effort, a group of friends or colleagues can come together and have great fun making collective investment decisions and boosting their savings.

By this time, you will see clearly how individual investors may do as well as the average professional investor as long as they apply logic to the choosing of shares and get at least average luck. There is still one advantage professional investors such as unit trust managers have over the individual however.

At the beginning of the book we noted that this one advantage is the ability to pool resources and spread many people's money over a wide set of shares. The investment club effectively secures this same advantage. For remarkably little effort, a group of friends or colleagues can come together and have great fun making collective investment decisions and boosting their savings.

▶ Action points

This chapter encourages you to speak to people who may be interested, prepare for the inaugural meeting of an investment club and call it.

CHAPTER 1

The case for buying individual shares

The logic of looking at shares as an investment option, not an alternative to the National Lottery

- The monstrous power of inflation
- Whether you like it or not, some of financial life is a gamble
- How the financial markets tell us about risk
- Is it best to do it yourself or give your savings to the professionals?
- Conclusion
- Exercises

Most people's first knowledge of the stock market comes from reading about spectacular rises and falls in particular shares. Poseidon, Polly Peck, the Maxwell empire and others give a glimpse of the huge potential gains and losses that are possible. The truth is more mundane and you should be clear about why you are considering equity investment and decide, in an informed way, on the level of risk that suits you.

The monstrous power of inflation

At this stage, it is worth continuing the arguments about the effect of inflation on fixed rate savings. Take the building society case seen in the Introduction and extrapolate a little further.

You have a capital sum of £10,000 available to invest in either a building society or in equities. Suppose also that it is part of your income, that is you are using the interest in the case of the building society or dividend in the case of the equities as part of your annual income.

Assume the following:

- inflation averages 3 per cent per annum during the next five years

- the total return from the equities is made up of 4 per cent dividend yield and 11 per cent capital growth

- the interest rate the building society is offering for this sum of money is 6 per cent.

When you consider income, you really need to think about it in terms of its buying power. Forward projections of income must be looked at in 'real' terms, that is having made adjustments for the impact of inflation.

Given all these assumptions, the real income from interest would have gone from £600 in the first year to £533 in the fifth year. Dividend income would have gone, in real terms, from £400 to £540. Looked at also in real terms, if the capital had been invested in equities, at the end of the period it would be £14,535, while, of course, if it had been put in the building society, the value of the capital would have been eroded by inflation and be worth just £8,626.

Look now at inflation from the point of view of a pensioner. Supposing a man retires aged 65 with a fixed pension of £15,000 (which we will assume to be average earnings) and the old age pension, which is currently linked to the Retail Price Index (RPI) and stands at, say, £4,000. This puts the pensioner some £4,000 ahead of the average earner. Now, if you make some assumptions about inflation and the annual increase in average earnings, you get the following picture.

Assume the following:

- inflation averages 3 per cent per annum for the next 20 years

- earnings increase by 5 per cent per annum during the same period.

In absolute numbers, the pensioner's spending power at retirement is £19,000, or 127 per cent of average earnings. By the time this pensioner is 75, his real spending power has reduced by 20 per cent to £15,161, while the average earner's spending power has increased to £18,181, also in real terms. That is, the pensioner is now living on 83 per cent of average earnings.

Suppose now that the pensioner is lucky enough (or unlucky enough depending how you look at it) to live to 85. His spending power reduces to £12,305, which is just 56 per cent of the real value of average earnings, which have, in the meantime become £22,036. For the record, in absolute terms, the pensioner is receiving £22,224 while average earnings are £39,799.

Everyone has their own way of looking at the monstrous effect of inflation, but for people planning to fund their retirement out of a fixed annuity bought from personal pension savings, this is as good a way as any.

The fact is, we have to plan into our savings the impact of inflation, and this leads inevitably towards investing in equities in some form or other. This is because a company's profits take account of inflation as it raises its prices to compensate. This increase in profit and dividend is then reflected in the capital value of the investment, thus saving us the severe erosion of capital that is inevitable in a building society.

Having made that decision, we can consider investing directly, by becoming a do-it-yourself personal investor, or indirectly, by buying unit trusts or any other of the many financial products on offer that use equities in whole or in part as a hedge against inflation. However, if we are in equities, we are bound to be taking some measure of risk.

The word 'risk' in financial terms is an expression of the level of certainty with which we can predict the outcome of events. You could decide to lend money to the government by buying gilt-edged stocks in the knowledge that you will be paid interest and that you will need the capital back in five years. There is a very high level of probability that the expected outcome for both income and the capital will occur. Such an investment would therefore be very low risk.

If, on the other hand, you prefer to invest in a start-up company in the technology business, it is much less easy to predict the outcome in both income and capital terms. This makes the investment a higher risk.

All uses of capital can be explained in terms of their risk.

Whether you like it or not, some of financial life is a gamble

Millions of people every week play National Lotteries of various kinds. In the UK, each pound 'invested' is split into prize money, tax, good causes and return for the retailers selling the tickets and the company running the Lottery. It is difficult to think of a worse way of investing money as the Lottery interferes artificially with rational investment.

Rational investment demands that risk and return should be directly linked. The greater the risk, the greater should be the expectation of generous returns. This explains why banks charge higher interest rates to the companies least able to afford them. The bank is insuring itself against the risk that, for example, smaller and more speculative businesses are more likely to default. It therefore charges more for accepting this increased risk.

The element of risk is a principle reason for the return on equities needing to be steadily higher than the return on safer forms of investment such as banks and building societies. The market value of the share will be set to reflect the investor's acceptance of the higher risk.

Going back to the Lottery, we can see what this distortion means if we consider the alternative offered by betting shops.

Taking away the charitable aspect of the Lottery, gives a higher, and more realistic in risk terms, return to gamblers: for example, as much as £100,000 for five numbers in the betting shop game, compared to £1,500 in the National Lottery. We are not, strictly speaking, comparing apples with apples here as there is no jackpot in the new game. (What this means is that punters will give up the 14,000,000 to 1 shot of winning more money than they could possibly need. You probably have a better chance of meeting a stranger at Paddington station and correctly guessing his telephone number than winning the jackpot.) However, it does give an indication of how the National Lottery distorts the normal risk/return relationship. Some would say that you should regard the playing of the National Lottery as a rather inefficient way of giving money to charity. The grand majority of people would be better off making the contribution to charity directly, perhaps splitting the tax saving with the good cause and saving the remainder another way. We say 'the grand majority of people' as there is a group of people who would be better off to prefer the lottery – namely the people who actually bring the 14,000,000 to 1 chance off and win the jackpot.

Moving some steps up the gambling route brings us to savings schemes such as premium bonds. Here the government borrows money and pays out interest annually of about 5 per cent on the amount borrowed. The trick is, of course, that it leaves to chance who is the recipient of the interest payable. In the long term, there is a reasonable chance that a premium bond holder will get the average payout of 5 per cent per annum, with the outside possibility of getting the million pound jackpot.

Another difference between premium bonds and the Lottery is that with the former, at least the Government has the grace to give you your capital back, whether you have been lucky or not.

However, in reality both of these schemes are gambles rather than investments and are better looked on as sources of fun. For serious savings aimed at protecting ourselves from poverty in old age or other longer-term projects, we need to start to look at other possibilities.

As we have seen, any fixed interest investment, such as bonds or building society accounts, cannot act as a hedge against inflation. Only equities do this, but, of course, the risk is higher.

Serious savers must therefore consider equities and decide on the amount of risk they wish to take. They can then use the models and techniques in this book to try to identify companies that will give them that amount of risk with a commensurate return.

How the financial markets tell us about risk

The *Financial Times* contains much that an investor needs to know about the market's view of a stock at any one point in time. The information does not appear in its entirety every day, but if you look at a copy of the paper each day for six days, you will see all the information displayed. Throughout the book we will make reference to this. To start with, readers need to learn, or recall, the key shareholder ratios that are listed on a daily basis.

The key shareholder ratios

In terms of hard data, we would argue that all business people have in their minds two, three or at most four financial ratios that they use to measure performance.

For example, the head of a consultancy will be concerned with the ratio of days billed to days available. A sales manager will be worried about orders taken to date as a proportion of the budget or target for that period of time.

This way of thinking is by no means limited to those in managerial or senior posts. If you ask a self-employed sole trader company in the building trade what their quick ratio is, they may find it difficult to tell you. However, if you ask the same person what money is owed to them, what money they owe to their suppliers, what their bank balance is and the amount and timing of their next tax bill, they will probably be able to tell you. This is, of course, in financial jargon, their quick ratio, but they do not need to know that.

These financial ratios are by no means the only indicators of the health of a business, but they are chosen by their owners because of their crucial importance to achieving success.

The job of an investor is to understand and be able to test businesses against the main *general* ratios and then read about or work out the particular ratios that are important to a specific manager or a specific type of business.

Investors are never in the position of a manager in a business who knows intimately how it is doing, but there are some ratios that allow investors to make well-informed assessments.

Two of the most crucial ratios are reported in the press daily and a third on a weekly basis. The first two are key shareholder ratios known as *yield* and *price/earnings* (P/E). The third regular indicator is the *dividend cover*, which is published in the Stock Exchange listings of the FT on Mondays. Let us look at each of these ratios in turn.

Yield

This is the return on investment that a shareholder receives in gross dividends expressed as a percentage of the current share price. The share prices are listed daily in the FT, which also gives the average for all the industry sectors on the back page. On 7 May 1997, the average for all shares was 3.56 per cent. (You can find the current figure by looking at the back page of the 'Companies and Markets' section of the weekday FT. The page is entitled 'London Stock Exchange' and we will have reason to visit it on many occasions during the course of this book. The title of the column is 'FTSE Actuaries Industry Sectors'.)

This means that, on average, £1,000 invested in shares will pay out £35.60 in dividends over the following year if the dividends are kept at the same level as the last payment. Most companies try to increase their dividends at least slightly each year so the real dividend return might be a bit higher than this.

If, however, the market detects reasons for the company to grow faster than in the past and therefore generate more profit that could be distributed to shareholders, it will buy the stock and thus force its price up. This, of course, has the impact of reducing the yield because the dividend used in the calculation is the dividend of the previous year. We can see the normal correlation between risk and return here. If a stock has a relatively high yield (but not so high as to be dangerous, as we will discuss in a moment), the market is not expecting average or above-average growth in the sales and profits of the company. If its dividend is maintained, we should therefore see little prospect for big capital gains. It is therefore a lower risk stock than one with a low yield.

Put another way, the market looks at the potential of a company to increase its profits and therefore its dividends. If the potential is poor, it will value the company less, thus increasing the yield. If it thinks that the company has real potential for growth, it will buy the shares, push up the price and reduce the yield.

Unfortunately, as happens so frequently with statistics and ratios, this cannot hold true in all cases. If the market believes that, due to problems or changes in the business, a company will be unable to maintain its dividend, then it will sell the stock until the yield becomes abnormally high. Just as a benchmark guide, 9 or 10 per cent in most cases signals danger to the current dividend. At this stage, the market is probably warning investors that the next dividend is likely to be lower or that the company is going to miss out a dividend payment or two.

Generally, investors looking for income will pick shares with a higher yield than average because that puts them into the lower risk situation described earlier. However, long-term investors may also look for yield. This is particularly true when they are investing in a tax-efficient way, as, for example, with a PEP. If investors are avoiding higher rate tax by sheltering their investments in a PEP, then they get a real boost to their savings by having shares with a high yield. Or, if you like, they are getting a higher return with an abnormally low risk.

We will discuss yield further when we consider investment decisions.

Price/earnings

Also known as the multiple, the price/earnings ratio reflects the market's valuation of a company expressed as a multiple of past earnings (profits). The calculation is:

earnings ÷ market capitalization (last year's profits ÷ the market value
of the company)

In fact, the calculation is more often stated by dividing both numbers by the number of shares, which brings you to the more usual formula:

earnings per share ÷ share price

The price/earnings ratios is listed daily in the FT, which also gives the average for all the industry sectors on the back page. On 7 May 1997, the average for all shares was 18.18 times.

Once again we will pay much more attention later to the price/earnings ratio, but for now, it is important that you understand the concept and its importance.

A local newsagents shop in a residential area is a rather stable and unadventurous business. How then should we value it?

Suppose we decide to value it solely on its ability to earn an income stream or profits. This gets rid of distorting factors such as the value of the property and its potential for development. Suppose again that the current owner of the business earns a bottom line of £25,000 per year. That is, after deducting the costs of the goods the owner has sold and all the expenses, such as heat and light, necessary to run the shop and having drawn an appropriate salary, the owner is left with £25,000. The owner may spend this money, save it or re-invest it in the business.

Consider now the potential for improvement in the performance of the business. If you were to buy it, whatever you did in terms of improving the use of space or changing the stocking policy would have little impact on the number of people passing the shop and, therefore, little impact on the ability of the business to generate profit.

Back now to the valuation. As potential buyers, we may look to retrieve our capital in about five years. This would mean offering £125,000 for the shop and business. This gives a multiple, or price/earnings ratio, of five times.

On the other hand, how would we value a business in the electronics industry shortly after it has announced a new and very competitive range of products? The possibility for rapid and substantial growth in sales and profits in this situation is very high. Judging it by its profits last year would therefore considerably undervalue it, and we would judge the price much more by its potential in future years. In this case, a multiple or price/earnings ratio of 30 would not be out of the question. The number is high because although the value is based on the future earnings of the company, the number is expressed as a multiple of past performance. Indeed on 7 May 1997, the average price/earnings ratio for the electrical and electronics sector was 21.39 times and that includes some fairly staid businesses, such as light bulbs and electrical appliance manufacture.

So, the market shows its view of the potential of an investment in a company by the price/earnings ratio. In simple terms, the higher the price/earnings ratio, the higher the potential return and the higher the risk. Why is the risk higher? We have said that risk is an expression of the likelihood of a predicted outcome occurring. If the outcome predicted is stretching and involves rapid growth, then the risk of its not happening has to be higher than an outcome of 'Much the same as last year.'

Investors looking for capital growth will look for shares that have a high price/earnings ratio. If the market has made a correct prediction, an investor in such a share should expect to see growth of sales and profits in the company.

Of course, the market sometimes gets it wrong and the most fortunate investor will buy shares with a low price/earnings ratio in the hope that further information will bring the stock into fashion and the market will buy the shares and send their price up. The price/earnings ratio follows and the investor banks a tidy profit. In terms of risk, it is probable that such an investor will try a number of companies before they find such a winner. Such a strategy may work if investors have the money and if they set an achievable objective. The risk is higher in one way, in that if they fail to identify such a winner they will fail in their objective. Risk and return going, as usual, hand in hand.

Whether such a strategy is gambling or investing is a moot point. Going on no further information than the price/earnings ratio would have to be seen as a gamble. Looking at other information about companies to find such a prospective win is called looking for value, or value investment.

Dividend cover

At this stage, a quick word about dividend cover. Dividends are paid out of profits, but it is also very important to retain some of the profits in the business to fuel expansion, fund new products and so on. We are thus interested in dividend cover for two reasons.

Dividend cover is the number of times *gross dividends* are covered by profits. Let's explain gross dividend. When a company pays out a dividend, it is required by the Inland Revenue to retain the basic rate of tax on the dividend in the same way that a building society deducts income tax from its interest payments. This retention is known as the *tax credit*. The gross dividend is the *net* dividend – the amount actually paid – plus the tax credit. Thus, if profits are £3,000,000 and the dividend costs £1,000,000, then the dividend cover is 3.0.

The Chancellor changed some of the rules on dividends and tax. These will eventually affect the private investor. Everyone will have to keep up to date with these changes.

Dividend cover is another useful indicator for investors. It helps them to understand the level of risk there is of the company not being able to continue to pay the dividend. It also tells investors if the Board is keeping enough money in the business to fuel expansion.

For example, many private investors recognise the long-term benefits of a growing income stream from dividends. If they are investing for the long term, therefore, they may very well look for shares that are out of favour with the current market and, as a result, have a high yield. It is quite likely that the capital growth of such a share may be very limited in the short or even medium term as the price reflects the market's view of limited potential for growth in earnings. But this slow growth at the early stage is less important if the dividend payments are worth having.

A problem arises where a high-yielding share has insufficient profits to continue to increase or even maintain its dividend. The number of times the dividend is covered by the profits tells us how easily the company will be able to keep up the payments.

The second thing that the dividend cover tells us is whether or not the company is in fact retaining profits in the business to fund new enterprises.

The average dividend cover for all shares in May 1997 was 1.9 times. As with any other ratio, reasonable cover depends on a number of factors. The age of the company, the industry sector and its requirement for research and development will all affect what the market regards as 'reasonable'. After we have introduced the next level of financial ratios in Chapter 3 we will give an example of the changing ratios, including yield, price/earnings and dividend cover of a company trading over a long period of time.

Where to find these facts in the FT

The two pages of figures about companies are entitled 'London Share Service'. The yield and price/earnings ratio are the last two columns on these pages and can be found from Tuesday to Saturday. Dividend cover is on the same pages, but on a Monday. When we come to the sections on choosing sectors and shares, we will return to this crucial source of shareholder information. There is an exercise on the topic at the end of this chapter.

Is it best to do it yourself or give your savings to the professionals?

Setting your own investment strategy and researching companies to find ones to invest in takes time. In this book, we try to show a way of doing this that makes the investment of time reasonable. Alternatively, the way to save all that time is to talk to salespeople and/or independent financial advisers and, after listening to what they have to say, decide which pension scheme, unit trust or other type of savings method suits your needs. Then you can forget about it.

This saving of time is certainly real and a good reason for leaving it to the professionals. The downside, of course, is that the professionals will charge you for the privilege. This means that your savings are being diverted into management charges, particularly at the outset of most plans.

Consider the placing of a lump sum into a unit trust that is a balanced fund of UK equities. A balanced fund is one that includes a mix of shares bought to yield an income and shares bought for their potential to grow. The fund managers will use your, and other savers', funds to buy the sorts of equities your own strategy might very well lead you to. What, therefore is the advantage of paying a 6 per cent initial charge and a annual charge of, say, 1.5 per cent? The answer is that, the professionals, by means of their full-time effort, very considerable experience and access to information, should, in the long term, defeat a do-it-yourselfer who is using a series of simple ratios calculated from published information.

The funds' costs in terms of buying and selling transactions are also lower than they are for the small investor; it is a competitive market and they have the clout. This furthers their claims that they are the obvious route for the private investor.

Let us examine this claim. The simplest proof would be to calculate by how much the fund manager will have to beat us to make up for their charges and produce the same result. We can then look at past performance to see whether or not the average fund achieves this.

To achieve a sensible comparison, we must assume that the portfolio obeys some 'safety first' rules. It has a good spread of risk, for example, and avoids putting too many eggs in one basket in the hope of fantastic returns.

Given this policy, we can test the professionals versus private investors.

BACKGROUND FACTS

A unit trust has high charges in the beginning. This means that its returns are very poor in the short term. This need not cause great problems, as we must agree that investment in equities is for the longer term. However, this does give investors an opportunity to try their skills against those of the professionals.

Assume the following:

- the comparison is for a period of five years

- the unit trust has an initial charge of 6 per cent and an annual charge of 1.5 per cent.

If an investor can achieve growth of 5 per cent per year during the period of comparison, they will have £1,276 at the end of the period. A unit trust manager would need to achieve a growth rate of approximately 7.5 per cent, or be 50 per cent better, to match that figure.

The choice is ours. Can we generate a total return that is at least better than the average unit trust over the long term with a reasonable chance of doing considerably better? We think this should be possible if we follow some logical rules and are not too greedy.

Market risk and the professionals

The answer to the question of whether it is better to do it yourself or not would be incomplete without discussing the fact that if you do it yourself there is the potential risk of massive downside and this can be avoided on the whole, by professionals who have an intimate knowledge of the economy, markets and the moods of markets.

Ken, one of the authors of this book, was impressed by a real story surrounding the Crash of 1987. A consultant was self-employed (nothing to do with finance or investing) and had a new client who was a stockbroker. Shortly after the Crash, he told Ken that the stockbroker was still on a long holiday and he was concerned that the new relationship would stop as the stockbroker would be running low in cash. (The consultant was well aware that the stockbroker himself had invested heavily in shares.)

On his return, the stockbroker revealed that all was well. He had known that this severe correction was likely to occur for some time and had completely sold out of the equity market some weeks before. Ken, who lost some 15 per cent of the value of his portfolio at the time, was indeed impressed. As this story shows there is, of course, truth in the fact that the professionals are close to what is going on and better informed in these matters than people in other professions. The question has to arise though, if the stockbroker sold the shares at or close to the top of the market, who bought them? The answer, at least to some extent, is that smaller private investors bought them. For the reason stated below, the herd instinct runs strongly among private investors. If we can avoid such instincts, though, we can beat the professionals in the long term.

Buy at the bottom, sell at the top, result happiness; buy at the top, sell at the bottom, result misery

In a rising market, publicity also rises, with people hearing of new highs in exchanges around the world. There are human interest stories of people making small fortunes. (Sorry, but we've just got to put in the oldest Stock Exchange joke here. Question: how do you make a small fortune on the Stock Exchange? Answer: start with a large one.)

More and more people are becoming interested, many for the first time. The marketers of financial products have noticed this and reflect such growing interest in hugely increased advertising. The advertisements can correctly point out what profits have been available in the short term. Private investors pour into the market. Dinner table talk encourages someone else to try – they hear how the host has made money – and more momentum is added to a bullish market.

All the overall ratios go haywire and the professionals can see that the market is bound to become overheated and suffer a sharp or, some would say, catastrophic drop. At this point we cannot say that only the do-it-yourselfer is buying, but it is probably fair to say that very few do-it-yourselfers are selling.

Classically the market now drops, the smaller investor sees erosion of their capital, panics and sells, probably before the bottom itself but certainly into a weak market. We hardly need to ask who is buying at this stage. Knowledgeable private investors, such as the stockbroker mentioned before, and the big funds are buying the shares back from the small investors they sold to at the top. Also buying are the private investors who are avoiding going with the tide.

We must remember that it does not need to be a cataclysm like the Crash of 1987 to have this effect, but any of the fairly sharp changes in fortune that happen on a day-to-day basis. Some fund managers, of course, will make as much of a pig's ear of a sharp correction as the private investor (you can see that clearly in their results). Unfortunately, most smaller investors put themselves at a huge disadvantage by being too exposed to a single stock or by slavishly following the herd.

The sensible investor's strategy is to be a contrarian. This involves selling stocks that are in high demand and buying stocks that are unpopular. In other words, buying at the bottom and selling at the top.

Buying at the bottom

Easier said than done. We can only really illustrate this by giving an example. Suppose you have decided that your portfolio requires a pharmaceutical stock that you are buying mainly to provide capital growth. The stock will have, at the time of purchase, a high price/earnings ratio and a relatively low yield. It will be in a big company because, again, that is what your strategy at this time demands. You have used some ratio analysis (covered in subsequent chapters) and identified two potential buys. Suddenly, one falls out of favour. There is a rumour of a court case or a stockbroker changes its recommendation from hold to sell or even just from buy to hold. Remembering that the underlying strategy and figures of the company still suit your bill, you decide to try to buy this stock at the bottom. You watch it go down and swoop when the price is where you think the floor is.

Spotting the *actual* bottom in this kind of situation is always going to be difficult, for many reasons, some of which are concerned with the logical performance of the company and some of which are much more to do with the market's effect on a share where some big holders feel overweight in the stock.

Taking the first case – the performance of the company – it is quite possible for some bad news to be followed by more, in which case the decline will continue. The law suit that threatened now looks even worse than the fears that drove the price down in the first place. A competitor announces a new product that threatens to damage the profits of the target company despite your happiness with its competitive strategy. It could be any of another million possibilities. So you can get it wrong. At one point in its past, shares in Eurotunnel were well over £11. We can imagine that many people tried to predict the bottom for this share and came in at any level between the £10 and ultimate low (to date) of around 64 pence. Bad news just tumbled in on other bad news.

In the second case, consider the psychology of an institution that has decided that the 3 per cent of a large company it owns is surplus to requirements. The news of this 'overhang' will probably elude the private investor, but its impact on the share price will be significant and possibly very prolonged. Obviously, to try and sell the lot in one go would massively reduce the price the institution would get. It will therefore, slowly but surely, release the stock on to the market as time and emotion allow. During this period of time, many small investors will also be selling as they see the downward drift in the price of the shares. Not so the contrarian, who could be buying if the share meets their requirements.

The thinking of a contrarian helps the investor to heed well the warning on all financial statistics and advertisements – past performance is not a guide to future performance.

Selling at the top

We will argue that there are fewer reasons for selling shares than there are for buying them. The investment strategy would have to change for a share that used to suit the bill to have no place in the portfolio. But such changes do occur. Perhaps the investor has reached an age when they wish to reduce the amount of risk in their portfolio. Perhaps the business cycle has turned and the share is in a sector the investor does not want. In these cases, and others, the investor will sell. Those who are contrarian in nature will, however, try not to sell the share into a weak market. When shares are racing ahead and the market is setting new highs, the contrarian will sell unwanted shares into a strong market.

Invest regularly

Another decision the investor needs to make before setting their strategy and starting to use value judgements about the underlying performance of companies is when and how often to invest. The mantra 'The time is never exactly right to invest' has its corollary – that it is always the right time to invest.

Putting of regular amounts of money into shares has two main benefits. First, it forces the investor, at least in part, to become a contrarian. That is, when market sentiment is low, the regular investor still makes investments, building their portfolio, in bad days as well as good.

The other benefit is so-called 'pound cost averaging'. Here is an illustration of this theory. It is particularly applicable if an investor has chosen investment trusts for their overseas stocks. Instead of going through the difficulties of buying foreign shares directly, a lot of investors use investment trusts as their vehicle for making sure their portfolio has a spread of shares abroad as well as in the UK.

BACKGROUND FACTS

In the long run, all markets rise. This is a result of inflation plus the inevitable growth caused by population and economic growth. It is hard to envisage capitalism failing to produce growth eventually. In these circumstances, pound cost averaging means that the regular investor is getting better value for money during a period of time than the average cost of the investment they are buying during this same period. All this means is that the investor is taking advantage of the fact that they are buying in a market that is continuously rising over time.

Taking an extreme example, in the course of three months, an investor buys, each month, £50-worth of a share that fluctuates in price from 150p to 100p and 300p, the average price of the share during that period would be 183p and the average price paid 150p.

This argument is used by sellers of financial products to encourage regular investment, but the real-life impact of pound cost averaging is normally pretty small. It is only in widely fluctuating markets, as above, that any significant advantage shows through.

The real advantages of regular investment are those of remaining calm when things are hectic, reaping the benefits of being a contrarian and avoiding the pain of trying to catch a share at its low, a very difficult thing to predict.

Conclusion

This book is about the private investor who is not seeing the stock market as a way of making huge short-term profits, but is looking for a sensible saving scheme to run by themselves. Such investors are willing to take risks, but want to take them in the context of the longer term and that of understanding what type of share will fit into an investment strategy before embarking on the exercise of identifying the actual companies in which to invest. We will also look for advantage in building the portfolio by minimising the cost of getting information, buying and selling transactions and holding the portfolio.

EXERCISES FOR CHAPTER 1

At the end of each chapter there is a series of exercises. You can do these using the sample forms in the book or you could create a series of spreadsheets to do them if you have the software and the expertise.

Apply some of the background facts

EXERCISE 1
Two 40-year-olds and their family spend £3,000 per month on living expenses, including mortgage, holidays and so on. Assume an inflation rate of 5 per cent per annum and an increase in earnings of 2 per cent above inflation.

What will they be spending per month in absolute terms at the age of 50, assuming there is no material change in their circumstances and that all pay increases are spent on increasing their standards of living?

This is the first part of the exercise for setting investment strategies.

EXERCISE 2
Make a rough estimate of your present spending and do the same calculation for when you are aged 50, or the age at which you intend to be fully or semi-retired.

Becoming familiar with financial information

EXERCISE 3
Pick three shares in different sized companies (measured by means of market capitalisation) from the same business sector in the financial pages of a newspaper. Plot the yield and price/earnings ratios for a period of a least five days. Can you explain the initial differences in these ratios by means of the nature of the risk of the enterprises? Do you see the reasons for any changes to these explained in articles in other parts of the paper?

EXERCISE 4
Do you have an idea of how much money you are likely to invest in the next five years? If so, make a first draft plan as to how to invest it, making sure that you obtain some of the benefits of regular saving. Perhaps you are going to start by taking a lump sum out of the building society and then investing regularly.

This is only the starting point for setting an investment strategy. Find out more in the next chapter.

CHAPTER 2

Setting the investment strategy

The objective of picking the right shares sits inside the strategy of what sort of share you require to fit into your personal portfolio

- The seven-step process towards identifying the right shares for your portfolio
- Setting personal objectives
- Establishing a strategy for risk
- Exercises

The art of do-it-yourself investment is to make considered decisions based on the knowledge of what you are trying to achieve. This chapter looks at reducing the overall risk of equity investment by making sure that an investment in one company supports previous investments and ones yet to be made. It is like building a wall rather than buying bricks.

The seven-step process towards identifying the right shares for your portfolio

There is a reasonably simple process by means of which you can make sure the shares you are buying are good value, in terms of the intrinsic merit of the company and their contribution to the overall strategy that is driving your portfolio. The seven steps are shown in Figure 2.1.

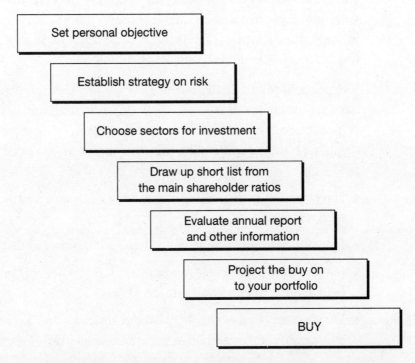

Fig. 2.1 The seven steps towards choosing the best shares for your portfolio

In this chapter we will look at the first two of these: set personal objective and establish strategy on risk.

Setting personal objectives

Many people find investing in shares a hobby in itself. They enjoy rooting around the press and other sources of information to try and outsmart the market and make good returns. Others stay clear because they are not convinced that they will be able to make money *and* expose their capital to only sensible risk. In both these cases, they would be well advised to take a step back initially and determine what they are trying to achieve.

The starting point

There is an old Chinese proverb that states that before you decide where you are trying to go – the objective – and how you are going to get there – the strategy – make quite sure you know where you are now. With this in mind, your starting point is taking a careful look at your current finances, in terms of both outgoings and income.

Independent financial advisers are required by their regulators to carry out a thorough examination of these things in their initial 'fact find.' If you have done one of these, ask the salesperson or financial adviser who compiled it for a copy. Failing that, the questions you need ask are the following.

- Have you got sufficient insurance – life assurance and all other types of insurance?

- Do your pension arrangements make good use of available tax reliefs?

- Do you have a sufficient fund of cash to allow for any unforeseen expenditure, such as house repairs?

- Do you need to have further cover against risk and a shortage of cash by investing, for example, in government securities?

- After your normal outgoings, how much could you afford to put by as savings on a regular basis?

This exercise does not need to be done to two decimal places – rounded figures will do, unless your financial resources are stretched to their limit and there is a danger of your having to borrow money or stop the investment strategy if the calculation goes wrong.

Let us assume that the result of that analysis shows that there is a lump sum available for investment in equities, and an excess of income over expenditure that allows a certain sum to be put aside on a monthly basis. The question now arises, 'What am I trying to achieve?'

It is very important to reiterate at this point that the assumption that you have money to save means that you are already retaining some money in cash for the rainy day when the roof needs repairing and you have made sensible use of the tax benefits of professionally run pension plans and that it makes sense to invest the excess remaining in equities. The strategy we are talking about is the equity investment strategy, not your overall financial plan.

Possible objectives

From time to time we will talk about the fictitious Darnley Village Investment Club. A later chapter in the book looks more closely at the topic of investment clubs, but suffice it to say at this time that the Darnley Village Investment Club (DVIC) is a group of some 20 individuals from in and around Darnley who have formed a club to pool their resources and buy an equity portfolio. The strategy of the club as we will see later is inevitably a compromise, not as tailored to each individual as it could be were each individual investing alone. But each member can live with it and, in most cases, the amounts of money involved on a monthly basis, are fairly small though, they become significant after a remarkably short length of time.

The point is that each member, even in this environment, has different motives for joining.

SCENARIO ### The individual objectives of members of the Darnley Village Investment Club

- The **Chairman** is a senior manager in a small company that has the potential to grow dramatically. She invests a modest sum in the Club even though she has a good income, but is prepared to increase it if the performance of the Club merits it. One of her main objectives is to learn about this form of investment without having to put in a lot of time, which she simply does not have.

- **Graham** is self-employed and not the main family bread-winner. He uses the Club as a form of enforced savings. He has never really saved before and the sum of money put by quite quickly becomes relatively significant. He is also attracted by the thought that he is much less likely to maintain saving in the alternative, a building society, as there he would be more tempted to withdraw it. He also understands that the returns in the Club could be superior.

- **Emily** is an entrepreneur and the Club handles a small amount of her money. She likes the Club because she has little to do with the investment strategy. She feels she spends enough time on commercial matters already and is happy to go with the tide.

- **Iain** and **Diana** are a married couple using the Club as part of their retirement planning. For them the Club is a serious fund that needs to build to some £60,000 by the time the couple retire at 60. They are currently 50.

Much more could be said about the members of the club, but the point is made. The reasons for buying shares are highly individual, and the key to it is knowing what you are trying to do.

In the next section on risk acceptance we will look at more detailed cases of savers looking to equities to reach different objectives.

How to set your objective

Let us assume that you have decided to put a certain amount of your savings into equities for the reasons we have discussed – as a hedge against inflation, to give a better return in the long run and so on. Now you need to choose your objective. The questions to ask to help you do this are as follows.

- *What are you saving for?* Try to be as specific as possible. Is it part of your retirement fund? Are you hoping to take a really big holiday in five years' time? Your setting of a strategy and ability to pick appropriate stocks does depend on your really knowing what you are trying to achieve.

- *What is the financial aim, what do you hope to have made at the end of the time period?* Now define the objective in money terms. At the end of this chapter you will have the opportunity to put this in cash flow terms, but for the moment give yourself a point to aim at.

- *Is it achievable or are you getting carried away by the 'get rich quick' bug?* When you work out the cash flow you will see what rate of return you will require from the savings you are investing to meet the objective. If the rate is higher than 15 per cent, you are hoping to achieve a higher rate of return than the market has done over many years. That is, you are hoping to pick shares that outperform the market as a whole. As the average unit trust does not do this, you may feel you are going too high. On the other hand, the aim needs to be stretching – after all we are in this business to take some risk and to do better than more secure investments.

- *What time period do you need to set?* At least five years if you are to have a realistic chance of success. If you achieve it earlier that's great, but shares are expensive to buy in terms of costs so you need to give them time to make profits.

- *How will you measure success on the way?* You need a system to plot your progress. This will be suggested later in the book.

- *What will happen if you do not make it?* Do not be too gloomy, but what would you do if the portfolio produced much lower returns? We are planning for success, but need to understand the downside.

Establishing a strategy for risk

We suggest that you consider as a basic model of investment strategy three levels of investment risk: high, medium and low. It is then the investor's job to allocate a proportion of the invested funds to each of these levels of risk. In most cases the model will be a pyramid shape as investors will wish to place more of their fund in the low-risk category that in the high-risk one. We will use a model that assumes that some 50 per cent of the fund will be in the low-risk area, 35 per cent in the medium-risk one and the remaining 15 per cent in the high-risk one. Of course, you can take a different view on the shape of the portfolio if you wish. For example, you could take more risk in the hope of more return. However, throughout this chapter and beyond we will assume the 50, 35 and 15 per cent model, illustrated in Figure 2.2.

Remember that we are also assuming that investors are in it for the long haul and that they will wish to limit their risk to a significant extent. We are not talking about speculating on the Lottery or putting money on the roulette wheel.

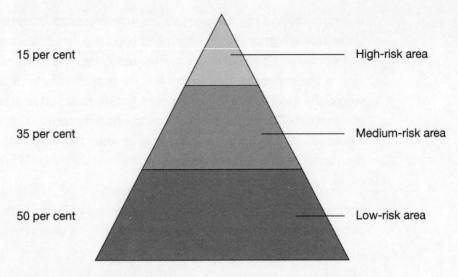

15 per cent — High-risk area

35 per cent — Medium-risk area

50 per cent — Low-risk area

Fig. 2.2 The standard risk model

A portfolio has to have a spread of shares to limit the downside risk. This implies that all investors should decide on their definitions of high-, medium- and low-risk areas and allocate money to each of these catagories. If the sums involved are to be more than a gambling pot, the investor must take some care to avoid losing the lot.

It is a cliché but nevertheless true to repeat that risk and return are in proportion. The higher the risk of something going wrong, then the higher is the expected return. Indeed, the whole emphasis of the stock market is to evaluate the risk of companies achieving their intended results and being able to maintain or increase past dividends into the future. Having evaluated this risk, the market sets the price accordingly. This evaluation is then echoed, as we have seen, in the price/earnings ratio and the yield.

Of course, the market and investors will get this evaluation wrong from time to time, but there are some fairly obvious rules that govern risk generally. It is probably true to say that a company in the FTSE 100 – one of the top 100 companies in the country measured by total share value or market capitalisation, is much less likely to become worthless than an option to buy a small company recently started and floated by venture capitalists in, say, the computer industry.

However, try telling that to people who bought or held shares in British

Gas or Hanson during the years of 1994, 1995, and 1996 who saw a dramatic fall in these shares. Most portfolios that had them as low-risk bankers must have suffered in terms of achieving their objectives at that time. Hanson never really recovered before it was broken into smaller pieces, British Gas clawed back a lot of the loss, but, at the beginning of 1997, was still a much more volatile share than investors in utility shares were expecting. Indeed, one of the reasons that the company was subsequently split in two was to isolate the part that was giving rise to speculative concern.

Nevertheless, all the private investor can do is to take a view on risk and make decisions accordingly. It is very individual. What is an acceptable medium risk for one person could feel like a wild punt to another. The technique is to work it out for yourself using our examples and techniques.

Let's look at three examples.

EXAMPLE ## The Fastlaners

John is a 28-year-old salesman of computer components. He works in a world of risk in his everyday life, selling commodity components the price of which change subject to availability, discounts and promotions on, literally an hour-to-hour basis. For a 28-year-old, he is reasonably well paid and so pays income tax at the top rate. He and his employers pay into a company pension scheme, although he does not really expect to be with the same firm for a protracted length of time.

His partner is self-employed as a recruitment consultant. She has no company scheme, but has taken out a personal pension plan that, of course, has the tax benefits of such schemes, but ties up the money until she is at least 50 years old. The Fastlaners have no children and no intention of having any in the short term.

They decide that, after their pensions and keeping a reasonable sum of money in a building society just in case, they can afford to invest £2,000 now and then 10 per cent of their net salaries in a portfolio of shares.

They set their objectives as follows:

- protect capital in a way which is consistent with objectives

- disregard income and, therefore, high-yield shares since they do not need the income and it would be taxed at top rate

- go for growth of capital by looking at speculative shares, such as takeover possibilities and even options.

The shape of their risk model is the standard triangle, but it is pitched at the upper end of the spectrum of risk. Their motto is 'You had better enjoy life, this is not a dress rehearsal.'

Their low-risk investments will be in large companies in a sector that is seen to be consolidating by merger and acquisition. For example, the financial sector, where insurance companies are plainly going to diminish in number and increase in size over the next few years. Trying to spot companies that are likely to be taken over requires a lot of study, so probably the Fastlaners will glean tips from the press and magazines.

They will also use a simple device that has a reasonable track record. They will look quickly at any share that is being bought by at least four of the company's directors in the same week. This information is published weekly in the FT. If the company passes some other tests in the value analysis stage, they will buy shares in it. Speed will be important here, for if the device works, others will come in and the price will, to begin with, rise artificially. This is particularly true if the company is small.

To spread their risk, while maintaining the strategy, they may decide to use a collective investment as their medium-risk option. This might be an investment trust specialising in venture capital. Such funds are big enough to back a whole lot of new ventures, knowing that the return will emerge from very few really high flyers.

At the high-risk end, they will punt on penny shares, shares in small companies in fast-growing sectors, such as telecommunications, and new companies bringing innovative products to market. They will find some such companies in pharmaceuticals, with biochemists working on totally new drugs, electronics, where many companies are trying to find out how to make money out of the Internet in new ways, and so on.

Also included in the high-risk sector is investment in share options, which we will describe in outline later. Suffice it to say here that the same rules apply as before – you need to try to discover good value in the company offering the shares you are speculating in, with the added ingredient of using a 'geared play', which allows you to gamble with money that you are, in effect, borrowing at zero interest.

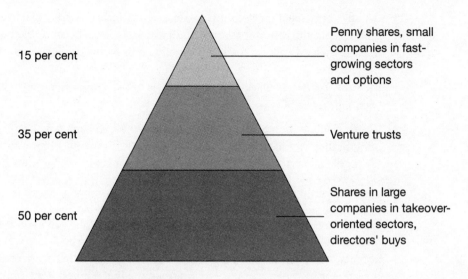

15 per cent — Penny shares, small companies in fast-growing sectors and options

35 per cent — Venture trusts

50 per cent — Shares in large companies in takeover-oriented sectors, directors' buys

Fig. 2.3 The Fastlaner's risk model

We will look at the Fastlaners as they go through some of the seven steps involved in building a portfolio. We will also look at the Lookaheads.

EXAMPLE

The Lookaheads

Mr and Mrs Lookahead are also in their late twenties. He is an architect and she is a part-time administrator for a small local business, although she is about to take maternity leave to have their first baby. Their clear intention is to have two children and their objective is to send them both to private schools, he because he did not go and regrets it, and she because she did have a private education and cannot envisage doing anything else.

The maths are daunting. They need the equivalent of £5,000 per child per year from the time each one becomes 5 years old, and £7,000 for secondary school. Here is their likely spend.

- 5 and 6 years from now, £5,000 per annum

- 7, 8, 9, 10 and 11 years from now, £10,000 per annum

- 12 and 13 years from now, £12,000 per annum

- 14, 15, 16, 17 and 18 years from now, £14,000 per annum

- 19 and 20 years from now, £7,000 per annum.

Mr Lookahead's pension is a company one, his wife's a small personal one. They are going to use a PEP shelter for their savings, thus getting the benefit of tax relief on both income and capital gains. Their objective, therefore, is a mixture of income and growth. Income because the tax relief maximises it and allows them, eventually, to draw the money regularly to meet the fees, and growth because they will eventually have to use the capital to pay the later fees, particularly when they come to the years when they will be spending £14,000.

They calculate that, with a growth rate, income and capital of 10 per cent per annum, they would need to invest some £5,485 annually from now. They can, however, only afford £5,000 per year, which, to achieve their objective, would mean that they need just over 12 per cent growth. In five years' time, they will be able to review this and possibly invest more if it is necessary.

Note that, for simplicity, we have left inflation out of the school fees and assumed a flat investment. If we were to assume that school fees were inflating at 5 per cent per annum and that the Lookaheads intended to increase their investment by 5 per cent per annum, then the initial investment would be about £6,800, assuming a growth rate of 10 per cent.

In the early years, they will have to go for growth, changing their strategy for income when the expenditure starts. They do not underestimate the usefulness of yield, however, in the long term and will, even at the start, be looking for shares with a higher than average yield.

The downside is that if the strategy does not work, they will, for some years, have to make other economies, such as not going up market in their housing, but that is a fall back position that they are willing to accept.

The level of risk they will take is that, in the low-risk area, they will buy FTSE 100 companies with a high yield. This will tend to mean those that are out of favour with the market at the moment. They will have to look carefully at each company they are considering to make sure that the high yield is not indicating an almost certain cut in dividend. However, as they do not need to draw money for some time, they can afford to choose a big company with problems that has a low share price at the moment while it is solving its difficulties. Assuming, of course – and this is the risk – that the company maintains its dividend.

In the medium-risk area, they will look abroad. It is, in any case, a good idea to have some of your portfolio overseas. There is an additional risk of adverse currency moves, but that can cut both ways. The Lookaheads will use investment trusts as their chosen vehicle for overseas shares. This gives them an instant spread of shares and makes the administration more straightforward.

In the high-risk area, they will invest in anything that appeals, from speculating on shares that have recently been purchased by a number of the company's directors to tips on takeover rumours they have picked up from the financial magazines. It is interesting to note that the high-risk area of the Lookaheads is very similar to the low-risk part of the Fastlaners' model.

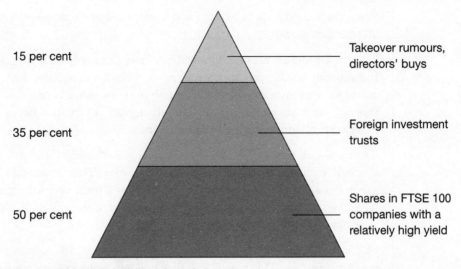

15 per cent — Takeover rumours, directors' buys

35 per cent — Foreign investment trusts

50 per cent — Shares in FTSE 100 companies with a relatively high yield

Fig. 2.4 The Lookahead's risk model

Notice how the Lookaheads have thought through their needs and so on in order to identify the size of the investment they need to make related to time, risk and rate of return. This is the exercise you will be asked to do for yourself at the end of the chapter.

Our last example is that of the Getting-on-a-bits, whose objective is different from either of the above two examples.

EXAMPLE

The Getting-on-a-bits

This married couple are both in their fifties. The wife will retire at age 55, or later, but the husband is in a fairly insecure position at work. Technology has led to the classic company strategy of downsizing and he may very well have to take early retirement, say in two or three years' time. His pension is not high enough to allow the standard of living that they currently enjoy, and things could become very tight indeed, given inflation and poor increases.

He has an interesting opportunity to top up his pension. A keen golfer all his life, he has been involved in the running of his local golf club in various offices, from captain to committee member. The current committee believe that there is a need for a part-time professional administrator and that the club's finances could stretch to it. Mr Getting-on-a-bit would be an ideal choice. The income this would generate, as well as the salary brought in by his wife, would enable them to live. They would only have to draw on his pension for special purchases, such as holidays. They believe that, with hard work for another few years, they could achieve savings and a pension that would allow them the lifestyle they want.

Their risk profile is set much lower than those of the previous two examples. Indeed, they will allocate much less, proportionally, to equities than, for example, the Fastlaners. However, for all the reasons we have already seen, they will use equities to keep up with inflation and to try for a better return than other savings during this period of their lives.

Their low-risk area will include large, stable British companies with a yield not much, if at all, above the sector or market average. Their motto will be, 'Buy the shares and then forget about them.' They will trade very infrequently, relying instead on the long-term growth of the dividend and capital to meet their objectives.

Falling within their medium-risk area will be the next 250 companies in the UK measured by size. This means that they will not invest in any company with a market capitalisation of less than £250 million. The reason for this diversification is to try to get a slightly higher rate of growth during the period from now until retirement. At retirement they may review even this level of risk.

For their high-risk area they will turn abroad, using investment trusts.

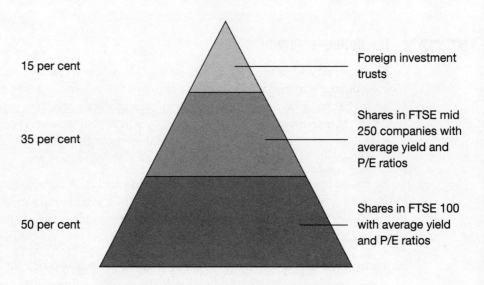

15 per cent — Foreign investment trusts

35 per cent — Shares in FTSE mid 250 companies with average yield and P/E ratios

50 per cent — Shares in FTSE 100 with average yield and P/E ratios

Fig. 2.5 The Getting-on-a-bits' risk model

These three examples set the scene for you so you can start to plan your own portfolio. Despite claims to the contrary, there is no golden rule for judging shares and making certain profits, no matter how carefully you examine value, charts or any other form of alchemy aimed at picking stock successfully. What they illustrate is the importance to all investors of choosing an objective that is relevant, understanding the standard risk model and thinking through what types of share would fit into your specific version of the model.

Some of the options

A simplified spectrum of the types of equity investment available might look like this.

BENCHMARK GUIDE **A spectrum of investment opportunities in order of risk**

Low risk

↑ FTSE 100 companies

FTSE mid 250 companies

Overseas shares

Shares bought for their growth potential

Shares bought for their recovery potential

Penny shares and shell companies

↓ Options

High risk

Each of these areas can be broken down further, but a short definition of each one follows.

FTSE 100 companies

The FTSE 100 index measures the rise and fall of a basket of 100 companies that are the largest UK companies, measured by their *market capitalisation* (market capitalisation is the market value of the company, calculated by multiplying the current share price by the number of shares). While it only lists 100 companies, together they represent some 70 per cent of the market capitalisation of the whole market. The total return from these shares has a relatively low risk, due primarily to the size and relative resilience of the companies in the index.

FTSE mid 250 companies

This index contains the next 250 companies by market capitalisation below the 100 given in the FTSE 100 index. Whether they represent a lower risk than large overseas companies is a moot point, but as they include much less currency risk, we have put them as, arguably, the second lowest risk.

Overseas shares

Investing in overseas shares in developed markets – USA, Japan, Western Europe and so on – gives you diversification from the UK and allows you to take an interest in other groups of very large businesses. The return here is complicated by currency fluctuations, but as we have argued that it is good to aim for diversification of UK shares in the portfolio, so we should have some exposure to overseas markets. Exposure to *emerging* markets, such as China or Latin America, however, carries a much higher risk.

It is generally very convenient to invest overseas by using one of the many investment trusts that specialise in all parts of the world.

Shares bought for their growth potential

There are always available to investors areas of particular growth. Technology is an obvious one, and investors can sometimes put a very high value on companies that are blessed with a technological advantage as it may make their shares grow rapidly in value. Such shares can produce a a very high return if you choose the right one, but a rather disappointing one if, for example, the technology is improved by someone else or simply fails to find an application or a mass market.

Shares bought for their recovery potential

In this case, the investor chooses a company the news about which has recently been bad and where its share price has suffered accordingly, but which offers scope for recovery. You can buy individual shares of this type or a collection of them in an investment trust.

Penny shares and shell companies

There is a particular fascination among private investors with penny shares. These are defined as shares with a very low price (say, less than 30 pence) and a high bid-to-sell spread. There are tip sheets by the score claiming powerful results from selecting penny shares the prices of which took off. In fact, there is very little logic in all of this. If a share goes from £1 to £2, it means that, in the short to medium term, the market expects the profit performance of the company to double. This is exactly the same if a share goes from 5p to 10p. There can also be problems with the liquidity of penny shares, which means that you may have trouble selling the shares when you choose to.

There is always a possibility that someone might buy the penny share company, or any other, as a *shell situation*. A shell situation exists when a company has low market capitalisation and some assets that could, preferably, be easily realised. If an aggressive entrepreneur wants to save the expense of launching a company on to the market, they may buy a shell company and 'back' the company to be floated into it. In this case, a share would increase in value very dramatically as it is increases hugely in size when it is 'taking over' a larger concern.

Options

An investor can buy an *option* to buy a share at a date in the future for a fixed price. They are gambling that the price of the share, when the time comes for the option to be exercised, will be higher than the sum of the price of the option and the fixed share price. This allows the investor to make greater gains than they would by buying the underlying share.

Suppose an investor buys in May an option to purchase in October shares in an oil company. The price of the share in May was £5.50, the fixed option price £6 and the option itself cost 50p. If in October the underlying share price has increased to £7.00, then the holder of the option can buy for £6, a total cost of £6.50, and then sell immediately for £7. The profit over a 5-month period is 50p per share for an outlay of 50p. In effect, the investor has doubled their money in 5 months.

It is sobering to think, however, that if the shares had only gone to £6.25 during the same period, then a similar calculation would show a loss of half of the original stake. And, of course, if the share had stayed at £5.50 or even gone to £6, then the whole investment would have been lost, as it would have been cheaper to have bought the share in the open market than exercise the option.

Options are not, as they say, for widows and orphans, but for those who can take a significant gamble in the high-risk area of their portfolio.

A summary and illustration

Within each of these types of investment there will, of course, be different levels of risk. Some will go across these arbitrary boundaries. For example, a company given in the FTSE 250 could well be a recovery stock if the company has been through a difficult period. A company in the FTSE 100 with a very high yield may belong in one part of an investor's risk model, and a company with an average yield in another. The key for small investors is to understand the possibilities and work out a pattern or strategy.

SCENARIO Darnley Village Investment Club

In a number of chapters, we will illustrate what has gone before by reference to an investment decision that the Investment Club is making. The club has set its medium-risk strategy as simply to invest in companies that are given in the FTSE mid 250 index. These are, by their nature, large companies, the 250 next biggest companies by market capitalisation after the top 100, have generally been around a while and afford a level of risk somewhere between safety first and excitement.

We will watch the members of the Club as they choose a share to fit into this strategy.

To start with, all we need to know is that their individual objectives have been worked into a strategy they can all live with, and that the medium-risk strategy is as above.

EXERCISES FOR CHAPTER 2

By the end of this chapter, you will have decided on your own investment objective and timescale, drawn your risk model and defined the types of investment that fit into each part of the model.

Becoming familiar with financial information

EXERCISE 1 Looking in a newspaper, find a list of the FTSE 100 companies at this time (you will find it on the back page of the FT in the column headed 'Major Stocks – Trading Volumes').

EXERCISE 2 Study the 'Unit Trust' section of the paper and get a feel for how the industry describes certain types of fund. For example 'Recovery and Smaller companies'. Think about the types of shares you will have in your portfolio and order the prospectus for a unit trust that covers one of these types. This will give you a feel for the names and types of companies invested in, and the reasons given by the fund managers for so doing.

Setting your own objectives

EXERCISE 3 Using the criteria above, set your objective. Use the SMART acronym if it helps. Is the objective:

Stretching

Measurable

Achievable

Recoverable if it fails

Time-targeted?

EXERCISE 4 Plot a cash flow forecast of your investment payments and experiment with the rate of return to find one that meets your objective in the time allowed.

Establishing your strategy

EXERCISE 5 Prepare your risk model triangle as follows:

On the 50, 35 and 15 per cent basis, decide on the types of investments you are going to make. Make sure they are consistent with the objective. You may have to do a few iterations of setting objectives and strategy to get a sensible answer.

CHAPTER 3

The financial starting point: an introduction

An introduction to the main financial ratios

- Introduction
- The key financial ratios
- Forty years in the life of a growth stock
- Conclusion
- Exercises

Before getting on to the detail of analysing an annual report, we need to understand the key ratios that can be used to reveal the characteristics of different businesses. Having looked at the key shareholder ratios in Chapter 2, we turn here to the key corporate ones.

Introduction

We have said that investors can never be in the position of a manager in a business, knowing intimately how it is doing, but there are some ratios available that allow us to make well-informed assessments.

After the *Financial Times* and the financial pages of other newspapers, as mentioned in Chapter 2, the next mine of information available to investors is the company's annual report. This offers some consistency of key indicators as the contents of the accounts are regulated by law and accountancy standards. Using these, investors can make relevant comparisons of one company with another, particularly if the companies are in the same sector.

Company reports are notorious of course for what they hide as well as what they reveal. It is possible, at least in the short term, for creative accountants and their boardroom masters to produce numbers that reflect more accurately their *aspirations* for the company than its *actual* performance. However, this cannot go on forever. As the business continues to perform in a certain way, the accountants will eventually force the Board to break the bad news to its shareholders.

Despite this caveat, the annual report does give some very usable information. The most useful of these ratios are *capital gearing, income gearing, return on capital employed* and the *pre-tax profit margin.*

Armed with these four ratios and the three covered in Chapter 2, investors are in a better position to make decisions. The problem is that many private investors think that this will be too time-consuming and they either make decisions based on less information than this or trust their money to the professionals who charge royally for the privilege.

This chapter endeavours to describe a quick method of getting to these numbers, and then, by means of an example of a company going through a 40-year lifecycle, show how the mix of the investor ratios and the key company ratios paints a picture of the health and prospects of potential investments.

If investors add a judicious reading of a Chairman's statement to discover the Board's intentions for the future, they are as well prepared as it is possible to be without becoming a full-time company watcher.

The key financial ratios

The four ratios covered below give an effective check on progress quite quickly. They are reasonably easy to calculate and, with practice take a matter of a few minutes to produce. Always work them out for the two years covered by the report so that you can look at the change. You can then check the directors' statements to see if they comment on changes that you regard as significant.

Frequently, the report will include a section entitled 'Facts for shareholders' or 'Five-year record', which will show some calculated ratios. The advantage of these is that they remove the need to do any calculations. Unfortunately there are also two disadvantages to relying on these that make them much less useful than detecting them yourself.

The first problem is that the published ratios are generally calculated in a way that suits each company. They will use figures that are not misleading or inaccurate, but give a gloss on its performance that the truly objective investor wishes to avoid.

The second problem is connected with the first. As companies use ratios that suit themselves, they do not use the same ones as each other. So, for the sake of consistency, it is better to become very familiar with four ratios that you work out for yourself. You also build a personal database of examples that gives you various benchmarks for examining and comparing any company. This is particularly true if you study only one, or at least a limited number, of business sectors.

One final point. The benchmark guides given below are useful as you learn to appreciate the significance of the ratios. They are guides only, however, and we will see later how their significance varies depending on the business the company is in and the stage it has reached in its lifecycle.

Capital gearing

Gearing involves comparing the amount of the company's external liabilities with the amount of money in shareholders' funds. High gearing means that a company's external liabilities, including borrowings, are high compared to its shareholders' funds. High gearing is more risky than low gearing because the company has a commitment to service the debt. However, high gearing could also mean that the company is pushing hard for expansion and needs high levels of debt to finance that growth. It is possible to calculate gearing in a number of ways, but one of the easiest to calculate is also one of the harshest measures of a company's exposure to the perils of high levels of debt and creditor dependence.

The ratio is a comparison of the total liabilities of a company with its shareholders' funds. The higher the ratio, the more likely it is that debt will become a burden. The more debt, the more interest, the lower the profits and, therefore, the ability to pay dividends is threatened.

The formula for the calculation is:

$$\frac{\text{Total liabilities}}{\text{Shareholders' funds}} \times 100 = \text{percentage}$$

If you are having problems finding the appropriate numbers, follow this step-by-step approach.

STEP BY STEP

Calculating the capital gearing ratio

- Find the current liabilities, often called 'Liabilities, amounts falling due within one year'.

- Now add 'Creditors: amounts falling due after more than one year'. Make sure you include everything, including provisions.

- Find the figure for total shareholders' funds. Do not include minority interests.

- Now divide total liabilities by shareholders' funds and multiply the result by 100.

- This gives you a percentage figure.

Comparing the capital gearing ratios

- Low gearing is less than 100 per cent.

- Medium gearing is between 100 per cent and 200 per cent.

- High gearing is above 200 per cent.

In 1994, Eurotunnel's gearing was 466 per cent, and getting worse.

Eurotunnel	£,000
Provisions	141
Current and long-term liabilities	8,113,322
Total liabilities	8,113,463
Total shareholders' funds	1,739,833

For this calculation and the others that follow in this chapter, we will show only the comparison of one year's results with the benchmark guide. In practice, you will want to compare last year with this year to get another important angle on the information. We will discuss this in more detail in the chapters covering the Sherwood Industries case study.

Income gearing

The total liabilities to shareholders' funds ratio has the limitation that it includes all current liabilities as well as debt. We therefore need another ratio that indicates the company's ability to service its debt. The income gearing ratio does this. It is the ratio of interest payable to the profits out of which interest is paid. It takes a bit more working out than the other ratios discussed, but has the merit of being impossible to fudge. Nowadays, many people regard it as the key gearing ratio.

The formula for the calculation is:

$$\frac{\text{Interest payable}}{\text{Profit before interest and tax}} \times 100 = \text{percentage}$$

STEP BY STEP

Calculating the income gearing ratio

- Find the interest payable for the year. You often have to look at the notes for this figure as the figure in the profit and loss account is 'Net interest'. Net interest is interest payable minus interest receivable, which is not the figure we want here.

- Find the earnings, or profit, before interest and tax. Often you will have to calculate this by adding the interest payable figure to the pre-tax profit shown in the profit and loss account.

- Then, divide interest payable by profit before interest and tax, and multiply the result by 100, which expresses it as a percentage.

BENCHMARK GUIDE

Comparing the income gearing ratios

- Low gearing is less than 25 per cent.

- Medium gearing is between 25 and 75 per cent.

- High gearing is above 75 per cent.

In 1996, BT's gearing was 10.9 per cent reflecting its low level of debt.

BT	£m
Interest payable	371
Profit before tax	3,019
Profit before interest and tax	3,390

Return on capital employed

This measure is a key indicator of managerial performance as it relates pre-tax profit to the long-term capital invested in the business. It is a good guide as to whether or not sufficient return is being generated to maintain and grow dividends and avoid problems of liquidity.

Over time, it tells us what we need to know about the health of the company measured by profits. Many people regard it as the key profitability ratio and the definition we give here is the one used by most commentators.

The formula for the calculation is:

$$\frac{\text{Pre-tax profit}}{\text{Capital employed}} \times 100 = \text{percentage}$$

STEP BY STEP   **Calculating the return on capital employed**

- 'Capital employed' means the same as total assets minus current liabilities, and this figure is often given in the balance sheet. If not, calculate it as long-term debt, plus provisions for liabilities and charges, plus any other long-term liabilities, plus shareholders' funds, plus minority interests.

- Now divide the pre-tax profit figure given in the profit and loss account by capital employed and multiply the result by 100, which expresses it as a percentage.

BENCHMARK GUIDE   **Comparing return on capital employed ratios**

- Low profitability is 0 to 10 per cent.

- Medium profitability is between 10 and 20 per cent.

- High profitability is above 20 per cent.

In one year, Hewlett-Packard's profitability was 21.4 per cent while Land Securities' was 4.8 per cent.

Hewlett-Packard	$m
Earnings before taxes	2,423
Long-term debt	547
Other long-term liabilities	864
Shareholders' funds	9,926
Capital employed	11,337

Land Securities	£m
Profit on ordinary activities before tax	245
Total assets minus current liabilities	5,120

Note: For relevant comparisons, choose companies in the same business.

Pre-tax profit margin

This reveals the profits earned per pound of sales and, therefore, measures the efficiency of the operation. This ratio is an indicator of the company's ability to withstand adverse conditions, such as falling prices, rising costs or declining sales.

The formula for the calculation is:

$$\frac{\text{Pre-tax profit}}{\text{Sales turnover}} \times 100 = \text{percentage}$$

STEP BY STEP
Calculating the pre-tax profit margin

- Take the pre-tax profit figure given in the profit and loss account.

- Divide it by the total sales revenues, often known in British reports as 'Sales turnover', and multiply the result by 100, which expresses it as a percentage. Where there are continuing and discontinued businesses mentioned, use the total of both.

BENCHMARK GUIDE
Comparing pre-tax profit margin ratios

- Low margin is below 3 per cent.

- Medium margin is between 3 and 8 per cent.

- High margin is above 8 per cent.

In one year, Seeboard's pre-tax profit margin was 11.9 per cent and Pilkington's was 5.4 per cent.

▶

Seeboard	£m
Profit on ordinary activities before taxation	142
Turnover	1,195

Pilkington	£m
Profit on ordinary activities before taxation	144
Turnover	2,676

Note: For relevant comparisons, choose companies in the same business.

Forty years in the life of a growth stock

There is no such thing as a typical company. Their different products, markets and management styles make each enterprise unique. It is possible however, to use the following fictitious example as a benchmark of the characteristics and ratios of a company over a long period of time.

Stage 1: from inception to ten years old

Turn back the clock to the time when telecommunications was in its meteoric growth phase. The sample company, Phoneco, was created by means of a flotation from its parent, where it had been a non-core business. The newly floated company, in the early stages, had the ability to generate a very rapid growth in sales. The market was eager for the new service and sales were there for the taking for any company that could lay down a telecommunications network.

Phoneco was very aggressive at this stage. It needed volume to cover its voracious appetite for cash as it invested millions of pounds in infrastructure. This made its competitiveness very sharp. It would, to a considerable extent, sacrifice profit for market share. It hired a salesforce of 'hunters', salespeople who enjoyed the challenge of getting new business in fast. These salespeople were good at closing business and handling objections. If they did not close business fast, they went elsewhere.

We would have expected to find high morale in the company at this time as the business and consumer markets flocked to the upstart.

The annual report and the Chairman's report

In the Chairman's report, we expected to see a reflection of this growth, and this was the case.

> 'May saw another milestone when the new connections rate for residential customers signing up with Phoneco reached 30,000 per month.'
>
> 'Our sales growth last year exceeded 50 per cent and, although this is likely to prove exceptional, Phoneco is confident of its ability to take further advantage of the expanding market over the next few years.'

The report's tone reflected the excitement and enthusiasm of the fledgling discovering success for the first time.

The financial ratios

The Board, at this stage, was running Phoneco by its cash flows rather than by its profit and loss account. It needed huge amounts of cash for capital investment and we expected to find very high levels of borrowing. This high gearing showed itself in both of the gearing ratios as there was a high percentage of debt and very little profit left over once the interest had been deducted.

Profitability was relatively low, measured by both return on capital employed and the profit margin.

Thus, Phoneco's ratios for stage 1 were:

- gearing   500 per cent
- income gearing   95 per cent
- return on capital employed   1 per cent
- pre-tax profit margin   1 per cent.

The investors' ratios

Investors at this time would have found that the market would only see Phoneco as having long-term potential, resting in the high-risk part of their portfolios. It would have been undesirable for the company to have paid large amounts in dividends as it would have needed all its cash to fund its expansion, so the yield would have been low.

The price/earnings ratio would have been very high as the market calculates future profit streams for a company as it gets into a position to exploit its assets. The dividend cover may very well have also been high, not because the profits were huge, but because the dividend was stingy.

Given all this, Phoneco's investor ratios for stage 1 were:

- yield   0.3 per cent
- price/earnings   35
- dividend cover   13.

Stage 2: from 10 to 20 years

Phoneco came of age in this period of its life. It survived the heady days of 30 per cent year-on-year growth and showed itself to be competitive. The company was, at this point, well into the FTSE 250 list of companies. It had a viable market share in the areas where it already operated and was looking for new opportunities to make further investment either in new markets, such as overseas, or in new product areas, such as telephone equipment.

This diversified growth still cost a lot of money, but the business then generated a healthy cash flow and was profitable. There was still a fair amount of risk in the company. It was vulnerable to making mistakes as it moved into new activities. No matter how good the prospects, it is always more risky to take old products into new markets, or new products into old markets, than to keep doing more of the same.

The annual report and the Chairman's report

We would have expected now to see the Chairman talking of some consolidation of its current affairs, although the emphasis of the report would still be on growth, looking for the new initiatives. Here are some of the things the chairman said.

> 'Our earnings per share before exceptional items grew some 22 per cent.'
>
> 'Our strengthening financial position allows us to explore new areas seeking basic telephone services, while at the same time consolidating our strategy to focus on those parts of the world where we are already strong and where our returns will be the greatest.'

The financial ratios

The debt ratios were still high at this stage. Almost certainly by this time, Phoneco would have been back to its investors to gain more cash by means of a rights issue. This, of course, would have radically reduced the debt to equity ratio, but it would have risen again to reflect further borrowing to continue investment.

Profitability had improved to what could be described as fairly safe levels. This meant that the current business would produce reliable profits, and only the new areas of activity would still have been high risk.

Therefore, Phoneco's ratios for stage 2 were as follows:

- gearing   200 per cent
- income gearing   75 per cent
- return on capital employed   10 per cent
- pre-tax profit margin   4 per cent.

The investors' ratios

Phoneco wanted to pay out some dividends of real worth. It probably had to make promises in this area when it made its cash call and it saw dividends as a sign of impending 'respectability'. Nevertheless, the yield was still well below the sector average, as the price of the shares was buoyed up by the market's expectation of further growth.

The price/earnings ratio was also still very high. It was probably less than other new entrants in stage 1 of their lifecycles, but it was well above the industry average.

The dividend cover was much more stretched than in the first phase. Investors were starting to ask when the return on their investment would start to come through, and there was no room for the very high dividend cover of the earlier stage.

So, Phoneco's investor ratios for stage 2 were:

- yield   1.6 per cent
- price/earnings   25
- dividend cover   3.5

Stage 3: from 20 to 30 years

The company had achieved respectability. It was, at this stage, at the bottom end of the FTSE 100 companies. It was then a complicated company and the analysts were looking for good statements of strategy to prove that the current management could run a cruiser, having been very successful in managing fast patrol boats and destroyers.

Its share price varied with the changes in the industry. A bad regulatory change, for example, would endanger profit growth significantly. Long-term planning was no longer a luxury, but a vital responsibility of the Board and its advisers.

It had some 'big names' on its Board, with the possibility of an ex-cabinet minister joining its numbers.

The risk it was exposed to in this phase had changed in its nature. The company could afford to make some mistakes without threatening its actual life during this time as the market saw the risk as being comparable to that facing other stocks in the sector. Investors would see reports of sell-offs of one share in the sector and swaps into other companies in the same sector as being recommended.

The annual report and the Chairman's report

It is unlikely that the annual report would claim that everything was rosy. Shareholders would expect more circumspect statements with admissions of error and promises of remedies. A careful look at the ratios the Chairman would choose to report could be revealing. For example, if he produced a graph showing that in the past 25 years the share price has consistently out-performed the market index, he would probably be trying to reassure the market that there was still plenty of growth potential there. He would not want the growth in share price to stall, although it would certainly have slowed.

Like the professionals, the private investor would be looking for a confident statement of comprehensive and long-term goals and strategies.

The Chairman noted the following in his report.

'We see alliances with other companies as an important contributor to our vision to be the supplier of choice for people seeking high levels of features combined with international coverage.'

'New technologies offer enormous opportunities to broaden the services available to our current customers. The convergence of voice, music, graphics, video and data will radically alter the way we conduct our lives.'

'The reorganisation that we completed during the year has ensured that we can carry through our promises of presenting a global image and relationship with our key accounts worldwide.'

The financial ratios

The ratios had now reached the mature end of industry averages. Gearing was at the low-risk end and less than a third of profits were required to pay the interest bill.

The measure of return on capital employed was as meaningful and reliable as any other large company's, and reflected the sorts of returns that were expected from the whole sector as opposed to the rapid growth part of the sector. The relatively high pre-tax profit margin showed the built-in profitability of the telecommunications sector that could exploit its expensive investment in infrastructure for many, many years.

Phoneco's ratios for stage 3 were:

- gearing   100 per cent
- income gearing   30 per cent
- return on capital employed   20 per cent
- pre-tax profit margin   8 per cent.

The investors' ratios

The dividend was an important part of large investors' portfolio plans. The yield would therefore tend to be around the average for the sector and even for the whole market. The price/earnings ratio was, similarly, near the average for the sector.

The dividend cover had gone sharply down as investors had started to make the returns they were expecting at this stage in Phoneco's lifecycle.

Phoneco's investor ratios for stage 3 were, therefore:

- yield   4.0 per cent
- price/earnings   18
- dividend cover   1.9.

Stage 4: over 30 years

The Board was, at this point, commanding a battleship or a stately galleon. Shareholders had stopped looking for excitement in the share and wanted long-term promises regarding dividends and the delivery of these promises.

It was in the top 20 companies in the FTSE 100 index and had high-profile Chairman and non-executive directors. You would frequently have heard its Chairman on the TV and radio talking about the company's performance, the economic situation, the regulatory environment and other current affairs issues.

Representatives of the company had a lot of power over standards bodies and supplier policies. Someone from Phoneco was one of the panel in any debate with a telecommunications context, from virtual reality shopping to home working.

The salesforce now had more 'farmers' in it than 'hunters'. The company had well-founded key account management techniques in place to develop and protect market share.

You would probably have found the Chairman complaining about the view the stock market took of Phoneco's shares. The company liked to think it was a growth and innovation enterprise, while the market saw it as primarily a utility, with limited opportunities for the sort of growth that would make a significant difference to its profit stream.

The annual report and the Chairman's report

There was an emphasis in the report on benefits to customers. The company took its dominant place in a number of markets very seriously and was anxious to show that it was not exploiting this. Phoneco would boast of new offerings to its customers, lower prices and a generally better service than its competitors.

The Chairman said the following in his report.

> 'Steady growth of sales, 4 per cent, and earnings 5.5 per cent, demonstrated our progress towards meeting the expectations of both our shareholders and our customers.'
>
> 'Against this economic and competitive background, Phoneco's strategy remains clear. We will develop vigorously in our traditional markets and at the same time establish ourselves in new markets for advanced services, both in our traditional areas and new parts of the world.'

The financial ratios

The ratios were all safer than the industry average and at the top end of the benchmark. There was no question in the short term that the company could maintain its market and profit growth, limited though that was. Investors were wary for any signs of decline. Regulations and new competitors represented the biggest risk.

Phoneco had already shown good control of costs, but it was necessary for this to be a continuing phenomenon and reflected in the profit margins.

Phoneco's ratios for stage 4 were:

- gearing   60 per cent
- income gearing   20 per cent
- return on capital employed   25 per cent
- pre-tax profit margin   10 per cent

The investors' ratios

The share was, at this stage, in almost all pension and private portfolios. The expectation was for dividend progress rather than capital growth and the yield and dividend cover showed this. The yield was well above the average and dividend cover was at a low level. Dividend cover probably wanted to stay around this level, except if there was an exceptional item affecting profits.

The price/earnings ratio was the sign that the company was like a stately galleon.

Thus, Phoneco's investors ratios for stage 4 were:

- yield   5.9 per cent
- price/earnings   13.8
- dividend cover   1.5.

A summary of all stages

There now follows a summary of Phoneco's ratios for the four stages of its development. While not a scientific benchmark, it provides a reasonable benchmark guide that can be used to make a preliminary judgement about any company. Look at the company's position in the stages of development, and then at its ratios. Look for inconsistencies with the benchmark and investigate from there.

Phoneco's financial ratios for the four stages were:

gearing	500 per cent	200 per cent	100 per cent	60 per cent
income gearing	95 per cent	75 per cent	30 per cent	20 per cent
return on capital employed	1 per cent	10 per cent	20 per cent	25 per cent
pre-tax profit margin	1 per cent	4 per cent	8 per cent	10 per cent.

Phoneco's investors' ratios for the four stages were:

yield	0.3 per cent	1.6 per cent	4 per cent	5.9 per cent
price/earnings	35	25	18	13.8
dividend cover	13	3.5	1.9	1.5.

Conclusion

While recognising that all businesses and, indeed, all sectors have different characteristics, we can already see pigeonholes that we can use to sort one kind of company from another. They require little working out, but are very helpful in determining whether a particular share is likely to fit into a certain investment strategy.

Suppose, for example, that our three case study couples had all decided to put a telecommunications company into their portfolios. If they had no more information than is above, they could still see clearly which stage of the long-term growth of a telecommunications company suited their strategy.

The Fastlaners would prefer a stage 1 company. This would present them with more risk, but they have the time to wait for growth, and no need for dividend payments. The Lookaheads would probably prefer a company at stage 2 or 3. At the outset of their investment plan, they are happy to go for growth rather than income, but, as time passes, they recognise that they will need to bolster their capital growth with income. So they need, perhaps, a company at stage 2 to begin with and to alter to one at stage 3 when their first child actually goes to school.

The Getting-on-a-bits would probably opt for the stately galleon company, at stage 4. They do not want the thrills and spills of high gearing, and they certainly do not want investments without an income return.

Notice how easy it is to spot the type of company that will be preferred in a particular situation if you have access to the figures for the three investors' ratios and the four key financial ratios.

SCENARIO | **Darnley Village Investment Club look for shares to buy**

Following their strategy for a medium-risk share, the members are looking for a share in a FTSE mid 250 company. In terms of the shareholder ratios, they decide to look for a company that has a yield that is above average for the market and its sector and a price/earnings ratio that is about average or even below average. This should fit in with their 'Buy shares and generally hold on to them' policy, give them income for reinvestment in other shares, but still have the safety of a share that is not expected by the market to produce thrills and spills.

Until they have decided on the industry sector they want, this is as far as they can go.

EXERCISES FOR CHAPTER 3

Becoming familiar with financial information

If you do not already have them, you need to acquire a number of annual reports. There are two main ways that you can do this. The first is to ring up or write to the companies themselves. In most cases, the switchboard operator will understand your request and either put you through to someone in shareholder relations, who will take your name and address, or the operator will take your name and address. Do not forget that the annual report, for most companies, is part of their promotional material and they are happy enough to send out copies. To find the addresses and telephone numbers, you will need a guide, such as *The Company Guide*, published quarterly by Hemmington Scott, which will give you details of companies' head offices. This guide is available in most reference libraries.

Alternatively, you can use the FT Annual Reports service. Look at the stock market reports at the back of the 'Companies and markets' section of the paper. Where you see an ace of clubs in the 'Notes' column, this means that the company is a member of this service. At the bottom right of the right-hand page, you will see the details of this service. You need to ring a number and give the FT code for the day. You will then be sent a copy of the report you have requested by return. We have used this service many times and it has worked well.

EXERCISE 1
Choose a business sector which you wish to study. Looking in the financial pages of a newspaper, try to identify, by using the price/earnings and yield ratios, four companies that could fit into one or other of the four stages of the four stage model described via the case study of the company Phoneco earlier in this chapter. Get hold of the reports for these companies and calculate the four key ratios. You should see a correlation between all these numbers and the four stages of growth. Where you see inconsistency, try to explain it.

Remember that we are using broad benchmark guides at the moment, which will prove satisfactory in most cases but fail occasionally.

Advancing your investment strategy

EXERCISE 2   Add the key ratio characteristics of companies that you would like to include in your different risk profiles to your strategy triangle.

CHAPTER 4

Designing the portfolio and choosing sectors

A portfolio must have a good spread of business sectors as well as shares to protect it from the risk of overexposure to one industry

- Introduction
- Choosing sectors for investment
- Designing the portfolio
- Exercises

Choosing sectors depends on the timing of the investment in terms of the economic business cycle, the investor's specific knowledge of different industries and the investor's view of the prospects for the industry.

Introduction

The timing of an investment in shares is a product of a number of issues. The main one, of course, is your strategy as a whole. If you have decided to invest regularly, then you are best doing this whatever is happening in, for example, the economy. For contrarians, even what is happening in the market as a whole will not prevent the regular investment being made.

Having decided to invest in equities, the next decision is which business sector you wish to put money into. In the *Financial Times* there are seven main sectors divided into some 36 business subsectors. The main sectors are:

- mineral extraction

- general industry

- consumer goods

- services

- utilities

- financials

- investment trusts.

A decision to investigate potential investments in a particular sector and subsector will depend on two main issues: the position in the economic cycle and what could be called trends, fashions and your own knowledge.

We will examine these points before ending with some comments on the size and design of the whole portfolio.

Choosing sectors for investment

The ebbs and flows of business success do appear to come in cycles, following movements in inflation and interest rates. In the past, these cycles have each lasted for around five years. The government watches the growing economy for signs of overheating that, if left unchecked, would lead to the monster of inflation, which is a key driver of government economic policy.

The business cycle follows the economic cycle, and some companies do better at different times within the business cycle. It is therefore worth thinking about how the economic cycle happens and its impact on businesses generally and sectors in particular.

The position in the economic cycle

At the beginning of an economic cycle, when inflation has been relatively low and interest rates likewise, business is in a growth phase. Consumers spend more and save less, export markets prosper and what has become known by political commentators as the 'feel good factor' is on the up.

During this period, it is wise to be in equities. Company profits are growing, and are seen to have the potential to grow further into the future, via increased sales and low interest rates. Following this growth, companies will have the ability to increase dividends. This adds to their capital value and the market tends to rise.

Near the top of the business cycle, which occurs as interest rates have started to rise as a result of government's concern about inflation, some investors will get out of equities in preparation for a period of high interest rates. The rise in interest rates then gives them two benefits: the return on cash is improving and they are avoiding losses in the capital value of shares as the market recognises that higher interest rates are going to inhibit growth and damage profitability. They are also out of the market at a time of uncertainty.

At this time in the cycle, the behaviour of consumers has changed. They are less certain about their job security. They will cut back on spending and try to pay down borrowings that were all right when interest rates were low but are hurting now. This, among other factors, has the effect of slowing down economic growth, which was the government's intention.

When interest rates are at their height, the business cycle is about halfway down its declining curve. At that point, the government or the Bank of England will think about taking the bite out of borrowing by starting the process of reducing interest rates. It can do this at such a time because the fear of inflation is much less.

Investors call this phase the bond phase. They get into fixed rate government bonds that will appreciate in value as other interest rates drop. As interest rates approach their nadir, business starts to pick up and the cycle has started again.

The equity, cash, bond cycle-type of investment strategy may be very sensible for large institutions with billions of pounds in funds. They can make adjustments to the amount of equity, cash and bonds they hold in a way that takes advantage of this cycle. It is more difficult for private investors, who know that if they come out of equities altogether, it will cost them some 5–6 per cent of their equity savings because of the costs of selling to get out of the market and buying to get back in. We will look at this in more detail later, but suffice it to say for the moment that the costs of making dramatic moves in and out of the market, combined with the difficulties of predicting the business cycle, probably push private investors into a simpler strategy. They decide what percentage of their savings to hold in equities and how much they are going to invest on a regular basis. That decision made, they buy equities and hang on through good times *and* bad, knowing that, in the long run, their investments will meet the objective they have set.

The main reason the business cycle can, however, still be very important to such investors is that it has a bearing on the matter of choosing sectors and timing purchases. Before looking at that, we need to take a quick look at the real difficulties of forecasting what the economy is going to do, which is a principle reason for the private investor not to follow the equity, cash, bond cycle.

Forecasting the future

The economy does give indicators of what is likely to happen to companies and their profits, but drawing conclusions from such economic indicators is notoriously difficult.

Even the professional economists have a poor reputation for getting forecasts right. The proof of this is easy to see by comparing different institutions' forecasts at the same time. Even over the short term, economists rarely agree, and they cannot all therefore be right.

Another way of proving the difficulty of predicting a national economy is to look at the forecasts for a year near the start of the year itself. The FT publishes such surveys, collecting the forecasts only two months before the start of the year in question and testing their validity once the year has gone by. Generally, it finds that the average of the forecasts, let alone the worst ones, is well outside the actual performance of the economy. This is true of indicators such as growth, measured by gross domestic product, and the trade balance. They prove to be much better on matters that, in the short term, are easier to predict, such as inflation and unemployment.

Many private investors feel that their own observations as they look for clues are as good a way as any to tell the future. Private investors talk regularly to friends who are consumers and who will give them intimate details of their financial affairs and their feelings. These are the grass roots of the business cycle and will sometimes outperform the biggest computer and the cleverest graph in predicting the economic future.

Indicators are divided into groups according to whether they 'lead' or 'lag' the economic cycle or coincide with them. We will only deal with some of the leading indicators because, by definition, they can give some clues as to the direction of the economy and, therefore, of business. Indicators can also be divided into groups by the length of time they lead or lag the cycle. Longer-term leading indicators, as we have already seen, include money market interest rates. They also include housing starts and changes in business optimism, measured by surveys such as those done by the Confederation of British Industry (CBI). Normally well reported in the financial pages of newspapers, these indicators may tell us when to buy certain shares that start a growth phase that coincides with different points in the business cycle.

Shorter-term indicators are also well reported and include new car registrations, rises and falls in consumer credit and other survey information, such as new orders. Economists measure, in average terms, the length of time that a leading indicator precedes the predicted change in the business cycle, but life is rarely so predictable.

Nevertheless, the Darnley Village Investment Club generally spends a little time on the economic situation prior to selecting a business sector that it wishes to study. We can join them as they do this.

Darnley Village Investment Club choose a business sector

Chairman: 'It does seem that most of the economic data tends to support the view that things are getting better in a way that seems more sustainable than, say, the last time we pulled out of a deep recession.'

Keith: 'Yes, unemployment is down, public borrowing is slightly less than the Chancellor had predicted and the car industry is gearing up for its best year ever in terms of new car registrations. And that's just this country. In the States, the worries about interest rates are much less than they were, with the slow down in growth lessening concerns about inflation.'

Chairman: 'There is no consensus now that the next movement in interest rates in this country will be up the way. The politics of the thing, as well as the economic situation, make nothing certain.'

Diana: 'What does that mean to us? I mean, we've had the debate about 'Do we come out of equities entirely if it looks as though there could be a crash in the market' and agreed that the answer is "no". We're in for the long haul and, in the end, the dividend income and eventual rise in capital values will bring us back at least to where we are now. So why do we bother debating economics, about which none of us knows much?'

Chairman: 'Well, it may influence our thinking about which sector to go into next. Where we are in the business cycle often makes the timing of investing in some shares significant. The problem is that we're all very unsure where we are in the business cycle at the moment. How long before interest rates start to rise? How long before consumers start to worry about their spending again? How high will house price inflation go? And we *have* to look some way ahead, because the market does.

'Suppose we assume that there are three more years of good growth coming along, then that will tend to push us into cyclical sectors, such as building and construction or even chemicals. Chemicals provides a very good example of a highly cyclical sector. At the moment, the sector is suffering a bit as people get jittery about whether or not the good times are coming to an end. That could make the timing of a buy into chemicals an interesting proposition. Similarly, precious metals have also started to wobble badly during the past year as the market sensed the business downturn. Precious metals obviously tend to fall at the thought of recession and rise some time before the boom or upturn comes along.'

Iain: 'Remember what type of share we are due to buy. It's a medium-risk share with good yield and a price/earnings ratio that is below the market average. We are looking for something a bit speculative but with our usual caution about how much risk to take with the underlying capital. This will tend to make us bet against the received wisdom about the business cycle and popular sectors. I like your analysis, Chairman, and would be prepared to go along with it. It even emphasises our wish to act like contrarians. What we would be doing is betting that the economy has further to go at a time when the institutions think they should be in cash and private investors are worrying about a major market correction down the way.'

Notice how difficult it is to keep to one reason for buying. It is inevitable that for one issue that pushes you towards a sector, there will be another that confirms or goes against such a decision. The club is picking a sector because of the position in the business cycle, but also they're looking for a share that is potentially undervalued and has a good yield.

Another way of looking at sectors is in terms of their defensive qualities. Defensive qualities are those attributes of a company that make it less prone to follow the business cycle, mainly because it is difficult, or impossible, to do without certain products and services. Companies that sell such products and services tend to be independent of the business cycle and have high security of earnings. The utilities, food retailers and food manufacturers are obvious members of this group, as are breweries and companies making household goods.

The opposite of this group have earnings streams that are in the 'nice to have' category for most consumers. *In extremis*, they can do without them. The obvious contenders here are leisure and hotels, engineering (vehicles), transport and media.

This leaves the rather variable earnings of banks, general retailers and others. They are difficult to place in one of the two categories above.

It is very tempting when starting a portfolio to opt for defensive sectors. Do not forget that, although you are picking a defensive sector, you can still choose a share that is in your medium- or high-risk category. Pharmaceuticals are in the defensive sector with a high degree of earnings certainty. But the up-and-coming pharmaceutical company may be extremely risky in its early stages. Your risk model will keep you on the straight and narrow as regards the bedrock of your portfolio.

Later on, once you have developed a good spread of shares in different sectors you are more likely to look at cyclical shares and those with more exposed earning streams. The reason for this comes back to the risk and return correlation.

So much for the influence of the business cycle on the choosing of sectors. There are other considerations.

Trends, fashions and your own knowledge

These are popular ways of choosing industries that the private investor thinks will do well. It is a matter of simple observation. You see a slight growth in the number of 'For Sale' signs in your street. Combine this with dinner party chat that reveals that a number of the guests would like to move but do not think they could sell their house at a price that would enable them to buy what they want. Such a trend will eventually affect the price of the shares of companies that do well in a rising house market with a relatively high number of properties changing hands.

A change in fashion in house decoration may give a clue as to when it is appropriate to make a move on building materials and merchants. In the 1960s and 1970s, it was very fashionable to rip the fireplaces out of Victorian and Edwardian houses while installing central heating. In the middle of the 1980s it was difficult to buy these things, which had been dumped as worthless only a few years earlier.

Such fashions are easy to spot with hindsight, but some very good choices of sector have been made on such slight foundations as noticing that the vogue for Artexing ceilings had given way to replasterboarding them. Also, the sudden rise of the fax machine and mobile phone made money for those who acted early enough. That, of course, is the nub of the opportunity: you have to see a fashion or trend *before* it is the subject of numerous press reports and special documentaries.

Choosing a sector by predicting trends and fashions is probably more likely if it is combined with your own expertise.

While it is not possible to be as knowledgeable about a company as its managers, your own job and other experience can give you an edge over other investors whose only source of information is published documents.

Whatever department you are in, you should be able to judge the strategy of your business and the likelihood that the sector it is in is on an upturn or not. We are talking here about the general health of the sector rather than any specific pieces of information. Buying shares when in possession of price-sensitive information that is not available publicly can be construed as insider dealing and this is illegal.

Your knowledge of the sector may lead you to buy your own company's shares, if you do not already own some as a result of a share purchase scheme. It may also lead you to buy shares in a competitor.

Look also for clues outside the sector that your business is in. In dealing with the people who work for your suppliers and customers, you will frequently receive well-informed general opinions about their industry sectors. If the factories are already working flat out to make the new product and the advertising budgets to promote it are fat, then you are too late. You have to see – some would say smell – what could happen in the future. In all this, though – we will say it once more to be sure – beware insider dealing.

Choosing a number of sectors leads to a reduction in risk and is an essential part of portfolio planning. If you have all your money in the technology sector, say, then you will have periods when it is doing very well. However, when that sector pauses for breath, you will have problems if your income and capital growth are so concentrated. Thus, we need to choose a number of sectors and, within them, a number of shares. It is time to consider just how many.

Designing the portfolio

We have now expanded our original identification of types of risk involved in equity investment. To market risk and specific company risk we have added *sector risk*. By sector risk we mean that, from time to time, some whole sectors will move against the market trend. This is reported every day in the *Financial Times*, which prints the winners and losers from the day before. However, how many sectors should we have shares in to achieve good diversification that protects us from individual problems?

In the rest of the book, we are going to work out how to choose companies that are likely to do well and offer good value to a buyer. However, often the sudden fall of a share or even the collapse of a company that passed all the tests of value occurs not because the business fundamentals were misrepresented or the analysis incorrect, but because there was a catastrophe that could not have been predicted from inside the company, let alone outside. High-profile incidences of this kind have occurred in the banking and financial sectors, where large sums of money have been found to have been lost due to the negligence or fraudulent behaviour of one of the bank's staff.

The movement to personal computers was a competitive move that the suppliers of mainframe computers did not believe would happen so quickly. Their shareholders paid for their overconfidence.

The same sometimes occurs positively. Obtaining a huge contract, discovering a new drug or inventing the next phase of software development can all lead to a sudden blossoming of a company and a sharp rise in its share price. When we diversify a portfolio it is to hedge the risk of failure with the possibility of success. In essence, diversification attempts to eliminate the risk specific to a company by balancing one possible outcome with another.

SCENARIO ## A business opportunity

The Queen and the President of the USA are due to pass down The Mall in London one summer's day. You have been offered the ice-cream concession. This would mean that you would be the only company selling ice-creams to the huge crowds expected to attend the walkabout. Given a hot day, you will make a fortune.

Alternatively, you could choose the umbrella concession, which will make a fortune if unexpected rain starts just before the event and continues throughout.

A good example of diversification would be to take *both* concessions rather than just one. It would mean more expense and therefore less profit, but more or less guarantees a successful venture.

If you reduce specific risk, then you are left, mainly, with market risk, over which you have no control. At some point, any further diversification will not add to your insurance against tragedy. There can be no hard and fast rule about this, but the following table gives a good indication as to the number of shares and sectors the average portfolio will have. Table 4.1, is the portfolio of the Lookaheads after some ten years.

Table 4.1 How the Lookaheads' portfolio looks after ten years

Sectors	No. of companies held	Cost	Percentage of total
Gas distribution	3	£10,376	17.4
Pharmaceuticals	2	£8,219	13.8
Healthcare	2	$8,067	13.6
Telecommunications	1	$5,636	9.5
Food producers	2	$5,030	8.5
Retailers, general	2	£4,836	8.1
Spirits, wines and ciders	2	£4,795	8.1
American Investment Trust	1	£4,760	8.0
Chemicals	2	£4,587	7.7
Building and construction	2	£3,132	5.3
	19	£59,438	100.0

Notice how the Lookaheads have generally invested larger sums in the defensive sectors. With their 10 sectors and 19 companies, there is a very reasonable spread of risk. Indeed, some people would say that it is not necessary to increase the number of shares held, and that the Lookaheads should concentrate on timing their acquisition of more shares in the same companies.

By the time the portfolio contains 19 different shares, the further spreading to more companies and sectors has much less impact on the degree of risk in the portfolio than it would have had earlier on. We will return to this in Chapter 9, but, for the moment, consider that if you double the number of shares from one to two, you are, if you have chosen the shares properly, roughly halving your risk. If you go from 99 shares to 100, you are not affecting your risk in any significant way.

It is generally accepted in the textbooks that between 15 and 20 shares achieves the objective of reducing company-specific risk to a level that gives satisfactory cover.

Darnley Village Investment Club and conglomerates

After due consideration, the members decide to buy shares in a company that has the characteristics of a conglomerate. In many ways, a conglomerate performs the process of diversification for you. The portfolio does not have one at present and, although conglomerates appear to be somewhat unfashionable at the time of the decision (the main talk is of 'getting back to core business'), it appeals to the Club's habit of behaving as contrarians.

The sector has somewhat underperformed in the market in the last few years. It has slightly shrunk in size, (measured by market capitalisation) as a number of large companies have been broken up and sold to more specialised companies.

The members note that the yield for the whole market is 3.52 per cent, whereas in the conglomerate sector – called in the financial pages 'Diversified industrials' – yield is 3.91 per cent. The average price/earnings ratio for the sector is 15.16 – a fairly low ratio compared to the rest of the market, which is 18.29. This reflects the role diversified companies can play in reducing risk by avoiding overexposure to a limited number of product types and markets.

A member finds Sherwood Industries. Its vital statistics are:

- market capitalisation   £280,000,000
- yield   5.9 per cent
- price/earnings ratio   12.9
- share price   150p.

The high and low points in the share price for the previous 52 weeks were 205p and 140p, respectively.

All these numbers make it a suitable choice for the Club. The share is towards its low at a time when most of those in the market are nearer their highs – another small step towards being a contrarian. The yield and price/earnings ratios are ideal and the market capitalisation places it at the bottom end of the FTSE mid 250.

The club now needs a copy of the company's annual report and one of the members is detailed to get this.

EXERCISES FOR CHAPTER 4

Becoming familiar with financial information

EXERCISE 1   Where do you think the economy is right now in the business cycle? What sorts of shares would be appropriate for what sort of investor in those circumstances?

EXERCISE 2   Using your own knowledge, define an area of business growth and, having thought through the implications of that growth, choose an industry sector that is growing.

Advancing your investment strategy

EXERCISE 3   If the sector you chose in Exercise 2 does not fit into or diversify your portfolio, choose another for whatever you regard as appropriate reasons.

EXERCISE 4   Remembering the profile of the company that you identified at the end of Chapter 3, find at least four companies that more or less fit that bill in your chosen sector. Make a request for their annual reports, either from the companies themselves or from the FT annual report service (see page 72).

EXERCISE 5   Write down the sector, number of shares held and planned value in each sector for your portfolio. If it is large enough, do it for the current time, but if it is still growing, work out projected figures for, say, three years ahead.

CHAPTER 5

What makes companies thrive?

Describing the potential of a company in words

- Annual reports
- Conclusion
- Exercises

Before investors peer into the murky waters of a company's finances, they should get an overall view of the company and its future from the annual report. In this chapter, we will concentrate on the textual part of annual reports.

Annual reports
·······················

The Chairman and directors of a company use the annual report as an advertising document as well as the means with which to satisfy legal reporting requirements. They are unlikely to open with a sentence such as 'We made a lot of mistakes this year and have to own up to a performance far below the potential of the business.' Scything through the propaganda is possible, however, for one very important reason. Unless engaged in actual fraud – luckily a remote possibility – they are bound to stick to the truth, albeit in its most acceptable form. The 'spin' is there, but, in most cases, a little detective work will reveal what we need to know.

Remember also that probably the key performance measure of a Chairman is their ability to deliver to the plan. This means announcing what the future of the business should be and then achieving it. This achievement of expectations is a principal concern of shareholders who have, as we have seen, set a strategy and decided on the type and qualities they want in a company they are investing in. The shareholders acknowledge, of course, that there is a risk that not all of these expectations will be delivered.

It is for this reason that you will, from time to time, hear of profit warnings. A Chairman who realises that the company is not going to be as profitable as they led the shareholders and analysts to expect, will tell them the moment the information is clear and the likelihood that the company will underperform is high.

This is particularly important in the case of dividends, which shareholders have been led to expect from previous performance or a statement of dividend strategy from the Board. In order to meet expectations on dividends, the company has to deliver to expectations in terms of profit and cash. It needs the profit to cover the costs of the dividends and what it requires to secure the future of the business, and it needs the cash to actually pay out the dividends. Shareholders will not take it in any other form and a bouncing dividend cheque is highly unpopular!

In Appendix 1 you will find the report and accounts for Sherwood Industries. Sherwood Industries is not a real company. It has things in common with a number of companies because it draws from real life, but it does not actually exist. We have also slightly simplified the report from real-life ones as this makes it easier to explain. One of the biggest differences with reality is the fact that we only report on the Group in the balance sheet. Real reports also report on the Company because it is the Company that is the legal entity in which shareholders invest. We will deal only with the Group statements here, however, as these give a much clearer picture of the day-to-day trading position of the enterprise.

For the sake of example, the case of Sherwood Industries contains these and some other simplifications. It does, however, conform to current legislation in almost every way. Some of the wordier parts, such as the text on corporate governance, are treated separately for the sake of clarity. Throughout this book, Sherwood Industries gives us the opportunity to transfer theory into practice.

Let us start with the front cover (see Figure 5.1). Notice how the statement of intent has been put on the front cover. It is a key vision and strategy statement, sometimes called a mission statement.

We can examine this vision statement in more detail and go on to compare it with similar, real-life examples. In the next few pages we will examine Tomkins and BT.

It is the intention of Sherwood Industries to grow a profitable business, diverse in its activities to reduce overexposure to particular products or markets, but having synergy between and within product groups.

Fig. 5.1 The front cover of Sherwood Industries' annual report

Sherwood Industries' vision statement

The statement shown in Figure 5.1 cleverly combines the benefits of a conglomerate – 'to reduce overexposure to particular products or markets' – with the more fashionable intention to build on core businesses, synergies and strengths – often called vertical integration. It is a slightly unusual vision and we will have to look carefully at the strategy for making it happen.

Already we can formulate questions that the report should answer, at least to some extent.

● Is the vertical integration real or a thought tacked on to pay lip-service to the fashion for returning to core business and the disposal of diversified divisions?

● How dependent is the diversification on acquisition?

● Is there a sensible structure that ensures that some managers are responsible for the current operation but others have time to look outside for opportunities?

● If you take a moment to think about the statement, you will come up with other good questions to ask. We should find that most of them are answered by the rest of the report.

If you look at the annual reports of a company for each of the last few years, you can actually trace the progress of the business, and the pressures that are being pushed onto managers, from the statements on the front cover or inside the front cover. Some of these are, to be honest, so broad in their range that they are virtually meaningless. In such a case, we would have to go further into the report to find out management's actual intentions. Mostly, however, even when the statement seems banal, it does tell us something that the rest of the report must back up consistently.

Here are two good examples of broad statements from which we can derive a number of good questions. What can you make of these?

Tomkins

'Tomkins is an industrial company dedicated to the revitalisation of underdeveloped businesses and their sustained growth.

'This is achieved by selective acquisition from a diverse range of low-risk technology manufacturing companies with unrealised potential.

'Acquired companies are revitalised as autonomous businesses by means of the injection of management expertise, capital for development and the application of tight financial disciplines.'

The second statement is broader still, but gives us the opportunity to understand the thrust of the Board and test its ability to deliver by reading the rest of the report.

EXAMPLE   ## BT

'BT's mission, our central purpose, is to provide world-class telecommunication and information products and services, and to develop and exploit our networks, at home and overseas, so that we can:

● meet the requirements of our customers

● sustain growth in the earnings of the group on behalf of our shareholders

● make a fitting contribution to the community in which we conduct our business.'

It can be rewarding to look at a number of consecutive annual reports for a company and to detect the switches in emphasis that have taken place from the first statements in the report, either on the cover or just inside. In the case of Sherwood Industries, the company was in the rapid growth stage four or five years ago, and then the plea on the front page concerned growth and volume in the current businesses. It then went through the earnings per share period, when the Board was stating that it wanted volume, but also intended to use the existing assets better and produce an improving profit stream. Now it is about growth by acquisition and the formation of a holding company with subsidiary divisions that are separate but some synergy connects them all up. This should leave the holding Board to look for ways to expand.

Page 1 is the table of contents and is reproduced in Figure 5.2. This chapter will look at all the sections of the report listed up to the financial statements. We will describe typical reports and work on Sherwood Industries' report. It is a good idea to have a real annual report to look at so that you can see how what you learn about Sherwood Industries is reflected in an actual report.

Annual report for the year ended 31 December

Contents

	Page
Financial calendar	1
Notice of meeting	2
Directors and advisers	3
The Chairman's annual review	4
Report of the directors	6
Review of operations	8
Directors' responsibilities	10
Auditors' report to the members of Sherwood Industries	11
Consolidated profit and loss account	12
Consolidated balance sheet	13
Cash flow statement	14
Statement of total recognised gains and losses	14
Statement of accounting policies and notes to the accounts	15
Group financial record	23
Operating divisions and principal subsidiaries	24

Financial calendar

Annual general meeting	9 April this year
Ordinary share register closed	28 April this year
Interim report – this year	August this year
Preliminary results – this year	February next year
Publication of this year's accounts	March next year
Dividend payment dates	
Final – last year	June this year
Interim – this year	November this year
Final – this year	June next year

Fig. 5.2 Page 1 of Sherwood Industries' annual report

The financial calendar

Sherwood Industries' annual report, page 1

The financial calendar (see the lower part of Figure 5.2) shows when dividend payments are made and the dates of the half-yearly and final announcements of the company's results. It will sometimes have the dates when advertisements will go into the newspapers giving a summary of performance for the quarter, half or full year.

Importantly, it also has the time when the shares will go ex-dividend, which is when the ordinary share register closes on 30 April. In order to simplify the payment of dividends to holders of shares, there is a period of time (normally between four and eight weeks) when shares are ex-dividend. If you buy shares during the time they are ex-dividend – or xd as it is written in the financial pages – the very next dividend payable will be paid to the person who held the share when it went xd. You will then receive the next payment, assuming you hold the share at least until it goes xd the next time round. In the case of Sherwood Industries, the calendar shows that the final dividend will be paid some weeks later, in June.

Dates of payment of dividends and the date of the last time the share went xd are given in the *Financial Times* on Mondays, as is the dividend paid in the previous 12 months in pence per share. Shares always go xd on Mondays and the price is adjusted down to allow for the fact that new shareholders will wait longer for their first dividend.

In some reports, there will be further data for shareholders on this page, often including the address and telephone number so existing and potential shareholders can ask for more information.

To follow the rest of the Sherwood Industries report you need to turn to Appendix 1 periodically as you read the rest of this chapter.

Notice of meeting

Sherwood Industries' annual report, page 2

A lot of annual reports contain the notice and agenda for the annual general meeting (AGM). If it is not in the report, it is probably sent out with it. The AGM is an opportunity for shareholders, no matter how small their holding, to listen to and question the senior officers of the company. Generally uncontroversial, they provide a useful forum for the Board to inform the shareholders of the way ahead and to set expectations of performance. It is also a useful forum for shareholders to 'eyeball' the directors and decide if they feel their investment is in safe hands.

The agenda in Sherwood Industries' report is typical. Any controversy there is will tend to occur in the first item, which concerns the acceptance of the directors' report and statement of accounts. At this point the shareholders can ask tricky questions about the amount the Board is paying itself or deal with matters of morality, such as supplying arms, or the protection of the environment. Indeed, many pressure groups deliberately buy shares in companies so that they can go to the AGMs and gain publicity for things of which they disapprove. Such meetings hit the headlines but are very untypical of AGMs, which are normally quiet affairs where the Board makes its presentations, the resolutions are passed unanimously and the meeting ends untendentiously with coffee and biscuits.

It is highly unlikely that any resolutions proposed by the Board will not be accepted. This is because, although there is a show of hands at the meeting, if the Board were to lose, it would then insist on a vote of all the shareholders present and not present. As they will have agreed the resolutions in advance with any major shareholders, who may control, say, 30 per cent of the votes, there is no doubt that the Chairman will get them through. Simply put, most chairmen have in their back pockets millions of votes before they even go near the AGM.

The higher profile of some aspects of corporate governance nowadays can make the AGM an opportunity for large shareholders to voice concerns and affect the running of the company. They are much more likely, however, to do this behind closed doors rather than courting controversy and possibly bad publicity at the public meeting.

It is at the AGM, or sometimes at an extraordinary general meeting called specially, that resolutions, for example, to issue more shares, are passed by the shareholders where their agreement is required.

If you have never done it, it is a good idea to attend one or two AGMs just to listen to how the people at the top of large organisations talk and present the affairs of their companies.

Directors and advisers

Sherwood Industries' annual report, page 3

Commonly this section contains exactly what it says. It has a list of the directors, quite often accompanied by well-produced studio photographs, and gives their roles in the company. For example, many companies and almost all large ones, will have a number of non-executive directors. These are not full-time executives in the company, but directors who are paid fees, not salaries, for preparing for and attending Board meetings. They also carry out agreed actions on the basis of their specialist knowledge or business, government or other important contacts.

A subset of the Board will be on the remuneration committee, which decides on the salaries to be offered to the directors and some senior managers. The members of this committee, often all the non-executive directors, will be identified on this page.

In the case of Sherwood Industries, there is a small holding Board at the top level consisting of three executives and three non-executives. As we will see further into the report, it is small because the company has just reorganised to empower the directors of the subsidiary companies to run the day-to-day affairs of their divisions, leaving the small holding Board to concentrate on strategy. More of this later.

Other information on this page includes the name of the Company Secretary, the address of the office where the company is officially registered and the name of the auditors. Sherwood Industries' report also lists, not unusually, the company's registrars – the people, or company, as in this case, who maintain the list of current shareholders and their bankers. Notice how large companies will have more than one banker to maintain the requirement for competitive performance.

The remainder of the information concerns the company's legal advisers, merchant bankers and the name of its stockbrokers. This last item can be important. The report of an analyst discussing a company that you will see referred to in the papers or you can obtain will probably be a stockbroker's report. It is important to know if it is the company's stockbroker or someone more independent who has written this report.

The Chairman's statement

Sherwood Industries' annual report, page 4

Called in Sherwood Industries' report The Chairman's annual review, this is always a key description of the intentions of the company. It is impossible to predict what will be in any particular statement, except that the Chairman will pick out the critical issues in the recent past and in the future. Often these critical issues are what shareholders have to form an opinion on.

The following are almost always covered in the Chairman's statement:

- last year's financial performance

- dividends

- the way ahead

- structure and people.

Last year's financial performance

Normally stated in terms of growth of sales and profits, this sets the scene for our analysis work.

EXAMPLE

Past performance at Sherwood Industries

The Chairman reports that sales were up substantially, but that pre-tax profits were down. He shows that the increase in sales was mainly because of the new Healthcare Division and helps us to understand where the Board sees the future – healthcare and electronics.

He has not really explained *yet* why pre-tax profits are lower, although we can infer that when you construct a new division and take over new companies, there is likely to be at least a temporary dip in profits. He moves on to explain why after-tax profits are also down by an even greater percentage than pre-tax profits – the unusually low tax burden in the previous year flattered last year.

The next two paragraphs describe how the business has changed over the last few years, what businesses the company has got out of and how its new structure of four divisions is going to work. He has already answered one of the questions we asked as a result of reading the sentence on the front of the report. 'Is there a sensible structure that ensures that some managers are responsible for the current operation but others have time to look outside for opportunities?'

He then picks a critical issue and comments on it. If you are going to grow a company by acquisition, you need quick access to money in order to seize opportunities as they arise. He comments immediately on his gearing and explains that, as it is low, he is in a position to get hold of capital quickly. Incidentally, when we get to the section where we calculate the company's gearing from the balance sheet, we will find it is not quite as good as stated here. The way he expresses gearing is fair but not as hard a test as the one to which we will put his balance sheet – a good example of the PR nature of the report and a good reason for our needing to learn to do these calculations ourselves rather than take them from material companies publish.

Also, as part of the historical performance, the Chairman will normally comment on the main trading issues of the past year. He or she will put them into the context of the economic situation in the main countries where the company does business and mention other factors outside the Board's control that have had an impact, normally a negative impact, on the past year's performance.

EXAMPLE Trading activities at Sherwood Industries

Notice how the Chairman deals with a part of the business that performed badly last year. There are two cases, Bradbury Pollock and Roland Bright Refiners. In both cases, we are told why things went wrong and, most importantly, what the Board has done to correct the problem. Once again, we have to use our common sense and business skills to make our own minds up whether or not the corrective action proposed will do the trick. He is extremely unlikely to say that the Board has no idea what to do and is hoping for the best.

Then he looks on the bright side and talks about the acquisitions in healthcare and what he regards as the major opportunities in this area. If we do not believe that it is timely to build a business in healthcare, we already know that this is not the share for us.

Dividends

In almost all cases, in the Chairman's statement you will see a comment that conveys the increase or decrease in dividends proposed this year, and this can be read as the Board's strategy for dividends in the future. We noted earlier that the biggest sin a Chairman can commit is to give shareholders surprises. This is particularly true where expectations regarding dividends are concerned.

EXAMPLE

Dividends at Sherwood Industries

We can understand from what is said here that while the Board would like to keep increasing the dividends annually, it will not do it if profits have not increased beforehand. It is more usual for the interim dividend to be held back in case the second half does not perform to expectations. Then, when the full year is known the dividends for the year can be announced.

As he raised the interim dividends, the Chairman was obviously expecting to be able to do better on the dividends for the whole year than he is now able. We are going to have to be convinced later in the report that the profitability is coming back or we may have to doubt if the current dividends can be maintained, let alone increased.

The way ahead

The Chairman here picks out the vital issues involved in the next period of trading. Look carefully at this as you are going to have to feel confident that the issue is actually what will drive performance and that you agree with the strategy suggested. In the case of Sherwood Industries, the section headed 'Prospects' is simply a summary of thoughts that have been expressed earlier.

In most reports the 'Prospects' section will reveal what the company believes is its main competitive advantage. Once again, you are going to have to decide whether or not it is a real advantage and, if it is an advantage, that it is relevant to future prospects. You can do this if you have some insight into the particular industry. Any private investor in any case can observe the world and think through what is likely to give companies competitive edge.

Structure and people

At this stage in the statement, it is very likely that chairmen will comment on the company structure and the quality of the company's people. They record their thanks to their people and end with a rallying cry for continuing hard work and success.

By the end of the Chairman's statement we will have a good idea of the financial summary of the previous year and the company's strategy for the future.

Report of the directors

Sherwood Industries' annual report, page 6

This report will contain a number of matters required by law. It may also include statements from the directors on the position of the company in a number of areas.

Principal activities

This is, as it suggests, a short statement of the principal businesses the group is in. As is usual, the paragraph in Sherwood Industries' report refers us to the more detailed review that we will find in later pages headed 'Review of operations'.

What is interesting about the Sherwood Industries example is that we should be able to detect the synergy of product groups mentioned on the front cover. Quoting part of it, it said 'but having synergy between and within product groups.' Well, up to a point. You will have to make up your own mind if the case for this is made.

Results and dividends

This is a full statement of the profit and dividend figures. This underlines the fact that the interim dividend was increased but the final dividend was left the same. The shareholders had almost no increase last year. This may or may not be important. It is more understandable in a situation where the company is looking for speedy growth by acquisition.

Research and development

The Board obviously considers the expenditure on research and development to be significant. It does not, however, say at this point how much it actually was. There is a statement on page 15 to the effect that R&D is written off during the current year, which is good housekeeping. Later in the notes to the accounts we will see the actual amount of money spent. From these two statements, we will form a view about whether or not it is spending enough in this area for a company of this type.

In the case of high-tech companies, for example, it is known that an expenditure of say 10 per cent of turnover on R&D is necessary just to keep the company up to date with its competitors' products or to maintain its competitive edge.

Land and buildings

Property is held on the Sherwood Industries' balance sheet at depreciated historic cost. The directors are confirming that this value approximates to its current use value as factories or offices. Notice the careful use of the word 'aggregate'. The Board is saying that while there might be some discrepancies about individual buildings, the overall value can be read as reasonable. Most major companies will re-value their land and property on a regular basis. We have not done this in the case of Sherwood Industries to maintain simplicity.

Acquisitions

This paragraph reveals the details about the Coden Laboratories. The deal was done for cash.

In a lot of acquisitions, there is a combination of cash and 'earn out'. A deferred payment of, say, 25 per cent of the pre-tax profits of the business for the next five years is offered to the previous owners. Such a deal is struck in order to maintain their interest in the success of the company for at least five years. This is beneficial to both sides, assuming that an accurate agreement has been reached on the real profitability of the taken over company now, and good estimates of its future potential. There have been some bad cases where acquiring companies have linked so much of the company's future profits to earn outs that the business itself has suffered. It is to be remembered that, however tight the rules of due diligence are in revealing the details of your business to a potential buyer, the people best placed to really understand the nuts and bolts of a business are always the managers who have been running it in the past.

In the case of Sherwood Industries, however, the whole payment was made in cash.

Directors

At this point there is a series of items of information about the directors, their resigning by rotation and how many shares they have in the company. There are also reassurances that the directors will honour the period of time when they are not allowed to purchase or sell shares. This period coincides with the time leading up to the announcement of interim and final figures. It is important that the Board does not deal at that time because, plainly, they have inside knowledge of the affairs of the company about to be made public. This would give them an enormous advantage over the rest of the market.

In the case of Sherwood Industries, we can see that the directors have neither bought nor sold shares during the last year. We also here get our first clue that the founding family is still involved with the company. The Chairman is Walter Sherwood and, unless there is a huge coincidence, which would probably be mentioned here, he is either the founder or a member of the founding family. The following paragraph reveals that he owns some 7.5 per cent of the shares, a significant shareholding but not one that gives him the great power of a holding of say 35 per cent or more.

A quick note on the 7½ per cent unsecured loan stock. We have seen that the capital of a company is a combination of share capital and loan capital. Loan stock, sometimes called debentures, are a sort of mezzanine floor between the two. On the one hand it very much has the characteristics of a loan, in that it has an interest payment attached not dividends, and it has, at some point in the future, to be repaid. The difference is that the loan stock, which has fixed interest, is traded on the Stock Exchange. Its market value will fluctuate partly according to the fortunes of the company and its likelihood of being able to honour its obligations for repayment, but more according to variations in interest rates. If general interest rates go down, then the value of loan stock will tend to rise as it has a fixed rate of interest. There are many variations on the theme of loan stock that can be issued in many different ways, as long as the characteristics of the loan are made plain to the original lenders and subsequent purchasers of the stock.

In many reports, rather than having the interests of the directors stated at this point, there is a reference to where this information can be found further into the report.

Shareholdings

Any person or institution that owns more than 3 per cent of a public company is detailed in the annual report. This item is particularly interesting in the case of Sherwood Industries as there are three very large holdings indeed, apart from Walter Sherwood's. What are the implications of the fact that the total holdings of Fremont Investment Trust, Reliable Assurance, Public Utilities Pension Fund and Mr Sherwood himself come to 31.2 per cent?

The major benefit to the Board is that it can very quickly get the attitudes of a third of the shareholders to a proposed action. Suppose, for example, that the Board wished to issue more share capital to pay for a new acquisition. With these shareholdings, in just three telephone calls Mr Sherwood can get an important feeling for how the shareholders are going to react. This helps him to move fast, a matter of importance in the speedy world of mergers and acquisitions.

It also means that if Mr Sherwood keeps these three shareholders up to date and 'on side' with his plans, then he can enjoy a relatively trouble-free relationship with his shareholders.

The downside of such an arrangement, from the Board's point of view, is that if any or all of the big three lose confidence in the Board's running of the business, they can equally quickly put plans in motion to change the behaviour of the Board or even change the Board itself.

If we are going very deeply into the affairs of Sherwood Industries, we may wish to check the investment policy of the Freemont Investment

Trust. A holding of such a size is probably there for the long term, but obviously if the Trust felt overweight in the share and wished to dispose of some or all of it, that would be a huge overhang of shares in the market and would depress the share price for possibly a considerable length of time.

Employment of disabled persons

There is frequently a statement at this point about the company's employment practices. Shareholders need to be sure that the Board is operating lawfully as regards employment and is unlikely to behave in a way that could bring it into conflict with individuals or trade unions. Sherwood Industries mentions disabled persons specifically, while other reports will talk about equal opportunities for women and ethnic minorities.

Employee involvement

It has become a cliché to say that the most important asset the company has is its people. (This is sometimes, ironically enough, found in a report that also talks about a large downsizing operation during the year in question.)

The directors will therefore make some reference to the way they treat their people. In the case of Sherwood Industries, they emphasise their communication policy, which is to keep employees up to date. One could imagine that the Board considers this important in an environment where lots of change is taking place. In Sherwood Industries, businesses are being bought and sold frequently. If staff are not kept in touch with what is going on, they could become nervous about their own positions. This leads to uncertainty and threatens performance. Another reason we should be glad that the Board emphasises this point is that it is linked to the restructuring mentioned in the Chairman's statement. One of the first questions that we asked after reading only the front page was whether or not the management structure would allow one group of people to run the day-to-day business while others looked after the strategy and searched for and found the types of businesses they wished to acquire. Here is some recognition from management that they at least know that this is an issue.

Other Boards may talk about the amount of training their people go through, if this is significant to their industry, or how well the company looks after people if their circumstances change – if they are injured or have personal problems for example.

The job of the potential shareholder is to decide whether or not the Board has policies in place that give a fair deal to both employees and shareholders and, most importantly, that look to the future.

While these statements about employment policies may seem obvious and even banal, we must remember that it is generally the completely unexpected that normally dramatically impacts a company's share price down the way. If a bank finds that a rogue trader has lost it some £50 million the share price will fall dramatically, not only because of the £50 million, but also because it reveals a lack of sufficiently tight controls. Similarly, if the world discovers that the company is using child labour abroad or is taking risks with health and safety regulations, then the effect on the share price could be significant. We need to know that the Board is aware of, and taking seriously, all its obligations.

Charitable donations

The directors report on money that they have given to charity or as political donations. This is a very sensitive area where a lot of shareholders think that it is not the job of a corporation to make such donations and that it should be left up to individuals, shareholders or not, to make their own decisions. Strangely enough, although the figure here is normally extremely small in relation to the finances of the company, it can be a point that is contentious and discussed at the annual general meeting.

Policy on the payment of creditors

This is as it says. It describes how the company agrees with suppliers the terms of their payment by Sherwood Industries. In the pipeline is a requirement to publish the settlement period of the company reporting. This will show how many days, on average, the company takes to pay its bills.

Auditors

A company's auditors have to be reappointed every year or replaced by others by a resolution at the AGM. The Board makes clear their intentions in this regard in their report.

Conclusion to the Report of the directors

The report is signed by the Company Secretary, who generally has some legal training and, in smaller companies, may very well be the most senior legal officer in the company.

Other items that you will find in this section of the report include references to resolutions, particularly with regard to the issuing of shares, that the Board intends to take to the AGM. At present, it also often includes a reference to how the company's shares are going to be traded in the future given the movement towards electronic registration and the abolition of share certificates.

Fashions and key issues change, of course, and with them change the contents of this report, although the basic contents, as discussed above, are, in the main, laid down by law.

Review of operations

Sherwood Industries' annual report, page 8

This is an important statement from which we derive the company's strategy. Detecting the overall strategy should not be too difficult. After all, the Board of a company is responsible for analysing possible future plans, deciding on the appropriate strategy and then communicating this to all the people who will be involved in its execution. Those involved in this are the staff, at all levels and in all functions. It is necessary that a consistent pyramid of plans ensures that what is happening on the shop floor and at the point of sale and delivery fits in with the plans of the directors. This communication is very difficult to get right, and its failure is obvious to staff and customers alike.

Put simply, if the staff are not aware of how their activities fit in with the grand plan, they are likely, even with the best will in the world, to be operating in a way that slowly but surely detaches itself from the rest of the business. In the worst case, you will see companies whose middle management, while complaining that senior managers either do not have a strategy or that it has not been conveyed to them, will second guess what the strategy should be and operate accordingly.

Given the truth of all that, it is logical to assume that the Board must be able to explain briefly what they are doing and what the plan is to another important group of stakeholders – the shareholders.

We need, however, a simple technique for detecting and documenting the Board's strategy. We can do this by means of the activity matrix. The review of operations will contain, in some form, statements of the company's products and markets' segmentation and we should be able to reproduce this in a simple matrix. The harder the exercise is to do, the less well, probably, is the Board explaining itself to shareholders and staff alike.

The company activity matrix

In the end, all businesses are concerned with taking products and services to various markets. The starting point of the strategic detective work is to understand the concept of the company activity matrix and use it to determine what managers are trying to do.

At its simplest, it looks like Figure 5.3.

Each cell of the matrix can be defined in a number of ways. The one we will concentrate on first is market focus. We must understand which products and markets are important for the company, which they are going to put energy and effort into, which they are abandoning and where they are looking to find new areas of operation. These we would like to style 'Develop', 'Phase down' and 'Explore'. Those that fit none of these we will designate 'Sustain'.

A single advantage that private investors bring to decisions on which shares to buy is common sense regarding what they believe will sell, what is fashionable and what is likely to be in decline. Would you buy shares in a company that intends to expand its operation in black and white televisions? Would you find it attractive if you read in the Chairman's statement that the company believed there was a mass

	Market segment 1	Market segment 2	Market segment 3	Market segment 4	Market segment 5	Market segment 6	Market segment 7	Market segment 8
Product or Service Type 1								
Product or Service Type 2								
Product or Service Type 3								
Product or Service Type 4								
Product or Service Type 5								

Fig. 5.3 A simple company activity matrix

market for motorbikes with a kick starter in Japan? On the other hand, a company that is switching more effort into finding ways of detecting disease in the food chain before the symptoms strike could be focusing on a real opportunity.

The Investment Club's members will try to build the activity matrix for Sherwood Industries, simply by reading the annual report.

Notice how it is not only the focus that is of interest, but also the *future* focus. Is there evidence that the Board recognises where its new products and markets will be found?

First of all, we find out what has happened during the last year. The first breakdown of markets is geographic for the whole company (this is found in a note to the accounts on page 16 of Sherwood Industries' report. From this can be calculated the first use of the matrix, as shown by Figure 5.4.

	UK	Other EU	Rest of Europe	Middle East and Africa	Australia, Asia and the Far East	North America	Others
Sherwood Industries' total (Sales in millions)	847.5	243.0	12.5	22.7	44.4	222.1	12.4
Percentage of total	60%	17%	1%	2%	3%	16%	1%
Change in percentage of total	−17%	6%	0	0	−2%	14%	−1%

Fig. 5.4 The locations of markets

If we drop into the meeting of the Darnley Village Investment Club, we can find out what they make of this knowledge generated from data in the annual report.

Darnley Village Investment Club discusses the strategy of Sherwood Industries

Chairman: 'Let us start with how well Sherwood Industries has protected itself geographically. As you can see, with the exception of the European Union, it is only recently that they have started to grow significantly outside the UK. Their presence in other markets is, to say the least, thin compared to the amount of business in their domestic market. And then along comes the acquisition and North America starts strongly.'

Iain: 'Yes, but it does go to show how quickly an acquiring company gets out of the starting blocks and expands geographically. If they have good advisers and can find companies to buy, these people could have a wide geographic spread very quickly. As the Chairman says, they have access to the money.'

Emily: 'Yes, but where is the expertise to run the new businesses? The answer is that it's in the new businesses. Are they not vulnerable to buying companies and then losing the managers who are capable of running them?'

Chairman: 'Good point, we will have to assume that the deals they are doing cope with that and somehow lock the managers in until their dependence on them has gone down. What do you think of the type of business they are growing in North America?'

Iain: 'Healthcare, it's dead right. With all the talk of everyone living longer, half the population ending up in long-term care homes, it's got to be the right area for the company to get good growth potential.'

Emily: 'Yes, but we could do that through a specialist company, not a conglomerate.'

Chairman: 'Well, to be fair, we have decided to buy a conglomerate, but it still makes sense to check that we agree with where the managers see the main growth areas. I am still concerned about the lack of overseas markets at present.'

Tom: 'But it's you who always says that you buy companies for where they are going, not for where they have been. While it is true that the main growth in percentage terms was in North America, we should not ignore the fact that they doubled their business in the EU, from 122.7 to 243.0.'

Chairman: 'Yep, you're right. In the end, the possibility for international expansion is always there, if the managers are able to take advantage of it and not drop the ball. There are an awful lot of instances of big companies, banks for example, buying abroad and regretting it greatly. But the point to keep in mind is that such expansion may not really be in the price of the share.'

Diana: 'How do you mean?'

Chairman: 'Well, if the market was really expecting Sherwood Industries to make huge progress and growth abroad, should we not expect the price/earnings ratio to be at least up with the sector average if not above it? Sorry, but again it comes down to "Do we believe that the new structure that the Chairman talks about, in terms of letting the managers run the businesses while he looks for new opportunities, is going to come off?" Frankly, from a geographic point of view, it is difficult to see much progress so far. Can we get any better information by looking at the next level of the activity matrix?'

Annual reports differ from one to another in terms of how much detail you can find about the activity matrices of companies. In the case of Sherwood Industries, we get some clues, but not really enough to do a full-blown job. Figure 5.5 shows us where the points of emphasis appear to lie.

Develop/Sustain/Phase down ('?' means we cannot be sure)	UK	Other EU	Rest of Europe	Middle East and Africa	Australasia, Asia and the Far East	North America	Others
Chemicals and Allied Materials Division	Sustain	Sustain	Sustain	?	Phase down?	Phase down	?
Precious Metals Recovery and Refining Division	Sustain	Develop?	Develop?	Develop?	Develop?	Develop	Develop?
Electronic Components Division	Develop	Develop	Develop	?	?	?	?
Healthcare Products and Services Division	Develop	Develop?	Develop?	Develop?	Develop?	Develop	Develop?

Fig. 5.5 Product group geographic emphasis

So, back to the meeting.

Darnley Village Investment Club discusses the strategy of Sherwood Industries once more

Chairman: 'Iain, just take us through how you derived this activity matrix for the product groups.'

Iain: 'The first one was easy. Essentially, Sherwood Industries wants to get away from being predominantly a chemicals company. That is the strategy and we got that from the Chairman's statement. They must, however, sustain the UK and European operations as they are going to be, for the foreseeable future, the backbone of the company. Last year, the Chemicals Division did sales of £610 million of the company's £1.4 billion, which is well over 40 per cent of sales. They speak about returning the Far East and North America to profitability, but against a background where the market does not seem to be improving, so they will have to scale down to get back the profits.

'As to precious metals, they talk about the opportunity for increasing volumes abroad, but do not state where. Don't forget that with £340 million in sales, this division is a quarter of the company. So, almost certainly, they need to sustain the UK operation. Incidentally, this is one of the few areas where you can see clearly the synergy between divisions. They can sell the precious metals to the new businesses in healthcare, which is mainly at the moment in dental laboratories.

'Then I moved to electronic components, which is a distribution business. Fundamentally the market for electronics is growing very fast, with a huge pressure on profit margins because of the competitiveness of the business. This puts a premium on first-class customer service, which is why the distribution system and its efficiency is so important.

Diana: 'Just a minute, how did you get that from this review of operations?'

Iain: 'Well, I didn't actually. I know something about it because, some months ago, my son went into the business of buying and selling electronic components. He seems to be under a lot of stress to find the best prices for his customers and to fix competitive delivery dates. I'm not sure how much he's enjoying it, but he is making a lot of money relatively speaking. It's a growth business without any doubt. I am not sure about geographic spread, though. It seems to me that they are likely to concentrate on Europe for transport reasons, but you can't tell from the report. Guessing, I would think that they will work hard on this business in the European market.

'And that leaves good old healthcare. We know they will develop that in the States. From what they say in the second to last paragraph, it becomes obvious what happened. They bought into Fleet Dental Services because of the synergies with precious metals and chemicals. They found, however, that it was a much bigger opportunity than just that, and changed the strategy accordingly.

'I don't think we can complain about the health strategy. It's a hugely growing business – almost limitless in growth if you think about it – and the States is the best place to be as it has a big domestic population and the wealth to afford more and more in terms of healthcare.

Chairman: 'Careful Iain, you are getting near "I've done the work so we must buy".'

Diana: 'What does that mean?'

Chairman: 'Well, we find a syndrome in these discussions. If people have gone to the sort of trouble that Iain has been to, they tend to favour a positive decision for two reasons. The first is that if you study a company, particularly by reading information supplied by the company itself, you start to get warm to it as you understand more about what it is doing. As you unravel a clue, you feel good about it and tend to transfer that feeling to the company itself. Also, if we don't buy, however logical it seems, you do feel that you wasted your time. It's simply human nature.'

Iain: 'I don't think I am doing that, but I do feel that this company fits our bill.'

Chairman: 'OK, that's fine, but it is important that we remind ourselves of "I've done the work so we must buy." But carry on with your analysis.'

Iain: 'Well, that just leaves profitability. The pre-tax profit margins look like this.'

In Chapter 3, we looked at this important measure of a company's profitability. It is the ratio of pre-tax profits to the figure for sales expressed as a percentage. Taking the numbers supplied on pages 8 and 9 of the report, we can calculate the profit margins of each division. These are shown in Table 5.1.

Table 5.1 The profit margins of Sherwood Industries' divisions

Divisions	Sales	Pre-tax profit	Profit margin	Percentage of total
Chemicals and Allied Materials	610.9	38.4	6.29	75
Precious Metals Recovery and Refining	340.8	–5.6	–1.64	–11
Electronic Components	195.6	4.7	2.40	9
Healthcare Products and Services	207.0	12.9	6.23	25
Discontinued	50.3	0.8	1.59	2
Sherwood Industries	1,404.6	51.2	3.65	100

Some explanation of all these numbers is needed. During the year, Sherwood Industries sold off some companies. The sales turnover and profits of these businesses are shown separately from the continuing businesses for the obvious reason that the reader can get a better impression of what might happen in the future if they take into account only the remaining businesses. As we will see when we read the profit and loss account, the profits here are stated before some transactions of the holding company that had an impact on the bottom line.

What will the members of the Club make of these figures?

Darnley Village Investment Club discusses the strategy of Sherwood Industries again

Emily: 'Now I know that we haven't checked these profit ratios with the industry average book, and that we need to do a more detailed analysis, but even I know that the profitability of these divisions, where they are actually making profits, is on the low side. So, Chemicals and Healthcare are doing a bit over 6 per cent. Given that Chemicals has been a core business for years it doesn't seem very good, does it? And if Healthcare is the cash generator that Iain makes out, a profit ratio of the same amount doesn't impress me. As for the other two divisions, the only thing that makes me warm to them is that they might, rather than be returned to profit as the report says, be taken over. Remember how that happened to another company we had? They had a very unprofitable division, a predator came by and bought the whole lot and sold off the profitable sections for about as much as they had paid for the whole lot and added the unprofitable division to one of theirs with the intention of beefing up its performance. We made a good profit by selling at the time of the takeover.'

Iain: 'That's interesting, so you think there is a chance of a takeover? I certainly don't think the company is too big.'

Chairman: 'Quite so, it is extraordinary how many very large companies, including some in the FTSE 100, are being talked about as possible bid targets, so Sherwood Industries certainly could be bought.'

Emily: 'I don't think we should buy Sherwood Industries for the *possibility* of its being taken over, that's not the spot we are trying to fill in the portfolio. It's just a bonus possibility if it passes all the other tests. Including, of course, profitability and the safety of the dividend.'

Chairman: 'Let's look at the dividend cover.'

As discussed in Chapter 3, dividend cover is the number of times the profit available for distribution to the shareholders 'covers' the dividends. It is a reasonable test of whether or not there may be problems in the future in maintaining or increasing the dividends.

The easiest way to find it out is to look up Sherwood Industries in the Monday copy of the FT, but it is possible to calculate it in this case as we have Sherwood Industries' report.

The profit for the financial year is shown on page 12 – in the Consolidated profit and loss account – as £21.8 million, and the dividends, shown on the next line, cost £13.3 million which is equivalent to £16.6 million gross. If we divide the former by the latter, we find that the dividend cover is 1.31.

Another way of getting to the same number is to take the earnings per share figure, shown in most profit and loss accounts, and divide it by the dividend per share. In the case of Sherwood Industries, we know the dividend per share to be 7.1 pence net, 8.9 pence gross as we read it in the Chairman's statement. Divide this figure into the earnings per share figure of 11.65 (it is at the foot of the column of figures headed 'last year' on page 12 of the report) and, once again, we get 1.31.

How does that grab the Investment Club?

<table>
<tr><td>SCENARIO</td></tr>
</table>

Darnley Village Investment Club discusses the strategy of Sherwood Industries a fourth time

Iain: 'Actually, the dividend cover is not too bad at 1.31, given that profitability is generally low and that two divisions are making no real profits at all. The average for the whole market is 1.9, or thereabouts, so this is not bad.'

Chairman: 'OK, that was a good discussion. Let's just recap where we have got to so far.

'We understand the businesses that Sherwood Industries are in and we can be comfortable that they have a strategy for the future that includes products and services that we think are growth areas – which is healthcare, being sold into a very buoyant market in the States. The growth can be supported by the core business, which has been around for a long time and is profitable and stable. After all, we are always going to need chemicals.

'Its profitability is held back by Precious Metals, which does not look likely to get much better, although the company promised to get it back to being at least profitable in the next year. The other business that shows promise is Electronic Components' distribution, which should be able to grow well but is in a very competitive area so may never be hugely profitable.

'The share suits us because we are looking for a diversified industrial with reasonable income and some hope for growth. The dividends look reasonably secure and the yield, at 5.9 per cent, and the price/earnings ratio, at 12.9, fit the bill. Indeed, we think the price/earnings may be unflattering to the company, so there is potential for capital growth. There is even a vague possibility of a takeover, of all or part of the company.

'Is it the belief of members that the share and the strategy are, at this stage in our investigation, promising?'

All: (Murmurs of consent.)

Emily: 'I'm afraid I come back to the management problem. Are we convinced that the current managers can actually carry out this strategy and that they can retain the loyalty of the new teams they take over? I wonder if we can get any more information about this man Moss. He's the one who has to first of all get out of the habit of running the businesses hands on and then work on the way ahead.

'The question is bound to arise, why didn't he do it before? I think that we should look carefully at the numbers but keep coming back to question as to whether or not this is a credible strategy.'

Chairman: 'OK, we shall now go on to the next task, which is to analyse the profit and loss account and balance sheet.'

We will come back to these numbers in the next chapter. For the moment we still have to look at the earlier parts of the annual report.

Directors' responsibilities

Sherwood Industries' annual report, page 10

This is a fairly recent addition to the contents of the annual report. It covers a number of issues. One of these is that there was some confusion as to what the individual responsibilities of the directors were in relation to the publishing of financial information.

To clear this up, a form of words was proposed to cover the directors' responsibilities, and this is set out on page 10 of Sherwood Industries' report. These words are exactly replicated in a lot of reports. Where there is a variation it is that instead of the statement saying what the responsibilities are, it says that the directors believe that they have carried out their responsibilities. The underlying responsibilities are the same.

It is a timely reminder to us that the figures we are about to examine in detail are based on opinions, best practice and the judgement of the Board of Directors. They are not facts in the same way as we would regard say, logarithmic tables.

It is to be hoped that this spotlight on what the individual responsibilities of the directors are has added to the dependability of the information in the financial accounts.

Auditors' report to the members of Sherwood Industries plc

Sherwood Industries' annual report, page 11

This statement is also nearly a standard one with few particular variations. It is here to record the fact that the auditors have done their job, how they did the job and what is their considered opinion of the prepared accounts. The usefulness of all these words to the private investor is questionable. We shall describe it in full below, but probably the most important part is that headed 'Opinion'. The report has four sections.

Introduction

The introduction merely records the fact that the audit has been carried out and identifies those pages of the accounts that are being reported on. The audit report does not cover the Chairman's or directors' reports or the review of operations.

Sometimes the auditors draw attention at this point to the way the accounts have been prepared by referring to the accounting policies.

Respective responsibilities of directors and auditors

The purpose of this section is to distinguish the auditors' duties from those of the directors, so that the reader of the accounts does not have unrealistic expectations of what the auditors are trying to achieve.

Notice the use of the word 'independent'. The need for independence is fundamental if auditors are to do their job properly. However, the company is the auditors' customer – one they do not wish to lose – and this can threaten the auditors' independence when contentious issues arise.

Basis of opinion

This mentions the standards laid down by the accounting profession.

The phrase 'examination, on a test basis' is referring to the fact that auditors cannot look at every item that forms part of the accounts because of the scale of the operations of major companies. Rather, they will need to work on samples. In fact, audit evidence consists primarily of three elements. First, the auditors will assess the company's financial controls and test the effectiveness of these. Second, the auditors will take samples of transactions and balances and confirm the validity of each item tested. Finally, they will perform analytical procedures to try to establish the consistency of the figures with other forms of evidence.

The paragraph continues, referring to 'significant estimates and judgements made by the directors'. Here, the intention is to remind the shareholder that accounts are not exact and cannot be said to be correct as such (although, of course, they could be incorrect). It is the directors who have the responsibility to make the judgements and the auditors to decide whether or not these judgements and the accounting policies selected are reasonable.

Moving on to the next paragraph, the auditors state that they gathered evidence sufficient to give *reasonable* assurance, not total certainty. Total certainty is not possible; the audit report is not a guarantee.

'Reasonable assurance' means that the financial statements are free from *material* misstatement, not all misstatement. A matter is 'material' to a shareholder if it would influence their decision.

Opinion

The auditors will normally report their opinion in the same words used in Sherwood Industries' report, that is, that the accounts show a 'true and fair view'.

Variations on this theme may be one of the following.

- A qualified report, where the auditors are disagreeing with the company's accounts in some way. In this case, the nature of the disagreement will be explained in the auditors' report.

- A qualified report, where the auditors have been unable to gather sufficient evidence.

- A modified report, where the auditors draw attention to an uncertainty but without qualifying their opinion. This is used, for example, where there is a significant level of concern about the survival of the company.

The first two are extremely rare for major companies as the auditors will work closely with their clients to try to avoid such a problem. The third situation does arise more frequently, but still rarely in the case of large companies.

Conclusion

Good judgement in investment decisions requires that the investor looks for good value in a share. Good value is revealed, in part, by understanding what the company's strategy for the future is. We now have in the activity matrix a quick way of getting to a summary of that strategy. With practice you will get better at determining that strategy and its feasibility.

This chapter has shown that there is a lot of information in an annual report that can help with this process. After we have looked at the hard data of the financial statements, we will come back to finding other sources of information to help make the decision.

Let's try to summarise the answer to the title of this chapter in a few words. Companies thrive if they are selling satisfactory products and services that are popular with their customers into markets that have good potential for growth. Their strategic planning should help them to identify those. They then need the capabilities, whatever they are, to carry out the strategy and change it when required. Finally, they need to manage the business in a way that unites the entire staff behind the strategy and keeps everyone in touch with what is required in a changing environment.

The investor forms an opinion on all these matters before making an investment.

EXERCISES FOR CHAPTER 5

Becoming familiar with commercial information

If you have got some annual reports, read through the Chairman's statement and the review of operations. Get a feel for how they are presented and become comfortable that you can find your way around the text of the report up to the point where the financial statements being.

EXERCISE 1 Take the report of a company in which you are interested and try to construct the activity matrix for the whole company or group. See if you can break it down a stage further by analysing the strategy of some or all of the divisions. Describe the markets in a way that is relevant. For example, it is not always a geographic segmentation that is required. The report will help you to understand what is relevant as the directors' review will point out what they consider to be the key issues and key markets.

EXERCISE 2 Look again at the yield, price/earnings ratio and dividend cover and evaluate these in terms of the company's strategy. It may help to do this if you go back to Chapter 3 and follow the route taken by the Investment Club members.

Advancing your investment strategy

EXERCISE 3 By now you should have narrowed down the number of companies that could fit in with your strategy. You know if the company would go into your high-, medium- or low-risk category, and that it is appropriate to purchase one in that category.

Using this approach, narrow the range further by testing the strategy against the issues we have discussed in this chapter, and choose those that you are going to take forward into the next chapter, where we will do the detailed financial analysis.

CHAPTER 6

Getting to the right numbers

Describing the potential of a company in figures

- Introduction
- The bookshop
- Identifying the information
- Conclusion
- Exercises

A refresher on the absolute basics of finance is our starting point. You will then go through the annual report of the case study – Sherwood Industries. You will identify the data you need from the slightly simplified case study before going on to look at the companies you have decided to study.

Introduction

In Chapter 1, we looked at the top two ratios that investors use as tools to aid them in making investment decisions. The ratios were yield and price/earnings.

Because of their importance to shareholders, we saw in Chapter 4 how the Chairman is obsessed with keeping the promises they made to investors in respect of profits and dividend payments. Thus, the need to pay the expected dividends and produce the profits and cash flow that allow it to be paid are important drivers of any company.

You may also recall that most managers have a small number (say two or three or four) ratios that they keep in their heads as key indicators of the success of their part of the business. Successful investing depends, to some extent, on the investor's ability to understand the ratios that keep the key people in the target company awake at nights.

We cannot emphasise too strongly the personal nature of these ratios. They are there because particular business objectives have been allocated to individual managers. Never assume, for example, that because you have read the views of one production manager that all production managers will use the same key indicators. There will, of course, be similarities and you will get better at anticipating ratios as you meet or read about more business managers.

Where we do get some consistency of key indicators is when we consider the published statements of different companies. These are regulated by law to a considerable extent and we can therefore make meaningful comparisons between the performance of one company and another.

Chapters 6 and 7 are intended to start you off or remind you of how to get useful information out of an annual report.

Learning objectives

This chapter concentrates on the basics of business finance and the identification of the data you need to calculate financial ratios for comparison purposes.

You will then do an exercise in identifying data before going on to the next chapter. There we will come to the meaning of the ratios themselves.

We will start here by going over the basics. If all the terms are familiar to you and you just want practice, miss out the section below entitled 'The bookshop' and go straight to the heading 'Sherwood Industries'. Otherwise go through the basics refresher before undertaking the case study. We have to learn where the data is before we can interpret the results.

First, a résumé of the basics.

The bookshop

The easiest way to explain the basics of finance is to, first of all, try to picture the numbers side of a business in a very physical form. Indeed, it is the ability to link the figures to what is actually happening in the business that defines a successful general manager.

So, taking something we can all recognise, let us assume that we are going to set up a bookshop.

Table 6.1 The Bookshop

Things the company owns	Money the company owes
Books	Suppliers' invoices
Invoices to customers	Overdraft
Cash	Dividends
	Tax
	Long-term loan
Shelving, tills, computers	
Motor vehicles	
Freehold shop	Owners' capital
	Profits

Table 6.2 Sales and expenses

Sales	Expenses
Sales of books	Cost of books sold
	Staff salaries and National Insurance contributions
	Directors' salaries
	Rates
	Rent
	Gas and electricity
	Telephone
	Postage and carriage
	Printing and stationery
	Repairs and maintenance
	Motor expenses
	Sundries
	Depreciation of motor vehicle, furnishings and fittings, and freehold shop

Note that each of the items in italics in the following section is shown either in Table 6.1 or 6.2, which contain a physical definition of the terms that we will later meet in actual company reports. Look where they are and this will explain the more jargon-oriented version of the same thing.

To start a bookshop, the first thing we will require is some *cash*. Before we can rent premises, we will have to pay a deposit and some rent in advance, so we need some cash. The first place to go is to our own bank accounts. The owners of the business – you and me – will put in enough *owners' capital* to get the shop running.

This we will use to pay the *rent* and *rates*. We then have to do the place up, and so will spend money on some consumables in the form of *repairs and maintenance*.

Some of the money will also buy the basic requirements of a shop that will allows us to trade, such as *shelving, tills, computers* and *telephone*. These will last for quite a while.

We need some *motor vehicles* – a van and, perhaps, a company pool car.

We are ready to trade now, so we must buy some *books*. We probably do not have much cash left, so we will get credit from our *suppliers*, and they will send *invoices*.

Even then, we are out of cash, so we will go to the bank and borrow some. The bank will not be impressed by the value of the business at this stage, so we will probably need some other collateral, such as our houses. We will try to borrow the money in a very flexible way by getting an *overdraft*.

We are open now and trading. Customers will buy books for cash, except where we get a bulk order from a school or library. Then they will expect credit and we will have to send them *invoices*.

Money comes in from the *sales of books*, and we have to record what were the *costs* of each of the books we sold in order to know how profitable each book we sell is.

There are more expenses than the ones mentioned earlier:

- *staff salaries and National Insurance contributions*
- *directors' salaries*
- *gas and electricity*
- *telephone*
- *postage and carriage*
- *printing and stationery*
- *motor expenses*
- *sundries.*

Do not forget that we own some vehicles and other assets that will last for some years and that we will have to *depreciate* as they get older.

At the end of the first year, we have done well and made a profit. Some of that profit we will pay in *tax*, some we will give to the owners in the form of *dividends* and the rest we will keep in the business to fund expansion. Do not forget that those *profits* belong, in the final analysis, to the owners of the business and are therefore part of *owners' capital*.

We expand, buy a *freehold shop* and run out of cash again. This time we will get a *long-term loan*. In fact, we will mortgage the shop. The bank still does not allow much recognition of the business as a going concern, so it will insist on a charge on the property as security for the loan.

And there we have it. We have just gone through the logical process of setting up a new business, and at the same time created the two main financial statements: the profit and loss account and balance sheet.

The profit and loss account

The top line of a profit and loss account is the sales made (see Figure 6.1) – called revenues or net revenues or *sales turnover*. Note that the word 'turnover' has a different meaning in the USA, where it is normally reserved for 'staff turnover'.

THE PROFIT AND LOSS ACCOUNT

Sales turnover
minus Cost of sales

= Gross profit

minus Selling and distribution expenses
minus Administrative overheads

= Trading profit (earnings before interest and tax)

minus Interest

= Net profit before tax

minus Tax

= Profit attributable to shareholders

minus Dividends

= Retained profit

Fig. 6.1 The bare bones of a profit and loss account

From this we deduct the actual costs of the products sold. In the case of the bookshop that is very simple. It is what we paid for each of the books we have sold. In a manufacturing company, it includes all the direct costs of producing the products sold. The jargon usually used for this is *cost of sales*.

This gives us the *gross profit*. From the gross profit we can calculate the gross margin. This is a vital piece of information for monitoring purposes. How we run the business is dictated to a considerable extent by how good our gross margins are. In fact, one of the most important characteristics of a business is its gross margin or, rather, gross margins as most companies sell a range of products and services that will probably have different margins. The gross margin of a product is the gross profit expressed as a percentage of the sales price.

If a product costs £100 to purchase from a supplier and the sales price is £125, then the gross margin is 20 per cent ((25/125) x 100)

If a manufacturer has direct costs of manufacture of £1,000 for a product and the sales price, governed by market forces, is £1,600, then the gross margin is 37.5 per cent ((600/1,600) x 100).

In most cases, there is a good reason for the margins that companies can achieve. For example, if a high level of after-sales support is required, then plainly the gross margin will have to be high. The costs of after-sales service come out of the gross profit.

A good example of the importance of gross margins can be found in the telecommunications industry. Most telecommunications companies operate in three different areas. First, they supply customers with the ability to make calls, second, many of them provide sophisticated data services to businesses and, third, most offer some private switching equipment that they buy in from suppliers. Consider the gross margin of these different product areas.

The high-margin area is, of course, the money they make from people using the network. It costs a fortune to put down, but once it is there it produces revenue with a lot of profit.

Their lowest-margin products are those commodities that are hardware-based and sold into a very competitive market. The best example is the private switchboards they sell at low or even non-existent margin. The equipment gives them some strategic benefits, such as a high profile with customers, but they do not make much money. Indeed, a number of operators are coming out of that type of business for just that reason.

In the middle, are the data products, which produce reasonable margins but nothing like those arising from the network.

It has been interesting to watch the computer industry make the traumatic change from very high-margin products, such as big mainframes, to tight-margin equipment in the competitive world of the personal computer. So difficult was that change that almost all of them failed to make it without falling into loss. Indeed, IBM lost some $9 billion by reacting too late and too slowly.

From the gross margin, we deduct the expenses. For annual reporting purposes they are divided into *selling and distribution expenses* and *administrative overheads*. You can see how the expenses we discussed for the bookshop fall into one or other category. In some businesses, this is a crucial distinction and some of the ratios in this area will be significant, but normally it is less important to distinguish between the two. We do not intend to pay too much attention to it here.

This gives us the *trading profit*, or earnings. This is often described as earnings before interest and tax or EBIT for short.

Now reduce this by deducting the *interest* and you get the *net profit before tax*. There is no golden rule, but this is generally the figure people talk about when they are making comparisons. In the business papers, when they say 'the profits are down' they are probably referring to this figure in the profit and loss account.

As we said in the bookshop example, we spend the profits on *tax* and *dividends* before finally crediting to the shareholders the portion we keep in the business. The *retained profit* is the item that connects the profit and loss account to the balance sheet, as we will see.

The balance sheet

Assets are what the company owns, and *liabilities* are what the business owes. These are listed in the balance sheet. Figure 6.2 shows the typical elements described in their formal language.

We group the assets by time considerations. Thus, *current assets* are those we are likely to turn into cash within the next 12 months.

In the bookshop we have the most common examples of current assets:

- *stock* (called inventory in the USA), which are the books

- *debtors*, which are mainly the amounts our customers owe us in the form of unpaid invoices

- *cash*, which is the most liquid asset of all.

Assets that will benefit the company in the longer term are called *fixed assets*. These are subdivided into *tangible* and *intangible*.

The tangible assets in the bookshop are the *furnishings and fittings*, which are depreciated in the profit and loss account, as we have seen. The bookshop also owns *motor vehicles*, which will be similarly depreciated, probably over a shorter length of time.

Assets	Liabilities
Current assets	Current liabilities
Stock	Overdraft
Debtors	Short-term loans
Cash	Creditors
	Dividends
	Tax
Fixed assets	Long-term loans
Tangible	Provisions for liabilities and charges
Land and property	
Plant and machinery	Shareholders' capital and reserves
Furnishings and fittings	Share capital
Motor vehicles	Share premium
	Reserves
Intangible	Minority interests
Goodwill	
Patents and licences	
Other	
Trade investments	

Fig. 6.2 The balance sheet in formal language

Depreciation is a method of charging the cost of an asset against profits over its useful life. It is frequently misunderstood, so it is worth spending a few minutes on the subject now.

Suppose the bookshop buys a new till for £650 at the start of its first year of trading. It is expected to have a scrap value of £50 in 5 years' time. The £600 fall in value of the till during this time needs to be charged against profits. It would be unfair to charge the whole £600 in one year, so the charge is spread over the five-year useful life of the asset.

The simplest way of doing this is by dividing the £600 equally, charging £120 per year. This is known as *straight line depreciation*, and is the most common method used in practice. Using this method, at the end of one year, the till will be included in the balance sheet at its 'net book value' of £530, which is the original cost less the charge of £120 for that year. At the end of the second year, the net book value will be £410, and so on.

Notice that there is no intention that the net book value should represent the selling value of a fixed asset because there is no intention to sell the asset in the short term.

Land and property can be different, as they are liable to appreciate in value. We may record that appreciation from time to time, based on an independent valuation, but between valuations, it is usual to charge depreciation on a property, as you would for any other asset.

Intangible assets are becoming less common features on balance sheets. There is a healthy suspicion of assets that are said to have a value but no substance. *Goodwill*, which arises on the purchase of a company, is probably an exception and you will still find that this is mentioned.

The other common type of fixed asset comprises *trade investments*. These are investments in other companies that the Board expects to be holding for the long term.

Now let us turn to liabilities.

Once again, the same period of time is covered by the word 'current'. Current liabilities are those liabilities that will have to be paid within the next 12 months. It is a strictly defined timespan. In fact, balance sheets use the expression required by the Company's Act, which is 'Liabilities – amounts falling due within one year.'

In this category we include:

- the *overdraft*, which the bank can recall at any time

- any *short-term loans*, which will have to be repaid within the next year

- *creditors* – including the most important item, 'trade creditors' – which are outstanding invoices.

If the company has announced that there will be *dividends* but has not yet paid them, they will be a current liability.

Tax is a common item that we need to pay within 12 months.

That covers current liabilities.

Long-term liabilities are also known as fixed liabilities. We can group them into long-term external liabilities, and liabilities to the shareholders. External liabilities include the following:

- *long-term loans*

- *provisions for liabilities and charges*. Most balance sheets have an element of these. They are liabilities that will probably have to be paid, but not within a year. The most common example is deferred taxation. Other examples would be possible liabilities arising out of restructuring or legal actions.

That just leaves shareholders' funds and *minority interests*. Shareholders' funds normally have three elements. First, there is *share capital,* which is the nominal value of the issued shares. In the case of most UK shares, they are valued at a nominal 25 pence. If, however, the Board were to issue more shares to raise capital, it would sell them at somewhere near the current market value. The difference between these two figures is recorded as the *share premium,* the second element. The Americans, slightly more plainly, call it 'Moneys paid above par'.

Third, there are the *reserves*, or retained profits which as we have seen, also belong to the shareholders. They build up over time, and companies that have traded for a long time will have a lot of money in reserves. One item that must be shown separately in the 'Profit and loss account' is the total of past retained profits. Another reserve you might come across is the *revaluation reserve*, which arises when assets are revalued.

The figure for minority interests is similar to that for reserves. It records what part of the reserves belong to minority interests, that is profits that have been made by companies within the group that have other shareholders apart from the parent company, which is presenting the report.

Identifying the information

The blank form shown in Figure 6.3 will enable you to note down the financial data you need from an annual report.

You will see that each item is identified by a reference letter, which will enable you to do the ratio calculations easily. We will start with a simple definition of the terms used in the form (see Table 6.3) and then make sure that you can complete the form for Sherwood Industries. From there you should find it relatively straightforward to move on to the real thing.

Completing a record of the information for Sherwood Industries

We now need to start the process of identifying the detailed financial data available in Sherwood Industries' report. There are, unfortunately, many ways of referring to the same items. To help with this, we have added the main alternative terms to the table of definitions and explained how the figures are normally found (see Table 6.4).

The members of our Investment Club have gone through the calculations and produced the data shown in Figure 6.4.

Company name:

Currency and units:

	Year	Last year	Previous year
Total sales turnover	A		
Net profit before tax	B		
Interest payable	C		
Depreciation	D		
Tangible fixed assets	E		
Intangible fixed assets	F		
Other fixed assets	G		
Stocks	H		
Trade debtors	I		
Total current assets	J		

	Year	Last year	Previous year
Trade creditors	K		
Short-term loans	L		
Total current liabilities	M		
Long-term loans	N		
Provisions for liabilities and charges	O		
Other long-term liabilities	P		
Total shareholders' funds	Q		
Minority interests	R		
Average number of employees	S		
Total of employees' remuneration	T		

Fig. 6.3 Form you can use to note all the financial details you need about a company you are investigating

Table 6.3 Definition of terms

Reference letter	Term	Definition
A	Total sales turnover	Sales outside the group, excluding VAT.
B	Net profit before tax	This is the profit before charging tax or any extraordinary items.
C	Interest payable	Gross interest payable.
D	Depreciation	A method by which the cost of an asset is charged against profit over the useful life of the asset.
E	Tangible fixed assets	Those assets – such as property, machinery and so on – that are used by the company to generate income or sales over a long period.
F	Intangible fixed assets	Fixed assets that are without physical substance. Examples are licences, goodwill, patents or other intangible assets that have been acquired.
G	Other fixed assets	Assets that cannot be classified as either fixed or current. Predominantly, these are investments or trade investments.
H	Stocks	Trading and sundry stocks, typically including raw materials, work in progress and finished goods.
I	Trade debtors	Amounts receivable from customers.
J	Total current assets	The sum of all assets that would normally be turned into cash within one year.
K	Trade creditors	Amounts owed to suppliers.
L	Short-term loans	Loans that are repayable within one year. This includes overdrafts and obligations under finance leases that are due within the next year.
M	Total current liabilities	The sum of all those liabilities that need to be paid within one year.
N	Long-term loans	Loans that are repayable after more than one year. This will also include obligations under finance leases due after one year.

Reference letter	Term	Definition
O	Provision for liabilities and charges	Includes deferred tax and other provisions.
P	Other long-term liabilities	Any other long-term liability not yet transferred to the information sheet should be included here.
Q	Total shareholders' fund	The total of capital introduced by shareholders, plus undistributed profits or reserves.
R	Minority interests	The interests of minority shareholders in non-wholly owned subsidiaries.
S	Average number of employees	The average number of people employed during the period.
T	Total of employees' remuneration	Wages and salaries, but excluding social security and pension costs.

Table 6.4 Filling in the form for Sherwood Industries, with alternative terms given

Reference letter	Term	Sherwood Industries' figures (£m)	Other terms found
A	Total sales turnover	£1,404.6 (Notice how the figures for continuing operations are distinguished from acquisitions and discontinued operations. Unless it would show a massive distortion, it is better to use the total figure. All the other numbers we use will be on this basis.)	Sales revenues Net sales revenues
B	Net profit before tax	£39.2	Profit on ordinary activities before tax Earnings before tax
C	Interest payable	£17.6 (In the case of Sherwood Industries, the profit and loss account identifies the gross figure payable. Frequently a company will show a 'net' figure that has been calculated as the gross payable figure minus the amount of interest earned from, for example, bank accounts. In such a case, you would need to go to the explanatory note for the item.)	Finance costs (Almost always in a note to the accounts.)
D	Depreciation	£26.0 (As is normally the case, the depreciation figure can be found by looking at the note concerned with operating costs or profits. In the case of Sherwood Industries, the note is number 1 and entitled 'Analysis of turnover and profits before tax'. The figure is normally in the list of items explaining how the profit figure has been calculated. An alternative place to look for depreciation is in the first note to the cash flow statement.)	Amortisation of fixed assets Depreciation of fixed assets You should include the depreciation of fixed assets held under finance leases

Reference letter	Term	Sherwood Industries' figures (£m)	Other terms found
E	Tangible fixed assets	£158.8 (In most balance sheets, this figure is clearly stated at the top under the heading 'Fixed assets'. If depreciation is given in the balance sheet, it is the accumulated depreciation and you should use the figure shown after depreciation has been deducted.)	Under the heading 'Fixed assets' as Tangible assets
F	Intangible fixed assets	(There are none for Sherwood Industries. In most balance sheets, this figure is also clearly stated at the top under the heading 'Fixed assets'. If depreciation is given in the balance sheet, it is the accumulated depreciation and you should use the figure shown after depreciation has been deducted. Very frequently companies do not have any intangible fixed assets.)	Under the heading 'Fixed assets' as Intangible assets
G	Other fixed assets	£0.3 (In Sherwood Industries' report, this number is shown as 'Investments'. In most balance sheets, there are some assets that are not defined as either tangible or intangible. The overwhelming majority of these are investments in other companies or associated undertakings.)	Under the heading 'Fixed assets' as Investments Trade investments
H	Stocks	£172.1 (Now we turn to current assets, which, you will recall, are assets likely to become cash within a year. Within that category, in most cases there is a figure for stocks. This represents the amount of money the company has tied up in stocks of raw materials, work in progress and finished goods. It is the total figure we want here.)	Under the heading 'Current assets' as Inventories Stock and work in progress

Reference letter	Term	Sherwood Industries' figures (£m)	Other terms found
I	Trade debtors	£258.4 (All balance sheets have a figure in the current assets column for payments to the enterprise that are outstanding. The number we want here is that which arises from the company's customers. Normally it is within the item 'Debtors', and you need to go to the note to find the figure for Trade debtors. Otherwise you would include figures that are not concerned with debt arising in the normal course of business. In Sherwood Industries' report the relevant note is note 8.)	Accounts receivable Receivables
J	Total current assets	£543.4 (Most balance sheets show this figure, which is the sum of stock, debtors, cash and other current assets.)	Sometimes the total is stated without the word 'Total' being explicitly stated, there is just a line and the total
K	Trade creditors	£185.9 (The definition of a current liability is one that has to be paid within one year. You will often see current liabilities expressed as 'Creditors: amounts due within one year'. Within this category you will find a term for creditors, either in the balance sheet or in a note. From the note you have to find the Trade creditors, that is, people to whom the company owes money in the normal course of business. In Sherwood Industries' report, this is note 9.)	Accounts payable Payables Trade and other creditors (In almost all cases you will have to go to the relevant note.)

Reference letter	Term	Sherwood Industries' figures (£m)	Other terms found
L	Short-term loans	£29.8 (Once again, you will often see current liabilities expressed as 'Creditors: amounts due within one year'. Within this category you will find a term for creditors, either on the balance sheet or in a note. From the note you have to find the short-term loans. Remember to add on overdrafts if these are shown separately. Again, to find this for Sherwood Industries, see note 9.)	Short-term loans can include: Bills payable Loans and overdrafts Finance leases (In most cases you will need the note.)
M	Total current liabilities	£333.2 (You need here the total of all the current liabilities, which will probably be stated in the balance sheet.)	Creditors: amounts falling due within one year. (Be careful not to take the figure for Net current assets.)
N	Long-term loans	£79.7 (Long-term liabilities are often known as 'Creditors: amounts falling due after more than one year'. You may have to go to the note to find the portions that are loans. Add in debentures and all other types of loan. See note 9 in Sherwood Industries' report – exclude 'Other creditors', which are included in 'P' below.)	Loans and finance lease obligations
O	Provisions for liabilities and charges	£2.1 (Most balance sheets include provisions for liabilities that are not due for payment within one year and, unlike Creditors, the amount and or the definite requirement for payment is uncertain. The total figure for provisions is normally on the balance sheet.)	

Reference letter	Term	Sherwood Industries' figures (£m)	Other terms found
P	Other long-term liabilities	£7.5 (Made up of the 'Other creditors', under 'Amounts due after more than one year', given in note 9 in Sherwood Industries' report. Most balance sheets include other long-term liabilities apart from loans and provisions, which you previously found. Include all other long-term creditors in this figure to ensure that you have transferred all the liabilities from the balance sheet to your model.)	Other creditors within the category of Creditors Amounts due after more than one year. (Remember that if you went to the notes to get the loans figure, the rest of the figures in the note will be included there.)
Q	Total share-holders' funds	£272.7 (The total shareholders' funds figure is found in the Capital and reserves part of the balance sheet. Include all share capital, share premiums and reserves that sometimes include a heading 'Profit and loss account'. Miss out Minority interests, which are picked up later.)	Equity share-holders' funds Total capital and reserves
R	Minority interests	£7.3 (Minority interests are the reserves of the company that belong not to the shareholders of this company but to the shareholders in a non-wholly owned subsidiary. They are normally shown in the balance sheet itself.)	
S	Average number of employees	10,896 This figure was found in note 3 of Sherwood Industries' report. (To work out the employee ratios, you need to find the average number of employees who worked for the company in the year in question. Make sure you find the	

Reference letter	Term	Sherwood Industries' figures (£m)	Other terms found
		average number rather than the number of employees at the year end. It is normally in a note near the information about directors' remuneration.)	
T	Total of employees' remuneration	£273.7 This figure is given in note 3 of Sherwood Industries' report. (To work out the employee ratios, you need to find the total remuneration of employees who worked for the company in the year in question. Make sure you use the figure for wages and salaries only – do not include pension and social security costs. The information will be in a note.)	

Company name:

Sherwood Industries

Currency and units:

£m

		Year	Last year (£m)	Previous year (£m)
A	Total sales turnover		1,404.6	1,041.9
B	Net profit before tax		39.2	48.7
C	Interest payable		17.6	10.8
D	Depreciation		26.0	19.9
E	Tangible fixed assets		158.8	160.4
F	Intangible fixed assets		0.0	0.0
G	Other fixed assets		0.3	7.8
H	Stocks		172.1	155.8
I	Trade debtors		258.4	200.4
J	Total current assets		543.4	470.1

		Year	Last year (£m)	Previous year (£m)
K	Trade creditors		185.9	148.3
L	Short-term loans		29.8	57.8
M	Total current liabilities		333.2	292.1
N	Long-term loans		79.7	52.2
O	Provisions for liabilities and charges		2.1	4.6
P	Other long-term liabilities		7.5	5.9
Q	Total shareholders' funds		272.7	277.2
R	Minority interests		7.3	6.3
S	Average number of employees		0.011	0.007
T	Total of employees' remuneration		273.7	144.3

Fig. 6.4 The form filled in for Sherwood Industries

Conclusion

Getting the financial data you need from published information is a skill that is easily gained. If you use the blank version of the form in Figure 6.3 and the one completed for Sherwood Industries as your guide (Figure 6.4), you should be able to identify what you need to know from any annual report.

EXERCISES FOR CHAPTER 6

Becoming familiar with financial information

EXERCISE 1   Take any one of the annual reports you have collected and abstract the data onto a copy of the blank form or build your own version as a spreadsheet.

Advancing your investment strategy

EXERCISE 2   As means of recapping what we did in Chapter 3, work out the four ratios – gearing, income gearing, return on capital employed and pre-tax profit margin – for Sherwood Industries and any other reports you have worked on.

In Chapter 7, we will examine these ratios in more detail.

CHAPTER 7

The key business ratios: an introduction

Calculating and interpreting more detailed ratios

- Introduction
- Profitability ratios
- Liquidity ratios
- Asset utility
- Gearing
- The employee ratios
- Growth ratios
- Calculating the ratios for Sherwood Industries
- Conclusion
- Exercises

Now that we have chosen the type of share to meet our strategy and looked at the business plans of contenders, it is time to go into a more detailed analysis of the historical performance of the business, measured by hard financial data.

Introduction

In Chapter 3, we looked at the main areas of business ratios and discovered them to be profitability and gearing. We now need to go into these areas in more detail. In this chapter, we will discuss further examples of profitability and gearing ratios and then move onto other ratios that measure the efficiency of the company's managers. The three areas we will introduce here are asset utility, liquidity and employee ratios.

Using the reference letters from A to T given in Table 6.3 we now need to calculate some other data essential for the production of the key business ratios. For the sake of completeness, this list also includes some figures that, although not used in the ratios covered in this chapter, will be required for some more advanced calculations used in comparisons of companies with industry averages (these are explained in Chapter 8.) The figures to be calculated are shown in Figure 7.1.

Table 7.1 defines the first column of new terms shown in Figure 7.1.

Company name:

Currency and units:

	Year	Last year	Previous year
Total sales turnover	A		
Net profit before tax	B		
Interest payable	C		
Depreciation	D		
Tangible fixed assets	E		
Intangible fixed assets	F		
Other fixed assets	G		
Stocks	H		
Trade debtors	I		
Total current assets	J		

Calculated figures follow

		Last year	Previous year
Tangible and intangible fixed assets	AA		
Total assets	BB		
Total liabilities	CC		
Net assets	DD		
Capital employed	EE		

	Year	Last year	Previous year
Trade creditors	K		
Short-term loans	L		
Total current liabilities	M		
Long-term loans	N		
Provisions for liabilities and charges	O		
Other long-term liabilities	P		
Total shareholders' funds	Q		
Minority interests	R		
Average number of employees	S		
Total of employees' remuneration	T		

		Last year	Previous year
Quick assets	FF		
Total debt	GG		
Tangible net worth	HH		
Pre-interest profit	II		
Net working capital	JJ		

Fig. 7.1 The expanded form

Table 7.1 Definitions of the terms extra to those given in Table 6.3

Reference letter	Term	How it is calculated and definition
AA	Tangible and intangible fixed assets	The total of tangible and intangible fixed assets (=E+F). While this number is not used in the ratio calculations, it can be of interest in some cases. For example, in an industry where the growth of fixed assets is a measure of the potential of the company, it is interesting to look at the growth of the assets from one year to another. The property business is just such an industry where obviously the tangible fixed asset growth in properties to be let is an important measure. You will recall that most companies keep intangible assets off their balance sheets, but in some cases, for example the newspaper business where the right to produce a title is a valuable asset, the growth of these assets can tell the story of the growth of the company.
BB	Total assets	The total assets are found by adding all the fixed assets to the current assets (E + F+ G + J). We will use the result of this calculation to work out how efficiently and profitably the managers of the business are using the company's assets.
CC	Total liabilities	Used in the advanced ratios, these represent all the liabilities of the company with the exception of shareholders' funds (M + N + O + P + R). If, for some reason, the company were wound up, all these liabilities would need to be paid before what was left could be distributed to the shareholders.
DD	Net assets	This is the figure for the total assets minus the current liabilities (BB – M), a figure often stated on the balance sheet itself.

Reference letter	Term	How it is calculated and definition
EE	Capital employed	This is the long-term capital employed in the business – both from shareholders and other long-term sources of funds, such as loans (N + O + P + Q + R).

At this point, we can carry out a useful check. Net assets should equal capital employed. Obviously, as net assets are calculated by means of the sum total assets minus current liabilities, this only leaves shareholders' funds, minority interests, long-term loans, provisions and other long-term liabilities or the capital employed. If they do not agree, it means you have not correctly copied all the figures over from the annual report. It should be simple enough to find your error. It is even simpler if the balance sheet includes the phrase 'total assets less current liabilities' as this is the figure you want!

Table 7.2 defines the second column of new terms shown in Figure 7.1.

Table 7.2 Definitions of the remaining extra terms to those given in Table 6.3

Reference letter	Term	How it is calculated and definition
FF	Quick assets	This is the figure for the total current assets minus the stocks (J – H). While the stock held by a company probably does have a value similar to that shown in the balance sheet, in order to turn it into cash it has to be sold. We are going to test the business's ability to deal with its short-term liabilities in two ways. The first will include stock and the other will exclude it.
GG	Total debt	This is the total of outstanding loans, long-term plus short-term ones, and is used in the advanced ratio calculations, (L + N).

Reference letter	Term	How it is calculated and definition
HH	Tangible net worth (Also written simply as 'Net worth')	This is total shareholders' funds less intangible fixed assets (Q – F). We have talked before about the 'unpopularity' of intangible assets, and in most balance sheets there are none. Where there are some, they are normally excluded from calculations concerning the return on shareholders' funds. That is, the net worth of the company is expressed as though the intangible assets were valueless.
II	Pre-interest profit	This is the profit that is available to meet the demands of shareholders for dividends and lenders for interest. It is calculated by adding the net profit before tax to interest payable (B + C). This figure is often called earnings before interest and tax.
JJ	Net working capital	This is total current assets less total current liabilities (J – M), and used in the more advanced ratios.

If the new form is filled in with the figures from Sherwood Industries, it looks like Figure 7.2

Company name:

Sherwood Industries

Currency and units: £m

Year		Last year (£m)	Previous year (£m)
Total sales turnover	A	1,404.6	1,041.9
Net profit before tax	B	39.2	48.7
Interest payable	C	17.6	10.8
Depreciation	D	26.0	19.9
Tangible fixed assets	E	158.8	160.4
Intangible fixed assets	F	0.0	0.0
Other fixed assets	G	0.3	7.8
Stocks	H	172.1	155.8
Trade debtors	I	258.4	200.4
Total current assets	J	543.4	470.1

Year		Last year (£m)	Previous year (£m)
Trade creditors	K	185.9	148.3
Short-term loans	L	29.8	57.8
Total current liabilities	M	333.2	292.1
Long-term loans	N	79.7	52.2
Provisions for liabilities and charges	O	2.1	4.6
Other long-term liabilities	P	7.5	5.9
Total shareholders' funds	Q	272.7	277.2
Minority interests	R	7.3	6.3
Average number of employees	S	0.011	0.007
Total of employees' remuneration	T	273.7	144.3

Calculated figures follow

		Last year (£m)	Previous year (£m)
Tangible and intangible fixed assets	AA	158.8	160.4
Total assets	BB	702.5	638.3
Total liabilities	CC	429.8	361.1
Net assets	DD	369.3	346.2
Capital employed	EE	369.3	346.2
Quick assets	FF	371.3	314.3
Total debt	GG	109.5	110.0
Tangible net worth	HH	272.7	277.2
Pre-interest profit	II	56.8	59.5
Net working capital	JJ	210.2	178.0

Fig. 7.2 The expanded form filled in for Sherwood Industries

We can now move on to calculating the key business ratios. The form for this is shown in Figure 7.3.

Company name:

	Last year	Previous year
Profitability		
Return on capital employed		
Profit margin		
Return on assets		
Shareholders' return		

	Last year	Previous year
Liquidity		
Current ratio		
Quick ratio (acid test)		

	Last year	Previous year
Asset utility		
Stock turnover		
Collection period		
Asset turnover		

	Last year	Previous year
Gearing		
Borrowing ratio		
Income gearing		

Employee ratios in round numbers		
Sales per employee		
Profit per employee		
Average wage per employee		

Growth rates	
Sales growth	
Profit growth	

Fig. 7.3 The form to be used when calculating key business ratios

Profitability ratios

As discussed in Chapter 3, in the final analysis, companies are in business to make profits. Here are the four most commonly used ratios to indicate to managers, shareholders and employees how well their business is doing in terms of profitability.

Return on capital employed

Term	Calculation
Return on capital employed	(Net profit before tax (B) ÷ Capital employed (EE)) × 100

This is often considered to be the main indicator of the profitability of a business. After all, the basis of enterprise is to take money in the form of share capital and loan capital and use it to earn profits. This percentage is a good guide to the performance of managers in terms of how successful they have been in producing sufficient returns. A sudden alteration in the ratio for better or worse would trigger further investigations to see what has changed.

In Chapter 3 we gave some examples, in terms of a simple benchmark guide, of what might be called high, medium and low returns. The real usefulness of this, however, arises, first, when you compare previous years' performance with the most recent historical figures, and, second when you compare that company's performance against other companies in the same business.

Return on capital employed is important whatever industry you are looking at.

Profit margin

Term	Calculation
Profit margin	(Net profit before tax (B) ÷ Total Sales turnover (A)) × 100

This ratio shows the profits made on each pound of sales. As businesses grow, their managers are concerned to maintain a good 'bottom line profit margin' over time. It is quite reasonable for peaks and troughs to occur, however. For example, where a company has been involved in a major expansion, it may take some time – measured in years – to get back to its original profit margin and then exceed it.

The figure you get is, of course, deeply bound up with the gross margin, which is the ratio of the gross profit to the total sales turnover. When there are concerns about the bottom line profit margin, you will have to look at the gross margin to see if the problem lies there or if it is the indirect costs that are causing problems. You will also need to read carefully what the managers say in explanation of any change or shortcoming.

Return on assets

Term	Calculation
Return on assets	(Net profit before tax (B) ÷ Total assets (BB)) × 100

This ratio is more important in some industries than others. Essentially, the clue to its importance is the amount of investment in fixed assets required to create a going concern. In a firm of consultants, for example, where there are few fixed assets as, arguably, the main assets are the people acting as consultants, this ratio will have little relevance.

Going back to our old favourites the telecommunications companies, the opposite is the case. Before they are able to make money from selling the use of the telephone, they have to invest heavily in creating the network. In such cases, managers will be very interested in the subsequent efforts of their people to squeeze profits out of these assets. 'Make the assets sweat' is the battle cry of a managing director who has invested a lot of capital in an enterprise.

If you take the case of a well-established company with little debt in its balance sheet, its performance in terms of return on capital employed may have become stable and reasonable. A better test of its ability to continue this into the future may very well be to examine its performance against assets. Indeed, if you can get close enough to a company to find out how its bonus scheme works, you may find that directors and/or staff are paid by the profit made on the assets.

In cases where this measure is important, the Board will frequently report on it in the annual report. If the calculation you have made does not exactly correspond with what the report states, check which measure of profit the company has used. In this model we use the figure for net profit before tax as tax is not entirely within the control of managers and may differ from year to year depending on circumstances. Sometimes the annual report will use net profit *after* tax in any of the profitability calculations we are discussing. Some calculations use earnings before interest and tax (EBIT), another frequently used profitability term.

Put simply, companies using their assets efficiently will have a relatively high return compared to those of less well-run businesses.

Return on shareholders' funds

Term	Calculation
Return on shareholders' funds	(Net profit before tax (B) ÷ Tangible net worth (HH)) × 100

This ratio measures management's ability to use the share capital in the business efficiently and produce good returns. There is a tendency to use this measure as a final measure of profitability. In some ways it is a more logical measure of return than is return on capital employed as the latter ratio is lowered by the inclusion of loan capital in capital employed. Some would argue that because the interest on loan capital has already been deducted from net profit before tax, the providers of the loan capital have already *had* their return and so should be excluded from the capital employed. That is the case with this ratio.

Using our benchmark guides, we would expect a return of 10 per cent to give room for the payment of tax and dividends and retain enough profits in the business to fund its growth.

In a small business, you could even use this measure to see whether or not it is worth while being in business at all. If a small business cannot produce, say, 5 per cent return on shareholders' funds, then the owners might as well put the money into a building society where it will, of course, be much more secure.

Liquidity ratios

We have mentioned previously how jobbing builders will know pretty accurately what their cash and short-term liabilities are. They are well aware that if they fail to complete a job, having bought the materials for the whole job and finished 90 per cent of it, they will not be paid. If there is a delay in payment, they will have difficulty buying materials or paying their people. So, they keep careful tabs on the 'liquidity' of their businesses.

Sometimes known as solvency ratios (though this is not technically accurate), liquidity ratios demonstrate a company's ability to meet short-term obligations.

Current ratio

Term	Calculation
Current ratio	Total current assets (J) ÷ Total current liabilities (M)

This ratio shows how well the current assets – assets that will be turned into cash in the next 12 months – cover the current liabilities, debts or obligations that must be met in the next 12 months. If the ratio is, for example, 1.5, it means that for every £1 of debt outstanding to be paid within a year, there is £1.50 in assets due to become cash quickly.

Remember always that it is management's job to move working capital round the business cycle as quickly as possible. This means that managers want to keep working capital to a minimum, provided that they do not get into short-term trouble with their creditors.

Large businesses, therefore, will run with a current ratio near to or even below 1. In the case of a company such as one that owns a chain of pubs and restaurants, it may very well work with a ratio of less than 1. The fact that they can rely on large amounts of cash coming into the business on a daily basis means that there is no danger that they will be unable to meet their short-term obligations, even though, at any one point in time, the working capital ratio is less than 1. Similarly, if the cash business works with stock, which they pay for after it has been sold, this situation will arise.

Large companies also have a great deal of power over both their customers and their suppliers. Consider again the telecommunications company. If a customer goes into arrears, the company can quickly turn off the service and then charge a fee for turning it on again once the account has been cleared. There is not much the customer can do to stop this. Changing to another supplier of these services will be difficult if they have a poor record of payment. This means that the credit collection period for such a company (see below) is pretty quick.

Its relationship with its suppliers also gives it great liquidity advantages. If a telecommunications company chooses to make a supplier wait an extra few days before making payment, there is little the supplier, which needs the volume of business that is available here, can do except wait. From these facts alone it is not surprising that the largest telecommunications company in the UK operates with a current ratio of 0.9. In effect, the company's credit period – the amount of time, measured in days, it takes to collect money from debtors (see below) – is shorter than its opposite, the company's settlement period. The settlement period is the amount of time, measured in days, a company takes to pay its creditors.

Our jobbing builders on the other hand probably have to have working capital, including access to short-term lending, which gives a ratio of say, 1.5. This gives them the cover against problems and ensures a continuation of their ability to pay the wages and buy supplies.

Simply put, the higher the ratio, the higher the security that the company has sufficient cash flow to met its short-term obligations.

Quick ratio or acid test

Term	Calculation
Quick ratio or acid test	Quick assets (that is current assets excluding stock (FF)) ÷ current liabilities (M)

A way to remember that there can be a huge difference between what the figures say and what the physical reality is, is the old story of the jobbing builder who claimed to his bank manager, through his balance sheet, that he had the fixed asset of a cement mixer and a stock of cement. In fact, when the bank manager visited the premises and looked around, he found that the cement mixer had hardened concrete in it.

So, while the balance sheet *was* accurate, the truth was that neither the fixed asset nor the cement held in stock had any value at all!

The value of stock is normally held at the lower of what the items cost and what they could be sold for. This should give a reasonably sensible statement of the value of the stock. However, of course, in order to turn stock into cash, you have to complete the work in progress and sell the finished goods. Company watchers therefore apply a more stringent liquidity test than the working capital ratio by taking stock out of the equation. This quick ratio, or acid test, is that more stringent test.

The importance of the working capital ratios to smaller companies is often heightened by their bank's willingness to lend being dependent on their maintaining an agreed level of liquidity. A bank may, for example, limit its overdraft facility to a small company to say 80 per cent of its outstanding debtors. Or it could refuse facilities when the current ratio has fallen below 1.

Asset utility

In the section on profitability ratios, we emphasised the importance of the managers of a business producing a satisfactory return on the money that shareholders and lenders have put in. The other crucial measure of the performance of management is to see how well they are 'sweating the assets.'

There are three key business ratios involved in this measurement.

Stock turnover

Term	Calculation
Stock turnover	Total sales turnover (A) ÷ Stocks (H)

In an ideal world, a company would buy in or manufacture finished goods just before they were due to be delivered to customers. This would minimise the cost of holding the stock in warehouses and, of course, reduce the requirement for working capital.

We can measure this from the report and accounts by dividing the sales by the current stock. This tells us how many times in a year the stock has been turned over. In simple terms, the more times management has turned over its stock the better.

It is, of course, very much dependent on the type of business that the company is in. We would expect a supermarket to turn over its stock very quickly, compared, say, with a manufacturer of aeroplanes. In the latter case, the length of time the product is in the work in progress stage, that is, is being built, is bound to be lengthy and therefore its stock turnover quite low. If you take a greengrocer, some of whose products become unsaleable within a few days of arriving as stock, you could expect a stock turnover of as much as 40 times per year. A company selling heavy engineering goods, on the other hand, may well be satisfied with four or five times.

You will sometimes see stock turnover expressed in terms of days. Sales divided by stock gives the number of times stock turned over in a year, so if you divide 365 by the stock turnover figure, you get the average number of days the stock was held. So, a stock turnover of ten times a year could also be expressed as 'Average time stock is held = 36.5 days'.

The calculation described here is a convenient one to do as the accounts will always show the figure for sales turnover and stock. A more accurate measure of stock turnover is obtained by using the figure for the cost of sales rather than turnover. This may be available in the annual accounts and, if so, it should be used.

The internal performance measures used by a company would provide a more accurate measure of stockholding efficiency as they, too, would use the figure for cost of sales rather than the turnover figure.

Further they would also look at stock turnover product by product. Depending on the gross margins on the various products, this could give a different picture from the one available to the public. This is simply another example of how the managers of the company are bound to be better informed than us. We should be conscious of the problem and look out for those areas where this could be significant. For example, the group accounts of a conglomerate would combine a variety of types of business, which would result in the stock turnover being averaged for the whole group.

Collection period

Term	Calculation
Collection period	The average time in days that debtors take to pay their bills is calculated as follows: Trade debtors (I) ÷ average daily sales (Total sales (A) ÷ 365).

Another crucial measure of management efficiency is the amount of time it takes to get money in. A poor performance, of say 110 days, probably shows that there is a problem in the company's business systems. It could, of course, be even more problematical if the real reason for delay is disputed amounts, where the customer does not agree with the figure given in their bill, or unmet expectations for delivery, where the customer is not satisfied that the supplier has delivered what was promised.

However, there can be valid reasons for seemingly poor performance. In high-tech companies, for example, a high collection period figure often arises because it takes time to make the product work to the customer's satisfaction. If the normal payment term in the industry being looked at is 30 days, then you should expect the collection period to be around 50 to 70 days. Less is a good performance, more reveals a likely problem.

Beware of doing this calculation for companies that do a lot of trade in cash. If, say, 50 per cent of its income involves no collection period at all, because the customer pays in cash, then we should really take that number out of the calculation to find the real collection period. Once again, inside the company, where they have the necessary information, they probably set collection targets taking cash sales into account. From outside the company, however, we may be unable to do better than look at the total sales figure as we do not know how much business involved cash. This does not invalidate the calculation entirely as we can compare the performance of management last year with its performance the previous year, and, as we will see in Chapter 8, we can compare the company with an industry average.

Asset turnover

Term	Calculation
Asset turnover	(Total turnover (A) ÷ Total assets (BB)) × 100. This is sometimes called asset utilisation.

We have said that the shareholders have given the managers of the business capital with which to earn a return. They have also given them an asset base to work with. A simple measure of their efficiency in using these assets is to compare the asset base with the total sales turnover.

As usual, this differs from industry to industry, so asset utilisation is high at the retail end of the spectrum, at, say, more than 250 per cent, and low in property letting, at, say, 20 per cent.

Gearing

High gearing carries a number of implications for companies and shareholders. If the company has a high level of debt compared to shareholders' funds, it is, of course, vulnerable to the effects of increases in interest rates. Whereas the income gearing, or interest cover, may have been satisfactory at the time the loans were taken out, such a ratio may become dangerous if interest rates go up sharply. Such potential effects of change should be taken into account when judging a company's gearing.

Low gearing is not in itself always a wholly positive sign either. If a company has little or no debt, shareholders may wonder if management is doing all it can to expand the business and take the well-informed risks that go with higher returns. Low gearing, however, means that there is the potential for borrowing if good opportunities arise. We need to ask ourselves if a low-geared company is becoming poised to raise money from lenders, for example, to make an acquisition. If you watch the financial pages, they will give you this information. Note that it is particularly useful to do this when a company you are interested in is reporting its annual or half-yearly figures as, around that time, the company's strategy will be announced and commented on in the financial pages.

In Chapter 3, we discussed two gearing ratios – total liabilities to shareholder's funds, which we will return to in Chapter 8, and income gearing, which we shall refer to again here. There is also another gearing measure – the borrowing ratio.

Borrowing ratio

Term	Calculation
Borrowing ratio or debt equity ratio	(Total debt (GG) ÷ Tangible net worth (HH)) × 100

This is an important ratio in determining the creditworthiness of a company and its potential to grow the business by borrowing further money. A profitable company will normally retain part of its earnings, after dividends, to help fund its growth and invest for the future. This addition to shareholders' funds allows the company to borrow more without increasing its borrowing ratio. Acceptable borrowing ratios, as usual, vary from one industry to another, but it is possible to suggest a benchmark guide.

Take a company with debt and tangible net worth (this, remember, is equity less intangible assets) that together come to £100 million. Here are three examples of how they might divide up.

Debt	10	50	90
Tangible net worth	90	50	10
	100	100	100

The borrowing ratios for each of these are therefore: 11% 100% 900%

The benchmark guide interprets these numbers as low, medium and very high.

Now a reminder of the income gearing ratio.

Income gearing

Term	Calculation
Income gearing	(Interest payable (C) ÷ Profit before interest and tax (II)) × 100

This ratio highlights the profits that are available to pay gross interest. It shows how easily interest can be paid out of profits and, therefore, indicates whether or not there is a possibility that the company will have problems paying its interest in the future. If a company has a good record of profits and there is an obvious upward trend in its profitability, this ratio may be more useful than the previously mentioned capital gearing ratio. For example, a management buyout may be highly geared at the outset as the managers have borrowed the money to buy the company. A strong profit trend and an improving income gearing ratio, however, should satisfy shareholders and even give scope for further borrowing if that is appropriate within the announced strategy. This assumes that the growth potential is still there. At some point, the shareholders and Board will probably prefer to pay down debt and increase the number of shares. At that time, the gearing will obviously fall.

Take a company that has produced earnings before interest and tax of £60 million. Depending on the amount of outstanding debt, the income gearing ratio could look like one of the following.

Profit before interest and tax	60	60	60
Gross interest paid	12	30	48
Income gearing for each of these is	20%	50%	80%

Thus, our benchmark guide is that these are low, medium and high ratios, respectively. You can easily see from this example how much less risk there is to lenders and shareholders alike in the low-geared company (the first one) where the profits cover the interest paid five times. It is a very different story in the third case, where interest accounts for 80 per cent of the profits. There is not much room left here to pay tax and dividends, and if profits were to dip slightly or interest rates go up a touch, then the income gearing ratio figure could easily rise to above 100 per cent and the existence of the company might then be threatened.

So far, we have studied the hard data revealed in the company report from a balance sheet and profit and loss account angle. There is one other important area to be looked at, which is the people who work for the company – often called 'Our greatest asset' in the Chairman's statement. We need to see how well, comparatively, the company is using its 'greatest asset' by looking at some productivity and remuneration ratios.

The employee ratios

The three main ratios used in this area are the sales per employee, profit per employee and average wage per employee. In order to get these numbers right, in round terms, you need to take into account what units you are working in. If, for example, the figures are presented in £ million (£1,564 representing £1.564 billion), then you will have to remember to adjust the employee ratio to allow for the different units.

Sales per employee

Term	Calculation
Sales per employee	Total sales turnover (A) ÷ Average number of employees in the year (S)

Let's work through an example to underline how important it is to get the units right.

Total sales turnover in £ million	£1,000
Average number of employees	10,000
Total sales per employee	(£1,000/10,000) x 1,000,000
	£100,000 (in round numbers)

There are big variations in the results for this ratio depending on which industry you are looking at. For example, the ratio for labour-intensive industries, such as services, is much lower than it is for automated manufacturing sectors, such as the computer industry. Thus, hotels could be running perfectly well with half the sales productivity of electronic manufacturers. As a benchmark guide, hotels may have ratios of less than £50,000 sales per employee and electronic manufacturers £120,000 or more.

The imporant thing is that if a company is falling behind its *competitors* in terms of its sales per employee, this could very well lead to a reduction in its profit. People are expensive, both to keep and to make redundant, so companies look carefully at this ratio to ensure they are keeping up their competitive edge, or at least not losing ground.

Profit per employee

Term	Calculation
Profit per employee	Net profit before tax (B) ÷ Average number of employees in the year (S)

Once more, what is a good figure will vary from sector to sector. Thus in the construction industry, profit per employee may be £4,000 or less, while in the property letting business, profits per employee could be five times that.

If a company has a competitive *sales* per employee figure, but a lower than average profit per employee figure, we may feel that its costs, direct or indirect, are not being controlled as well as those of its competitors.

Lack of competitiveness in the profit per employee ratio is a signal to shareholders to examine the Board's plans for the number of people it employs. Such a situation will have to be countered by increasing sales and improving profits or by decreasing the number of people employed. In a competitive business environment, it is not possible for such a situation to continue unchanged.

Average wage per employee

Term	Calculation
Average wage per employee	Total of employees' remuneration (T) ÷ Average number of employees in the year (S)

Once again, the importance of this ratio lies in how it comments on a company's competitiveness. If a company pays below the normal market rate for its people, it will tend, in the long term, to have a poorer quality workforce than if it paid them more, as it will fail to attract the best in the market or retain its own best people.

It is important to make sure that you are comparing like with like. If, for example, you compare two companies operating in the same kind of business, but with one the great majority of its people are based in the UK and with the other a large number of its staff are in South-East Asia, you may find that the wages per employee figure is much higher in the former than the latter. This, though, may not indicate an inconsistency as the latter is operating in an environment where, at least at the present time, the wages are generally much lower than they are in the UK.

Growth ratios

We spoke earlier in this chapter about how the figures in an annual report only really become useful when you make comparisons. The first and easiest comparison to make is of last year with the previous year. It is a good idea if you are following a company closely to gather more than two years' data and look at the ratios over, say, a five-year period. However, to start with, there are two more ratios that it is useful to calculate from the figures given in any annual report. They are sales growth and profit growth.

Sales growth

Term	Calculation
Sales growth	((Last year's Total sales turnover – The previous year's Total sales turnover) ÷ (The previous year's Total sales turnover)) × 100

Most companies need growth in sales to prosper. The level of growth necessary to achieve this is going to vary from industry to industry and obviously it will be higher during times of high inflation. In some ways, the best measure of whether or not the growth is sufficient is to look at what was said in the Chairman's statement. The important thing, to reiterate what we said earlier, is that the growth is on target.

Profit growth

Term	Calculation
Profit growth	((Last year's Net profits before tax – The previous year's Net profits before tax) ÷ (The previous year's Net profits before tax)) × 100

How to read them

The major comparison we would make here is between profit growth and sales growth. Boards will always attempt to avoid times when sales growth is outstripping profit growth. In the long term, it is untenable; in the short term, it saps morale. If the people in the business find that they have gone through all the trauma of making, say, 20 per cent more sales, but that profits have stayed the same or only increased modestly, they are going to wonder whether or not all the extra effort was worth while. And so are the shareholders. Most chairmen comment on this comparison in their statements.

Remember, though, that the Chairman also has to evaluate whether or not if sales had not increased enormously they would even have maintained, let alone increased, last year's profit.

Having learnt how to extract the relevant data in Chapter 6 and calculate the key business ratios in this one, it is time to return to Sherwood Industries to see how well its ratios are faring.

Calculating the ratios for Sherwood Industries

Using the reference letters from A to T and the calculated figures AA to JJ, we can produce the key business ratios for Sherwood Industries. Iain, the Darnley Village Investment Club member charged with analysing Sherwood Industries, has done the calculations and presents these to the other members, as shown in Figure 7.4 (note that the employee ratios in Figure 7.4 have been calculated using the exact number of employees rather than the rounded numbers used in Figure 7.2).

Company name:

Sherwood Industries

Profitability	Last year	Previous year
Return on capital employed	10.6%	14.1%
Profit margin	2.8%	4.7%
Return on assets	5.6%	7.6%
Shareholders' return	14.4%	17.6%

Liquidity		
Current ratio	1.6	1.6
Quick ratio (acid test)	1.1	1.1

Asset utility		
Stock turnover	8.2	6.7
Collection period	67.1	70.2
Asset turnover	199.9%	163.2%

Gearing	Last year	Previous year
Borrowing ratio	40.2%	39.7%
Income gearing	31.0%	18.2%

Employee ratios in round numbers		
Sales per employee	128,910	152,503
Profit per employee	3,598	7,128
Average wage per employee	25,119	21,121

Growth rates		
Sales growth	34.8%	
Profit growth	−19.5%	

Fig. 7.4 The form for recording the key business ratios filled in for Sherwood Industries

Darnley Village Investment Club looks at the key business ratios for Sherwood Industries

Chairman: 'Thank you for your good work Iain. How did you get on with the new spreadsheet version of the ratios model? Was it easy enough to use?'

Iain: 'You bet. The best thing about it was that when I put in the numbers for the average number of employees, I got the units wrong and ended up telling the computer that Sherwood Industries had 10.896 million employees! Because it gave such a stupid answer for the employee ratios, I saw the mistake immediately and was able to correct it quickly. The same happened when I miscopied some numbers for the long-term liabilities and Net assets did not equal Capital employed, which it should have done.

'Let's look at the figures line by line. Perhaps the best thing you can say about the profitability numbers is that there are no surprises. We noted earlier that profits had fallen this year and, of course, all the ratios calculated reflect this fall. Frankly, working on our usual benchmark guides, they have dropped from the low end of satisfactory to the high end of unsatisfactory, if you see what I mean.

'I then looked to see if all the ratios had gone down more or less pro rata and came up with something that might be interesting.'

Table 7.3 The percentage falls from last year to this year in the profitability ratios for Sherwood Industries

Ratios	Last year	Previous year	Percentage fall
Return on capital employed	10.6	14.1	24.8
Profit margin	2.8	4.7	40.4
Return on assets	5.6	7.6	26.3
Return on shareholders' funds	14.4	17.6	18.2

The figures Iain has calculated are shown in Table 7.3. He has taken the four profitability ratios and calculated the percentage falls from last year's figures to those for this year.

Darnley Village Investment Club continues its discussion on Sherwood Industries

Iain: 'For example, return on capital employed has gone down by nearly 25 per cent which is similar to the fall in return on assets – 26 per cent – and not too far from the return on shareholders' funds at 18 per cent. However, the drop in the profit margin is dramatically higher, at 40 per cent.

What I think this means is that the volatility in profits is more to do with the day-to-day running than with significant change in the business. To check this, I then decided to do a comparison between the change in gross margin and the margin after the indirect costs. This completely backed up what I am saying and, I think, what Sherwood Industries' Chairman was saying as well.'

Table 7.4 Analysing Sherwood Industries' profitability further

	Last year	*Previous year*
Sales turnover	1,404.6	1,041.9
Cost of sales	1,008.6	773.0
Gross profit	396.0	268.9
Gross margin	28.2%	25.8%
Indirect costs	347.8	215.6
Indirect costs as a percentage of sales	24.8%	20.7%

The second set of figures Iain has worked out are shown in Table 7.4. He has taken the gross margin (gross profit divided by sales turnover) and worked out the rate of change that has ocurred between the years. He has then done another, and slightly unusual, calculation in order to express the indirect costs and distribution expenses plus administration expenses as a percentage of sales.

SCENARIO

Darnley Village Investment Club discuss Sherwood Industries some more

Iain: 'You see, the gross margin has actually gone up from over 25 per cent to 28 per cent. This has got to be good news. I think it must mean that the gross margins in the healthcare part are a good deal better than the two divisions that are losing money. Now the indirect costs as a percentage of sales have gone up from nearly 21 per cent last year to nearly 25 per cent this, so the more controllable part of the business is where the profitability problem lies.'

Diana: 'How does that back up what the Board is saying?'

Iain: 'Well, remember how easily they passed over the problem of restoring profitability to the Precious metals and Electronic components divisions? What they said on page 9 of the annual report, in the first case, was that they would return to profitability "... from a reduction in costs resulting from the rationalisation of facilities on to one site." In the case of Electronic components, they said "... coupled with a number of internal changes that are currently in progress, should result in a return to profit this year." So, the acquisition strategy based on the divisional managers' running of the day-to-day business starts to sound reasonable and is, to some extent, backed up by the numbers, assuming that we agree with the Chairman's optimistic view on gearing.'

Chairman: 'Does it make sense, in trying to understand your analysis, to move straight to gearing and come back to asset utilisation later?'

Iain: 'I think so, yes. At first I thought I had got the numbers wrong. In the Chairman's statement, Walter Sherwood says that "net borrowings [are] representing only 19 per cent of shareholders' funds." Our calculations put the borrowing ratio at 40 per cent – quite a difference.
'In fact, *both* figures are correct, although, to be honest, I think ours is a more stringent test of gearing.'

The difference between the two expressions of the borrowing ratio is the cash that Sherwood Industries has in the bank. The calculation Iain has done using the model given in this chapter uses the total debt figure – short-term plus long-term, expressed as a percentage of shareholders' funds. Walter Sherwood reduces the debt figure by the cash he has in the bank. Figure 7.5 shows this calculation.

Shareholders' funds		272.7
Borrowings		
Short-term	29.8	
Long-term	79.7	
Total		109.5
Gross borrowings to Shareholders' funds		40.2%
Cash	57.4	
Net borrowings		52.1
Net borrowings to Shareholders' funds		19.1%

Fig. 7.5

Let's listen to the members of the Darnley Club discussing the rights and wrongs of this.

Darnley Village Investment Club talk some more

Diana: 'This is one of those times when I wonder if all this detective work has any point. Is the borrowing ratio of Sherwood Industries 40 per cent or 19 per cent, which is less than half of the first figure?'

Iain: 'Both, actually. You have to take a view. Walter Sherwood uses the 19 per cent figure to support his contention that he is in a position to move fast on an opportunity to buy a company because his borrowing ratio is low. This means that it would be easy to get the banks to lend more money as, even with it, the gearing will still be at a feasible level. Now, the reason for his taking the cash away from the debt is because he can argue that he can use the unused cash as part of the buying price of a company.

'We may think that is fair enough or we may argue that the cash in the bank is a buffer in case anything goes wrong in the short term. A sudden drop in sales, for instance, or a bad and significant change in exchange rates could leave the company temporarily having to use the cash up to support its short-term requirements. You have to think about this in the context of a big business. How likely is it that enough could go wrong in the short term to make a significant dent in its cash mountain, or, if not mountain, at least its cash hill?'

Chairman: 'Just to interrupt for a moment, Iain, is the liquidity ratio not relevant here?'

Emily: 'Yes, it must be, because from others that I have looked at, this liquidity at 1.6 is higher than I would expect of a company of this size. This would tend to back up the Chairman's view of gearing.'

Iain: 'Mmm, yes, but in any case folks, let's remember that even if our calculation is the more accurate version of the position, 40 per cent is by our benchmark guide, well below what we take to be medium gearing. So his statement in terms of flexibility and readiness to act looks reasonable in the circumstances.'

Chairman: 'Assuming, of course, that you don't worry about the income gearing, which, because of the drop in profits, all but doubled last year from 18 per cent to 31 per cent. We would have to take as gospel the company's statements that it is going to fix the profitability problems. If the position were to worsen by that amount again this year, the strategy would be shot.'

Iain: 'I know there is no such thing as a certainty, but you have to give a business this big and this old the benefit of some doubt. It must be able to put right a profit problem that is based on the need to rationalise some costs following a change in gross margin and a change in the pattern of demand. Now I know it sounds a bit upside down, but the fact that the employee productivity figures have gone down supports this view.'

'Sales per employee have dropped from 152,503 to 128,910. It must have known that that was going to be the case when it went through with the takeover. The number of employees went up to 10,896 from 6,832. This is a rise of 60 per cent. This was a massive change and we must expect it to take time to get the profitability back to where it should be. And the sales per employee figure seems high, although we won't really know about that until we have done the comparisons with the industry averages. Profit per employee is hit with the double whammy of a drop in profits *and* a rise in employees.'

Chairman: 'Well, it all seems to be plausible. You do seem to be able to explain the strategy in terms of the numbers from the last two years. Before we summarise, though, is there anything significant about the asset utility numbers?'

Iain: 'Once again, it's interesting because all these numbers improved. The stock turnover did, although this could simply be the difference caused by their being in somewhat different businesses. Maybe the new ones, by the nature of the company's business, have a higher turnover. I suppose you could really say the same about the other two ratios. The collection period has gone down by some 3 days, or 4 per cent – not inconsiderable when you are talking about daily sales of nearly £4 million. Using our benchmark guide, this has gone from the top of what we would regard as a medium performance to the bottom of what we would regard as doing well. It *may* be important, but it's difficult to know, given the change in the nature of a large chunk of its business.'

Diana: 'Talking about differences, have you seen the change in average wage per employee?'

Iain: 'Yes, but, again, that must be because the new businesses have much higher earners than the old. I mean, it's a swing from chemical manufacturing to healthcare. I am sure that this year we will see that that rise is not repeated if everything stays the same.'

Diana: 'But how do we know that will happen? It would be jolly useful to have next year's numbers before we make the investment!'

Chairman: 'Ain't that the truth Diana, but that's the nature of the Club! We are trying, within the bounds of our experience and logic, to guess the future. We could, of course wait until next year and see how Sherwood Industries has fared, but if it goes well and the market does re-rate it because of a series of successful takeovers, we will have missed the boat.

'When we had finished our look at the company strategy's, I summarised by saying that the share suited us and that we could live with the strategy in terms of what products and services it wanted to develop and where it wanted to develop them. There were acts of faith involved at that time. The first was that we had to do the financial analysis to see that the figures stacked up against the strategy and gave a good indication that, while pursuing that strategy, it would continue to pay the current dividend at all times or, better still, improve it. I think the work that Iain has done and this discussion has done just that. There *is* a risk that the dividends or the strategy could go wrong, of course, but that is the nature of the investment business. The figures are reasonable and seem to back up the statements of the Chairman and directors. We have more to do, in that we normally compare companies' numbers against some sort of industry average. I think we should still do that, although its being a diversified industrial makes it difficult to know what average to compare it with.

'Keith, will you take that task away with you, and maybe Graham could give you a hand?

'That still leaves the other act of faith, which Emily raised when we were nearing the end of our discussion on strategy. Are these the right people to manage the new strategy? Can Mr Moss keep his hands off the current business, find new businesses to buy and then keep the new managements to grow the divisions by selling more products and services more profitably? It's the big question on which we will have to take a view at the end of our deliberations.'

We will leave Darnley Investment Club there for the moment, and come back to them in Chapter 8, when we deal with industry averages.

Conclusion

We said at the beginning that the reading of a balance sheet and profit and loss account has elements of the detective story about it, and during this chapter we have tried to unravel the mystery of Sherwood Industries. It is a question, first of all, of understanding and buying into the physical strategy for the business and then using common sense in the main part to see whether or not the figures as they are at the moment support the managers' ability to deliver the promises set out in the business plan.

The argument goes from one ratio to another as you interpret the numbers and link them back to the physical world. For private investors it is almost certain to be more productive to do the analysis with at least one other person. A conversation pushes you to ask the right question next and keep away from the esoteric in favour of the practical. Two minds are more likely to get to the bottom of the puzzle than one. That is why investment clubs can offer such promise to the private investor. We shall look more at them and how to set them up in Chapter 10.

Project the buy on to your portfolio

At this point, as a choice of share is imminent, investors should check the impact the shares would have on their portfolios were they to buy them. Because of the way we have chosen which sort of share to go for, in terms of risk, this should be no problem. However, if the portfolio has changed since the analysis was started, investors need to take another look. Simply add the new shares into the portfolio's risk model and check that the profile of shares will stay in accord with the risk strategy.

EXERCISES FOR CHAPTER 7

Becoming familiar with financial information

EXERCISE 1 The more familiar you become with identifying financial data and calculating the ratios, the quicker you will become. Take as many annual reports as you have time to analyse and find the relevant data. Refer back to Chapter 6 if you need to as a refresher.

EXERCISE 2 If you have not already done so, take the data for Sherwood Industries from the annual report (see Appendix 1) and make sure you understand how the ratios were derived.

Now take copies of the data forms given in the book, or work on them on a computer if you have inputted them, and calculate the key business ratios for the reports you have gathered together.

Advancing your investment strategy

EXERCISE 3 By now, you will have a short list for the sector you have decided to invest in and pared it down to only two or three possibles. Take each of them and try to ally the ratios with the business strategy you identified at the end of Chapter 5 in the exercise you did ther under the heading Advancing your investment strategy.

EXERCISE 4 Are the details in the Chairman's statement consistent with what the numbers tell you?

Does the strategy derived, in the main, from the report of the directors still seem feasible now that you have understood the figures?

Can you see any financial reasons that indicate that the strategy may not be implemented?

If you had to choose just one of the shares to buy, which one would it be?

CHAPTER 8

Some advanced ratios and the rest of the annual report

What comes after the financial reports can be as important as the figures themselves

- Industry averages
- Some advanced financial ratios
- Some other ratios and measures
- The annual report
- Conclusion
- Exercises

Previous chapters covered the main parts of the annual report. We need to look, at least in summary, at the other items in the report and at some advanced ratios that allow you to compare a company with its competitors and keep up with the latest theories of value investment.

Industry averages

So far, in looking at published figures to assess value for investment purposes, we have limited our examination to a comparison of the current year's performance with that of the previous year. However, there are other comparisons we can make that give further clues in our pursuit of value.

In a similar way to the *Financial Times'* report on the back page, which calculates average yield and price/earnings ratios for a sector, so there is available a wealth of information on the key business ratios for different sectors. This can be found in the reference sections of a lot of libraries or you can subscribe for a book of them, which is updated at least annually.

Quite simply what the publishers of the books do is to take all the profit and loss accounts and balance sheets of a business sector, consolidate them into one set of figures and calculate the key business ratios to give an average for the sector.

The problem with such averages is deciding to which business sector the company you are interested in belongs. Most large companies have developed differently and find themselves with divisions or subsidiaries that make sense in some way with the Board's strategy but do not follow the parent into exactly the same industrial sector. This was more prevalent in the 1980s, when the fashion was diversification, than in the 1990s, with its clarion call to return to core business.

Assuming you feel comfortable that the comparison you are making is of apples with apples, then good information will come from such an exercise.

You can, of course, create your own industry ratios by deciding which company you think will give the most useful comparison. Run that company through the ratios model and you can then compare your target companies with it. If you then follow all of these companies over a period of time, you may find yourself joining those investors, often large fund managers, who leave investment money in a particular sector and switch the emphasis from one share to another depending on how the strategy and performance figures read. You will often read of stockbrokers advising their clients to switch from Barclays to Natwest or from BP to Shell or vice versa, say.

Another step further down that line is to take the sector in which you are interested and obtain the reports of several or all the companies operating in it. You can then aggregate the inputs and use the result to calculate your own industry average. It does not take long, it costs almost nothing and it takes your skill in doing the calculations and interpreting the results to an even higher level.

Down at Darnley Village Investment Club, they are doing just this to finish their analysis of Sherwood Industries.

Darnley Village Investment Club return to a consideration of Sherwood Industries

Chairman: 'Right, the continuing saga of Sherwood Industries. We left it, I think, with Keith and Graham about to go ferreting around the industry averages books to compare the main issues with companies in similar businesses. How did you get on?'

Keith: 'First of all we ran into the problem Iain had hinted at – with what companies do we compare Sherwood Industries? We actually found an average for diversified industrials, but decided that it was not relevant as Sherwood Industries efforts in that direction are so relatively recent. I also found it difficult to believe in the validity of such a comparison except in one area. The thread that runs through the strategy of all conglomerates is their desire to acquire other companies. Acquisition occurs from time to time as the last purchase is integrated into the group and the cash availability comes back to normal or even well above normal.

'You will recall our discussion on the gearing of Sherwood Industries, and the fact that the Chairman was claiming to be in a good position to buy companies. His argument settled round the liquidity of the Group, which gave them the power to go on the prowl. So, we decided to compare the liquidity of Sherwood Industries with the industry average first of all, and then with another company known to be well set for acquisition.'

Chairman: 'And the result?'

Graham: 'The calculation of total debt to tangible net worth, or the borrowing ratio, would seem to support Sherwood Industries. The ratio was 40 per cent using our calculation, which, by our normal benchmark guides, was relatively low. In fact, the same ratio for the average conglomerate was 145 per cent at the last count, which our benchmark guide says is above neutral. I then took a large organisation that is in the news for being predatory right now and found that its borrowing ratio was still slightly over 100 per cent. I think we have to give that one to the Chairman of Sherwood Industries, he looks financially capable of carrying out his strategy at least in the short term.'

Keith: 'We decided to ignore any comparisons of profitability. We knew without doing them that they were bound to be poor. After all, one of the reasons we think we may have found shareholder value in the company is because its profits are low right now and we have decided to believe management when they say they can fix it.

'However, we did look at the sales per employee ratio. At 128,910, this seemed at the time high and it still does. The comparison is probably not terribly accurate, but this is as good as anyone in the chemicals business and not far behind, distributors, which, particularly with the Electronic components business, is what Sherwood Industries claims to be good at.'

Chairman: 'Well done. We must not rely too heavily on these things, but where the comparison with some sort of rational benchmark confirms your initial feelings about a company, it does make you feel more comfortable that you have got it right. I think, incidentally, that the way Keith and Graham looked for a small number of particularly relevant indicators is the only way to make the averages figures work for us.

'So, we like the strategy, the company fits our needs, the key ratio analysis supports our view, as do comparisons with other companies. The downside looks limited, in that if the new strategy does not make the company thrive it can always go back to what it has a track record of being good at, albeit with a new Chairman and Chief Executive. The downside of that would be a drop in value in the share and probably a long period of time for it to come back into favour, but it would not be curtains. The yield should continue anyway.'

Emily: 'So that leaves the management. Do we believe in it? Can it deliver the promises it is making. That's still the key.'

Chairman: 'I agree. We have done a good analysis, and we know that when we have done that we tend to make better investments than when we respond to some tip and hope for the best. However, in the end, it's up to the people working in the business to make it successful. The time has come: do we buy Sherwood Industries as a long-term member of our Investment Club funds or do we find something else?'

Good point. We'll withdraw from the good folk of Darnley's meeting. After all, these things are personal. Would *you* buy the share?

Some advanced financial ratios

If you look at some of the more popular books of key business ratios you will find some ratios that we have not covered. Here are some examples:

- fixed assets to net worth

- current liabilities to net worth

- current liabilities to stock

- sales to net working capital

- creditors to sales

- capital employed per employee.

We are grateful to Dun & Bradstreet, the regular publishers of *Key Business Ratios* for giving us permission to use these ratios, which are in addition to our model. To be consistent and to help you to become familiar with the language such publications use, we have also, by kind permission, used their definitions and interpretations.

First of all, three ratios that are mainly to do with the financial viability of a company when compared to its strategy.

Fixed assets to net worth

Term	Calculation
Fixed assets to net worth	(Tangible and intangible fixed assets (AA) ÷ Tangible net worth (HH)) × 100

You will recall that net worth in this definition is equal to shareholders' funds less intangible fixed assets. The proportion of net worth that consists of fixed assets will vary greatly from industry to industry, but, in general terms, a company is undercapitalised if fixed assets exceed net worth. In this case, it is possible that the company has too much debt, and it should therefore be examined with care. If, on the other hand, fixed assets are much lower than net worth, the company is overcapitalised and is either extremely cautious or in a position to expand. Thus a ratio either well in excess of the median (as defined in the Dun & Bradstreet industrial averages) or well below it, means that the company should be looked at with care.

Current liabilities to net worth

Term	Calculation
Current liabilities to tangible net worth	(Total current liabilities (M) ÷ Tangible net worth (HH)) × 100

This ratio contrasts the funds that creditors are temporarily risking with a company with the funds permanently invested by the owners. The higher the ratio, the less security there is for the creditors. Care should be exercised when selling to any company that has a ratio of creditors of less than one year that exceeds two thirds of its net worth.

Current liabilities to stock

Term	Calculation
Current liabilities to stock	(Total current liabilities (M) ÷ Stocks (H)) × 100

This ratio gives an indication of the extent to which the business relies on the disposal of stocks to meet its debts. If the ratio is high, indications are that stocks are not a problem. On the other hand, if all short-term debt is being utilised to finance stock – a low ratio would indicate this – there is a strong possibility that the company is failing to sell its products and may be faced with financial problems.

Now, two asset utility ratios.

Sales to net working capital

Term	Calculation
Sales to net working capital	Total sales turnover (A) ÷ Net working capital (JJ)

This ratio indicates whether or not a company is overtrading (handling an excessive amount of sales in relation to its working capital). Companies with substantial sales gains often reach a level where their working capital becomes strained. Even if they maintain an adequate total investment for the volume being generated (in their assets to sales ratio), that investment may be so bound up in fixed assets or other non-current items that it will be difficult to continue to meet all their current obligations. A ratio falling into either an extremely high or low position may indicate potential problems.

Creditors to sales

Term	Calculation
Creditors to sales	(Trade creditors (K) ÷ Total sales turnover (A)) × 365

This ratio shows how a company is paying its suppliers in relation to the volume of sales being made. A high number, or one higher than the industry norm, indicates that the firm may be using suppliers to help finance operations. This ratio is especially important to short-term creditors as a high number could indicate potential problems in paying vendors.

(As with the stock turnover ratio discussed in Chapter 7, this calculation is a convenient one to do as the figures are available in the accounts. A better measure of the payment of creditors would use purchases rather than sales figures and the good news is that this information is now required in the directors' report.)

Finally, here is an additional employee ratio.

Capital employed per employee

Term	Calculation
Capital employed per employee	Capital employed (EE) ÷ Average number of employees in the year (S)

This ratio shows the value of the assets employed per employee. The higher the ratio, the greater the capital intensity.

Some other ratios and measures

Underlying shareholders' decisions to buy particular shares is their view as to whether or not the strategy the company has in place will be successful, and whether or not the management team that is going to implement the strategy has the necessary skills, leadership and application, and, of course, the money to implement it.

It is this last point that makes it useful to look at the historic ratios to check that the dividends policy as well as the business plan or strategy is viable.

The measures we have discussed in this chapter and the last have stood the long test of time. There are, of course, others that come along. They may be promulgated by a firm of consultants, they may hit the headlines and they will all have some merit in helping the investors to make their decisions.

We list some of them below, for you will hear of them. They are not necessarily a new truth in the measurement of a company's potential, but they give some further indicators. Much has been, and continues to be, written on these topics by consultants and academics. We will limit ourselves to defining the following and making a short comment on each:

- economic value added

- market value added

- added value

- total shareholder return.

As regards the last one, there is no doubting the long-term usefulness of it and we will take it further in Chapter 9. For the others, it is important to remember that, while many things affect a company's share price in the short term, only its real performance as a thriving business guarantees its share price in the long run. It cannot be right to give managers targets based on the share price alone because, put simply, it is too tempting to try to manipulate the price in the short term without improving the underlying performance.

Economic value added (EVA)

This is also known as economic profit, and is defined as the difference between net profit after tax and the cost of the capital employed in the business. This is said to be an important indicator of managers' real created value. It certainly has a benefit internally as managers who target their efforts on improving the EVA are forced to realise constantly that all capital has a cost.

Popular in some places, this measure also has its detractors. The problem is how to calculate the cost of capital. When used internally, an average cost of capital is calculated and applied to all investment, irrespective of whether or not the actual capital has been raised by means of loans or shares. When used by an investor, you have to calculate a 'notional' cost of capital. Crucially, you have to ask the question 'How do you take a long-term view of the company if you use this measure?'

Managers can, on a one-off basis, improve the EVA by reducing the cost of capital employed figure by failing to invest in assets. Profit can also be manipulated in the short term by suspending discretionary expenditure on training, for example. Internal measures that use EVA need to look over a longer period of time than a single year.

Market value added (MVA)

Very much linked to EVA, market value added takes the market capitalisation of a business and subtracts from it the total of its capital employed. Assuming this is positive, MVA is said to put a value on the 'stock market wealth created'.

In summary, EVA tries to show the return to shareholders on an annual basis, while MVA attempts to show the total return.

Added value

This is the difference between the market value of a company's outputs and the cost of its inputs. An improving trend here should augur a successful performance. The main problem is getting the necessary data to make the calculation from published material.

Total shareholder return

This measures the return to shareholders from dividend income and capital gains in the value of the shares. It can take time into account by discounting income and gains made to the present value, and is a very useful tool for comparing one share with another.

This is a significant topic in Chapter 9.

The annual report

We will continue our examination of the report by covering the rest of Sherwood Industries' annual report, and then some matters that were left out of the Sherwood Industries example for the sake of clarity, but which occur in the real reports that you will read.

The cash flow statement

Sherwood Industries' annual report, page 14

We have already noted the importance of the cash situation of a company, which can be dramatically different from its profit situation. For example, we noted that it is essential for a Chairman who is going to carry out promises regarding dividends to have the cash as well as the profit to pay the amounts expected.

Here is a simple example of a company that has unquestionable profitability, but a cash position that not only threatens its ability to pay dividends, it threatens its ability to survive.

EXAMPLE ## Going bust *profitably* 1

Here is a company that is making a healthy profit. In fact its return on capital employed is 20 per cent.

Its gearing is nothing untoward. Its income gearing is 30 per cent, which is at the bottom end of what our benchmark guide describes as medium gearing. The profit and loss account is shown in Figure 8.1

Long-term debt		60.0
Shareholders' funds		40.0
Capital employed		100.0
Return on capital employed		20%
Profit before interest and tax		20.0
Interest rate	10%	
Interest		6.0
Profit before tax		14.0
Tax rate	25%	
Tax		3.5
Net profit after interest and tax		10.5

Fig. 8.1 The profit and loss account for going bust *profitably* 1

EXAMPLE ## Going bust *profitably* 2

Unfortunately, Figure 8.1 shows only one of the implications of debt, which is the interest payable. The other two are security (not relevant here) and repayments. Let us assume that the term of the loan is five years. The cash flow now looks like that shown in Figure 8.2.

Long-term debt		60.0
Shareholders' funds		40.0
Capital employed		100.0
Return on capital employed		20%
Profit before interest and tax		20.0
Interest rate	10%	
Interest		6.0
Profit before tax		14.0
Tax rate	25%	
Tax		3.5
Net profit after interest and tax		10.5
Repayments		12.0
Net cash outflow		−1.5

Fig. 8.2 The profit and loss account for going bust *profitably* 2

In small companies, the cash flow is a frequent (even daily) calculation as the firm tries to expand without running out of cash. Even in a large company like Sherwood Industries, the cash position and gearing are important issues in the company's ability to achieve its strategy.

Net cash inflow from operating activities

The cash flow statement starts with the net cash inflow from operating activities. To tie this back to the profit and loss account requires you to go to the first note on cash flow, which in the case of Sherwood Industries is note 13, which is on page 20 of the report. This note reconciles the top line of the cash flow statement to the profit and loss account showing what non-cash items, such as depreciation, have been 'added back' to the cash flow. It also records the changes to working capital that have occurred during the year.

Returns on investment and servicing of finance

You are then told, in note 14, on page 21 of Sherwood Industries' report, how much was paid and received in the servicing of finance – the interest paid and received. Dividends paid to minority interests fit here, although the dividends paid to shareholders in the parent company are given later.

Tax

Returning to the cash flow statement (page 14 of the report), now comes the next cash item, tax. In the case of Sherwood Industries, it is only one number, but there will normally be a note distinguishing UK and overseas tax.

Capital expenditure and financial investment

This figure covers investment in and disposal of fixed assets and trade investments and note 14 (on page 21 of the report) adds the detail behind this figure.

Acquisitions and disposals

Where a company has taken over or sold the whole or a major part of a business, it shows the cash implication of that at this point in the cash flow statement. In note 15 (on page 21 of the report) you will find the figures for the balance sheet items that were bought or sold. Obviously this has an impact on the Group's balance sheet at the end of the year and could, in the case of Sherwood Industries, be very important because of its declared strategy of acquisition. Notice how cash outflows are shown in brackets.

Equity dividends paid

This next entry in the cash flow statement is the sum of dividends the company has paid to its shareholders. There is usually a difference between the figure near the foot of the profit and loss account and this number. This is because the cash flow statement shows the dividends actually paid during the year, which will include the previous year's final proposed dividend, but exclude the current proposed dividends, which will be paid during the following year.

The profit and loss account records the dividends related to the current year's profits, irrespective of whether or not they have been paid.

We could have made the same point earlier with respect to the interest paid and received, tax paid and capital expenditure. In every case, the cash flow statement records the actual amount paid or received, whereas the profit and loss account records the amounts payable or receivable.

Financing

This entry in the cash flow statement records the change in the capital employed. In the case of Sherwood Industries, this is due to a small issue of shares and repayment of loans. These details are given in note 14 on page 21 of the report.

Increase/decrease in cash in the period

This, the bottom line of the cash flow, shows, in the case of Sherwood Industries, a positive annual cash flow last year, although it was an outflow the previous year.

Reconciliation of net cash flow to movement in net debt

This section of the cash flow statement, together with its note, explains in detail changes in net debt. The reconciliation was introduced in 1997 to help link the cash flow statement to the balance sheet. The reconciliation shown on page 14 of the report is best read in the context of the detailed note 16 (on page 22 of the report). You should be able to link the figures given in note 16 to the relevant balance sheet headings and notes. If you recall, Walter Sherwood measured gearing using this net debt figure.

What the cash flow statement tell us

It gives an indication of the relationship between profitability and the ability to generate cash. As we have seen, profits without cash lead to ruin. Analysts will often develop models to assess the value of a company by reference to the present value of its future cash flows. The historical cash flow statement is useful in two ways. First, analysts will be able to use cash information rather than just profit information in their models. Second, they will be able to use the historical cash flow to check the accuracy of past predictions.

Statement of accounting policies

Sherwood Industries' annual report, page 15

There are different ways to treat a number of financial issues. Take, for example, fixed assets. Companies may choose to include most fixed assets at net book value, as described in Chapter 6. Alternatively, for some assets, the company may follow a policy of regular revaluation. If a policy of depreciation is adopted, then the method used (straight line, reducing balance and so on) will be shown in the accounting policies part of the report, along with the depreciation rates used or the useful lives of the assets. Revaluation usually only applies to properties, and in this case the company will show details of the values and the method of valuation used.

The statement of accounting policies declares the particular conventions and practices the company operates under. Once adopted, a policy should be followed consistently, unless there are sound reasons for change. Most of the items normally found are shown in the Sherwood Industries report.

Taking one example of how this information can be important, you can see how Sherwood Industries treats research and development: it writes off expenditure in the year it was incurred. There have been occasions when a company has not done this and got into problems. If, on the not unreasonable argument that the results of R&D are going to benefit the company over many years, the Board decides to depreciate the expense over a period of years, it is required to show that here. Were it to be concealed, the shareholders would have a blurred view of the assets of the company. The Sherwood Industries note is very much the current standard.

Most accounting policies in most companies are identical. Indeed, over the last 25 years, the accounting profession has published accounting standards that have reduced the choices that can be made. For example, the standard on research and development will only permit expenditure to be carried forward if a number of stringent conditions are met. A policy that goes against the requirements of an accounting standard should be easy to spot – it should be highlighted in both the accounting policies and the auditors' report. The requirement to highlight such policies means that such situations rarely arise in practice.

It is more difficult to identify the situation when a company is following an acceptable accounting policy that is unusual when compared with competitors in the same industry.

When comparing a number of companies in the same sector, check that they all have identical policies and if not, try to identify the effect of the differences.

One other thing you find by quickly going through the statement of accounting policies is any particular issues that affect the company in question or its industry. A good example is decommissioning. In, for example, the oil industry, decommissioning of fixed assets such as oil production platforms is an important area. It is expensive and under close scrutiny from the government and environmentalists in terms of how the decommissioning is done. In this section of the report you will see the financial treatment of this issue declared by the Board.

Notes to the accounts

Sherwood Industries' annual report, page 16

The main purpose of the notes is to present in more detail the information held in the main part of the report. In collecting the data for our financial analysis model, we have had to go into the notes to the accounts quite frequently. Indeed, in so doing, we have probably already looked at the most useful information the notes contain. At this point, we will simply pick out the following few from Sherwood Industries as being typical, and sometimes topical, areas covered in the notes:

- analysis of turnover and profits before tax and analysis of costs between continuing and discontinued operations

- directors' remuneration

- tangible assets

- group financial records.

We will take these one by one.

Analysis of turnover and profits before tax and analysis of costs between continuing and discontinued operations

We have already made good use of some of the information in the analysis of turnover and profits before tax (note 1, page 16 of the report) in our attempts to define the product and market strategy for the company. The distinction between the costs of the continuing business and the costs of the businesses the company is selling will, from time to time, be important for a business like Sherwood Industries. We can see that the figure for the turnover of discontinued operations given in the profit and loss account of 50.3 (page 12) had a cost of sales figure of 39.9 (note 2, page 16). This gives a gross margin of 10.4, which is 20.7 per cent. The acquisition figure is over 30 per cent. It's only a benchmark guide, but by this test, again the company is moving into businesses with higher margins and disposing of those that are below par (see Table 8.1).

Table 8.1 A comparison of the figures for the businesses Sherwood Industries has discontinued, continues to run and those it has acquired

	Discontinued	*Continuing*	*Acquisition*
Sales	50.3	1,209.5	144.8
Cost of sales	39.9	867.5	101.2
Gross profit	10.4	342.0	43.6
Gross margin	20.7	28.3	30.1

Once again we can use common sense to check the performance and prospects of the business.

Directors' remuneration

In the recent past, in the UK this has been a major talking point, and shareholders are questioning the salaries of the Board. Because many times the question has been raised in privatised industries, it has also become a political issue. More details are now required than are shown in Sherwood Industries' report (note 3, page 17 of the report).

Tangible assets

Given in note 6 of Sherwood Industries' report (page 18), this provides us with the details behind the fixed assets figure in the balance sheet and also shows the depreciation of the assets over time.

Group financial record

Sherwood Industries' annual report, page 23

Looking at the figures for the past five years together like this emphasises again the changes in strategy that have taken place at Sherwood Industries. The turnover stayed much the same (£1,060.6 to £1,041.9) in the four years up to last year. Then comes the change and the big jump from £1,041.9 to £1,404.6 in the last 12 months.

Note how the report ends as it began with an emphasis on the borrowings figure, stated as part of the springboard from which Sherwood Industries will forge ahead.

Other statements

All annual reports now include statements regarding corporate governance. There is a summary of what you will normally find in these statements (which are usually fairly standard) in Appendix 2.

Conclusion

After all the financial analysis done in previous chapters, here we have taken time out to compare the results with published averages. Given a sensible use of such information, you can re-examine the validity of the conclusions you drew from the two years of ratios on their own.

EXERCISES FOR CHAPTER 8

Becoming familiar with financial information

EXERCISE 1 In a library, examine the various directories available that give details of industry averages.

Advancing your investment strategy

EXERCISE 2 Take the company you are at present favouring and consider what numbers are worth comparing with the industry average. Remember that what you are looking for is a guide to the future, not a record of the past. The comparisons you want to make are those that test management's ability to carry out the strategy you identified in earlier chapters.

EXERCISE 3 See if you can work out some of the ratios given in this chapter for your chosen company.

CHAPTER 9

Keeping score

The private investor needs a system that is simple and quick to use to track the progress of investments

- The documents you need to keep score
- Conclusion
- Exercises

The lengths the investor can go to in order to track progress could make it into a full-time job. However, any or all of the forms and techniques outlined in this chapter could be used, without too much effort, to give an indication of which shares are performing well and how the portfolio is progressing.

The documents you need to keep score

At the beginning of this book you set yourself a personal objective for the equity savings you had decided to accumulate. In order to monitor your progress towards this objective, you need to keep records of transactions and progress. This chapter covers the main records you can keep, from the very simple to the mathematically clever. We will cover

- buying and selling transactions

- register of shares held

- risk profile and spread

- dividend expectations

- individual share performance – income and capital gains.

The system proposed here can be kept manually, but it is also designed in such a way that you can easily enter it into any of the popular spreadsheet systems available.

Buying and selling transactions

Let us assume that you wish to buy and sell shares on a regular basis. You can do this in a number of ways, but we will stick with one of the most economical and relatively easy to use – an execution only service from a stockbroker. The stockbroker will not only supervise the buying and selling transactions, but will actually hold the shares on your behalf via a nominee company. The 'execution only' part means that you will receive little if any investment advice from the stockbroker. As we are trying to make our own decisions in any case, this is not a problem and it has the added bonus of saving us the costs of an advisory service.

There are advantages and disadvantages to this method and you should shop around carefully to choose the one that suits your purpose. Here are some of the questions you should get the answer to to help you decide with whom you will work.

- What are the costs of using the nominee to hold the shares? This is often an amount per share held.

- What is the percentage commission for buying and selling transactions?

- What is the minimum charge for a transaction? Often this will be set high enough for the minimum to be charged until the transaction size reaches over £1,000. For example, if the transaction charge is 1.5 per cent for buying and the minimum charge is £20, then an investment of just under £1,350 will result in a transaction charge that is just over this minimum amount.

- Will the firm send you a copy of the annual report of any company in which you have shares that are being held in the nominee account, and does it charge for this?

- Will the firm accept a bank account that will automatically be used for debiting the money for a buy or crediting the money for a sale?

- In opening such a bank account, you will be given an unsettled deals limit. This is set by your bank and is dependent on your creditworthiness. It should be set high enough to cover your anticipated dealing activity over, say, a month. What would yours be?

- How often will the company send you a portfolio valuation, and would there be any charge for doing this more often if it were required?

- Does the company send you, free of charge, a composite tax voucher at the end of the tax year, showing the dividend income and income tax that has been deducted? Is this suitable simply to be attached to your tax return?

There are, of course, other considerations and the services change over time. Generally, they are improving as the business is very competitive, particularly for large personal investors.

Any share transaction has associated costs. First, the investor has to pay the marketmaker's *spread*, typically between 1 and 2 per cent. This spread, or *touch*, is the profit for the marketmakers, which are like share wholesalers. They make money by selling shares for more than they will buy them. If the mid-price were 100 pence, the market maker might be selling at 101 pence and buying at 99 pence.

Next, investors pay the stockbroker, or the retailer, who is the person investors contact directly in order to deal. A stockbroker will charge a commission of around 1.5 per cent to investors, both when they are buying and selling. Added to this is tax. The government imposes stamp duty on the buying transaction only of 0.5 per cent. This leads us to the sobering realisation that buying and selling shares costs at least 5 per cent of the value of the money invested. The share has to improve, in capital terms, by that amount before the investor starts to make a profit.

We should learn two lessons from this. One is that, normally, you buy shares to hold for the long term. The other is that being clever and trying to get out of equities just before a sharp downward fall in price is only a good idea if your timing is perfect and the drop in value is greater than 5 per cent of your investment. This is assuming that you want to go back into shares after such a fall has taken place, of course.

What you will get from the broker after each transaction is a contract note with the following information.

Contents of a contract note

These include the following:

- bargain reference and your reference number

- your associated bank account

- whether the transaction was a buy or a sale

- what the company concerned was and what type of share was involved

- date and time of the transaction

- quantity involved, the price at which the transaction took place and the value of the transaction

- percentage and amount of commission

- stamp duty for buying transactions only

- total charges and the total of the transaction and charges

- settlement date, which is the date on which your bank account will be debited or credited with the amount involved in the transaction.

This is not a complete list, but, does contain the main elements included in the form. You should check these details carefully as mistakes happen quite often. Mostly the stockbroker picks them up and sends out a replacement note very quickly. Then you should keep them in, as they say, a safe place.

Register of shares held

The key record you need to keep is the assets register for the portfolio. A blank version of the form is shown in Figure 9.1.

Most of the data entered on the form comes straight from the contract note, but the following figures also need to be calculated.

- The *average price paid*, which is the total cost, including transaction costs divided by the number of shares.

- The *net selling value*, which is the number of shares involved multiplied by the current selling price. You will probably use the mid price quoted in the business pages. To be more accurate, however, you can calculate an approximate selling price by reducing the mid price by 2.5 per cent to allow for stockbroker commission and the marketmaker's spread.

- The *profit or loss to date*, which is the difference between the total cost and the net selling value.

- *Change during month*, which is exactly what it says.

If you hold this information on a computer, updating the pricing details is a simple process. If you are keeping it manually, you will have to copy it and calculate the figures as and when you wish to. In most cases, a monthly update should be enough, although you may want to do it more often if you are about to make significant changes.

The main difference between the form shown in Figure 9.1 and the portfolio valuation form sent by an execution only stockbroker is that it

Name of company	Last date bought	Number of shares	Average price paid	Total cost	Selling price	Net selling value	Profit or loss to date	Change during month

REGISTER OF SHARES

Date _____

Total realisable value of securities

Fig. 9.1 Example of a register of shares held form

contains a calculation of the profit or loss to date and of the change during the month. This gives a view on any progress and change that has occurred during the month, which enables you to compare how your portfolio is doing against the market. You can easily have a feel for how the market moved in the last month, and this form lets you know if you have under- or over-performed in that period of time.

The form has limitations, however. For example, it does not take dividend income into account and, as it holds, for convenience, only one entry per share, it does not allow for the fact that you may have bought the shares on more than one occasion, with some period of time between one transaction and the next. In summary, it does not take into account the time cost of money. To do this, you require a statement of the value of a share that uses discounted cash flow techniques in order to make realistic comparisons between one share and another. We will cover this later in this chapter, under Individual share performance – income and capital gains.

EXAMPLE ## The Getting-on-a-bits review their portfolio

The Getting-on-a-bits had some money to put into their portfolio immediately after they had developed their strategy in Chapter 2 as part of Mr Getting-on-a-bit's early retirement package was paid in a lump sum. They did not put it all into the portfolio immediately, but, rather, invested a set amount each month after an initial lump sum had been used to get things started. Figure 9.2 shows how their portfolio has grown over a period of about three years. It has not been spectacular, but then that was not the strategy. It is now outperforming the average unit trust on a rolling year basis. They check this against the figures given in the FT on a Saturday. Rather than the names of the shares themselves the form has the sector for the share to demonstrate the breadth of the portfolio they have chosen.

REGISTER OF SHARES

Date   February, Year 3

Name of company	Last date bought	Number of shares	Average price paid (£)	Total cost (£)	Selling price (£)	Net selling value (£)	Profit or loss to date (£)	Change during month (£)
Oil Integrated	Nov, Year 1	284	4.84	1,373.35	6.84	1,941.14	567.79	95.14
Distributors	Jan, Year 1	762	1.81	1,375.97	1.15	877.82	498.15	−76.20
Banks, retail	Jan, Year 1	352	3.91	1,375.38	6.19	2,177.12	801.74	103.84
Insurance	Feb, Year 1	412	3.33	1,370.27	4.89	2,012.62	642.35	107.12
Telecommunications	Jul, Year 2	617	3.84	2,370.53	4.29	2,643.85	273.32	117.23
Chinese inv. trust	Nov, Year 1	485	1.08	522.05	0.92	446.20	−75.85	26.68
Food producers	Jan, Year 1	311	4.42	1,373.83	4.92	1,530.12	156.29	−18.66
Paper, pckg., printing	Apr, Year 2	810	2.96	2,398.82	4.27	3,458.70	1,059.88	291.60
Electronic and electrical	Oct, Year 2	501	4.07	2,038.96	3,75	1,878.75	−160.21	77.66
American inv. trust	Apr, Year 1	361	3.81	1,373.73	4.40	1,586.60	212.87	79.42
Gas distribution	May, Year 2	903	2.43	1,515.71	1.79	1,611.86	96.15	−22.57
Pharmaceuticals	Jan, Year 2	269	9.26	2,491.66	10.19	2,739.77	248.11	75.32
Retailers, general	Jun, Year 1	333	4.13	1,375.88	4.80	1,598.40	222.52	38.29
Spirits, wine and cider	Aug, Year 1	347	3.97	1,377.08	4.67	1,618.76	241.68	22.56
Spirits, wine and cider	Aug, Year 1	652	2.11	1,376.88	2.35	1,528.94	152.06	120.62
Chemicals	Jan, Year 3	355	7.87	2,794.59	7.58	2,689.13	−105.47	−124.99
Healthcare	Nov, Year 1	1,007	1.37	1,376.62	1.67	1,676.66	300.04	10.07
Food producers	Jan Year 3	5,882	0.17	1,024.94	0.18	1,044.06	19.11	−54.41
Building and construction	Jan, Year 2	1,333	1.50	1,998.90	1.39	1,852.87	−146.03	166.63
Media	May, Year 2	287	7.10	2,037.48	7.65	2,194.12	156.64	93.28
Engineering vehicles	June, Year 2	1,420	1.41	1,998.79	1.51	2,144.20	145.41	−56.80
Electronic and electrical	Jul, Year 2	178	4.33	771.34	4.04	719.12	−52.22	−40.05
Chemicals	Jul, Year 2	750	1.03	774.00	0.97	723.75	−50.25	33.75
Engineering	Oct, Year 2	1,625	0.85	1,375.98	0.88	1,421.88	45.90	8.13
Transport	Jan, Year 3	414	6.15	2,546.35	6.29	2,604.06	57.71	0.00
Gas distribution	Jan, Year 3	903	0.76	682.00	0.69	618.56	−63.44	0.00
European inv. trust	Jan, Year 3	1,200	0.77	920.00	0.74	891.00	−29.00	0.00
Emerging inv. trust	Jan, Year 3	1,097	0.84	919.00	0.84	918.74	−0.26	0.00
				£42,930.09			£4,218.66	£1,053.49

Total realisable value of securities   £47,148.75

Fig. 9.2 Example of a completed register of shares held form

The Getting-on-a-bits continue to review their portfolio

Helping in the reviewing process is the Getting-on-a-bits' daughter, Lana. She is, by profession, an accountant, and a brilliant one at that, and has agreed, somewhat reluctantly, to help with the review. She was not too keen because she did not want her parents to accept her advice as professional advice in the formal context of the word. She makes this clear at the start.

Lana: 'Look, Mum and Dad, I know it's important so I am happy to help, but I am no expert and no financial adviser. I have taught portfolio management in the classroom, but I've never pretended to understand it.'

Mr Getting-on-a-bit: 'No, no we understand your position, we just want to bounce some ideas off you.'

Lana: 'Yes, that's a good way of looking at it. I'll just make sure you have asked yourselves all the right questions.'

Mr Getting-on-a-bit: 'Take, for example, the number of shares in the portfolio. It's got 28 shares in it and Mum thinks that's too many. I quite like adding shares as it spreads the risk. When we first started and only had a few, it was frightening when anything went wrong with one of them – it seemed to set us right back where we started or worse.'

Lana: 'Yes, some people would regard that as excessive, particularly when you consider that some of the transactions are relatively small. For example, £522 is well below the sum at which you go over the stockbroker's minimum, so you paid the minimum of £20 plus about £2.50 in stamp duty. That means you paid well over 4 per cent of the cost of the shares in transaction charges. But, coming back to the risk issue. The rate at which risk diminishes slows down in indirect proportion to the number of shares you hold. For example, if you add a second share to a single shareholding, you – all things being equal – roughly halve the risk. When you go from 99 shares to 100, however, the difference this makes to the overall risk is minimal. These are complicated matters on which there is no definitive answer. Quite an accepted, but unguaranteed, benchmark guide, is that 15 shares in a small portfolio, properly spread, gives investors reasonable protection without the administration problems of holding large numbers of different shares.'

Mrs Getting-on-a-bit: 'Good, d'you see Stephen, I've been saying that for a while. I think we should remove some shares that are not doing well and use the money to add to ones we already hold to bring them up to a decent size.'

Mr Getting-on-a-bit: 'OK, when we get to looking at the individual performance of shares, I'm sure you're right and we'll find a number that we would be better without. Coming back to what Lana said about buying small numbers and paying high costs; we did that, of course, to limit the risk in some high-risk areas and because they were shares that we thought we might buy and sell quickly. The trouble is, if a share does do well quickly, it's hard to sell it. You feel there may be more growth there if you wait, and we've always said we were inclined to buy a share and forget about it, that is we don't particularly look for reasons to sell it.'

Lana: 'Yes, I do agree with that. Don't forget that it costs 5 to 6 per cent of the value to sell one share and buy another. I mean, suppose you thought the market was going into a severe correction and you sold your shares, found you were right and the market did fall. Then after a period of time, you felt that the market was starting a real recovery and you went back in. That would have cost you 5 per cent of £50,000, which is £2,500, at least, and you would have lost the dividends for the period you were out of the market. Of course, the loss of dividend is more than compensated for by the interest gained from having the cash in a savings account. You have to ask yourself if it is worth the hassle and, of course, the risk.

'You would think about selling when there has been a long bull run and the pundits are talking about markets all over the world being overheated. It could go horribly wrong, though, if you don't time things right. Suppose you come out and the market continues to rise, albeit more modestly, over the next six months. Talk of overheating is subsiding because the main rapid growth happened some time ago. You think, 'False alarm', and go back in, having paid the costs and the modest rise in the shares you are buying back. Then the market corrects itself by, say, 10 per cent. Your loss is compounded by the costs and the higher prices you paid. Looking back, you would have to say you would've done better to stay in and take the hit. After all, the market would recover at some point in all probability.

'It is quite different, of course, if you are actually cashing in and have no intention of reinvesting in equities. Then you try to sell as near to the top as you dare.'

Mrs Getting-on-a-bit: 'Well, that makes me feel much better. The market last month made us over a thousand pounds, as you can see, and I was just wondering if we shouldn't cut and run.'

Mr Getting-on-a-bit: 'Yes, it's interesting. You can't do it accurately because we did some buying last month so we wouldn't be comparing like with like, but I wanted to see if we were doing better or worse than the market. During the month, the FTSE 100 went up by a phenomenal 4 per cent roughly, while we only managed a more modest 2.5. It's very difficult to beat the market, although we are doing well – as you'll see later – against the average unit trust.'

Lana: 'OK, let's take a look at your spread of risk.'

Risk profile and spread

Going back to the start of the process, we divided our shares into the high-, medium- and low-risk parts of our triangular risk model in Chapter 2. The profile for the Getting-on-a-bits was

- low-risk area, FTSE 100

- medium-risk area, FTSE 250

- high-risk area, overseas investment trusts.

The definition of such a strategy allows investors to calculate the appropriateness of a share by plotting the new situation on to the existing position. The same shares can now be recorded in a different format to check the risk profile and plan the next purchase. Figure 9.3 shows this.

By using a spreadsheet it is easy for the Getting-on-a-bits to display their shares in a chart, showing the close adherence to their strategy.

Date					
Name of investment	Risk	Number	Cost (£)	Price (£)	Value (£)
Oil Integrated	L	284	1,373	6.84	1,941.14
Distributors	M	762	1,376	1.15	877.82
Banks, retail	L	352	1,375	6.19	2,177.12
Insurance	M	412	1,370	4.89	2,012.62
Telecommunications	L	617	2,371	4.29	2,643.85
Chinese investment trust	H	485	522	0.92	446.20
Food producers	L	311	1,374	4.92	1,530.12
Paper, packaging, printing	M	810	2,399	4.27	3,458.70
Electronic and electrical	L	501	2,039	3.75	1,878.75
American investment trust	H	361	1,374	4.40	1,586.60
Gas distribution	L	903	1,516	1.79	1,611.86
Pharmaceuticals	L	269	2,492	10.19	2,739.77
Retailers, general	L	333	1,376	4.80	1,598.40
Spirits, wine and cider	L	347	1,377	4.67	1,618.76
Spirits, wine and cider	M	652	1,377	2.35	1,528.94
Chemicals	L	355	2,795	7.58	2,689.13
Healthcare	M	1,007	1,377	1.67	1,676.66
Food producers	H	5,882	1,025	0.18	1,044.06
Building and construction	M	1,333	1,999	1.39	1,852.87
Media	L	287	2,037	7.65	2,194.12
Engineering vehicles	M	1,420	1,999	1.51	2,144.20
Electronic and electrical	H	178	771	4.04	719.12
Chemicals	H	750	774	0.97	723.75
Engineering	M	1,625	1,376	0.88	1,421.88
Transport	L	414	2,546	6.29	2,604.06
Gas distribution	L	903	682	0.69	618.56
European investment trust	H	1,200	920	0.74	891.00
Emerging investment trust	H	1,097	919	0.84	918.74

Summary of portfolio risk

Total risk	Total cost (£)	Percentage of portfolio	Value (£)
Low	23,353	54.4	25,846
Medium	13,272	30.9	14,973
High	6,305	14.7	6,329
Total	42,930	100.0	47,148

Risk profile

Low 54%

Medium 31%

High 15%

Fig. 9.3 Example of a form showing the summary of a share portfolio to check the risk profile

The Getting-on-a-bits review their portfolio some more

Mr Getting-on-a-bit 'Right, we've got 54 per cent in the low category, 31 per cent in the medium category and 15 per cent in the high. The portfolio is pretty well balanced and the pie chart clearly shows that the next purchase probably needs to be in the medium-risk area.'

Lana: 'I'm glad to see that the percentages and chart are calculated from the cost of shares column. This is a much better guide than using the current price. If you use the current price, you will distort the portfolio. For example, suppose a high-risk share fell by 50 per cent. This would tip you towards buying more high-risk shares if you were using the current price as the method of monitoring the portfolio. You avoid that by using the cost price at all times. The share was bought to be in a certain risk category, and whatever happens you should leave its cost there.'

Mr Getting-on-a-bit: 'It was Julia's mathematical background that helped there. She pointed out that if we didn't do that we could end up buying more and more high-risk shares that lost money, at the expense of anything else.'

Lana: 'There doesn't seem to be much of a pattern about the sum you invest in each category of risk.'

Mr Getting-on-a-bit: 'True, that depends on how real we perceive the risk to be and, to be honest, how much is in the pot when we make the decision to buy. For example, you can see we have put £1,374 into an American investment trust, but only £522 into a Chinese one. We simply believed the risk to be higher in the case of China, so we risked less money. Now, as time passes and the amount of money in the portfolio rises, the packages of shares are bound to get bigger. Otherwise we'll end up with hundreds of different shares, although you seem to think that we already have too many. You can see the growth in dividend expectation from the next form.'

Dividend expectations

For a number of reasons, it makes sense to make a chart of the timings and amounts of dividend payments. The form for the Getting-on-a-bits' dividends is shown in Figure 9.4.

To keep this record up to date, you have to note down each dividend payment as it comes in. Where a share is new and you have had no payments, you have to make an estimate based on the information given in the business pages. You will recall that the net dividend in pence are shown for all shares in Monday's issue. Multiply the figure for the

Date		Summary of investment performance											
							Dividends (£)						
Company	Annualised return (%)	Jan	Feb	Mar	Apr	May	Jun	Jul	Aug	Sept	Oct	Nov	Dec
Oil Integrated	36		14.20			12.07			12.07			14.20	
Distributors	–16			25.00							35.00		
Banks, retail	23		56.46					29.01					24.31
Insurance	21							46.76					
Telecommunications	11		58.74							79.41			
Chinese investment trust	5	35.71							20.67				
Food producers	11					34.52						16.17	
Paper, packaging, printing	23				15.33					6.97			
Electronic and electrical	–27	40.00						40.00					
American investment trust	10					39.57						29.31	
Gas distribution	6							47.02					67.79
Pharmaceuticals	10					50.35					50.35		
Retailers, general	10	10.99							37.97				
Spirits, wine and cider	12				42.62						20.30		
Spirits, wine and cider	17			9.78							15.97		
Chemicals	–6				66.00						44.00		
Healthcare	19		7.05						15.11				
Food producers	–8					46.66						5.88	
Building and construction	14										26.66		
Media	18						27.00					29.80	
Engineering vehicles	18							25.00				42.60	
Electronic and electrical	–15					3.00					5.00		
Chemicals	–5		5.00								12.25		
Engineering	3	36.01					21.00						
Transport	11	16.00						41.00					
Gas distribution	–10			23.00					27.00				
European investment trust	–3			16.00						24.00			
Emerging investment trust	–4						16.00						24.00
Shares sold 1	–30												
Shares sold 2	15												
Shares sold 3	14												
Shares sold 4	56												
Total £1,644	Totals	139	141	74	124	186	64	229	113	110	210	138	116

Fig. 9.4 Example of a form showing a summary of the dividends

company you have invested in by the number of shares you hold and that gives you the net dividend for the year. The same paper, or the annual report, gives the dates when the interim and final dividends are paid. You can estimate that 40 per cent of the net dividend will be paid at the interim date, and the rest, 60 per cent, at the final date as this is likely to be what will occur. You can then improve the accuracy of your record by entering the real numbers as they are actually paid.

The Getting-on-a-bits review their portfolio once more

Mr Getting-on-a-bit: 'One of the things we take into account in our buying strategy is that it's as well to get a smooth flow of dividends over the year. When we will be looking to draw income from equities, that should be helpful don't you think?'

Lana: 'Yes, I'd think so, but beware of making that too much of a driver in an investment decision. You are trying to build a value portfolio, so the underlying company and its potential must be the main reason to buy.'

Mr Getting-on-a-bit: 'Oh, here's something I always meant to check with you two. This form also allows us to monitor what the yield is on the investments we have actually made. To date we've spent £42,930 on the investments we're currently holding [see Figure 9.3]. The total expectation of return at the bottom left of the dividends form stands at £1,644 [see Figure 9.4]. This gives us a return of 3.83 per cent on the amount invested. I think this figure will be interesting. It reminds us that, over time, increases in dividends mean that we are catching up with what would have happened if we had put the money in a building society. The return is only a bit above the market as a whole, but it's rising.'

Mrs Getting-on-a-bit: 'Yes, and remember that the figures recorded here are the historical dividends and that some of them will increase in future payments. This means that if, on average, dividends in the portfolio go up by say 8 per cent, the total will be £1,775 and the return on the original investment will be 4.13 per cent. That's actually a more accurate picture.'

Lana: 'So I assume you will keep the portfolio going for at least the next two years. This would make it the five years that is generally regarded as the minimum for equity investment. Your dividend expectation will grow and, whatever your capital position, your dividend income should be coping with inflation with a bit on the top.'

Mr Getting-on-a-bit: 'That's the theory. Right, before we come back to the annualised return column on this form, we need to look at how we monitor the individual performance of each share.'

Individual share performance – income and capital gains

To get a true comparison of the performance of shares, it is necessary to take into account how much was invested, what the dividend income has been and, most importantly, when the transactions took place. If you compared 2 shares, 1 of which had doubled in price and the other had gone up by only 20 per cent, you would get the wrong answer if you were unaware that the first share had been held for 10 years and the second for 10 weeks.

The only way to track this is to use something like the form shown in Figure 9.5.

An explanation of the investment record

This record will be cumbersome if you try to keep it manually. It is possible, of course, but the record needs to have a monthly entry added for as long as the shares are held. To be able to make the calculation, even after, say, two years of holding the share, you still need to have the information on when the original purchase was made.

The heading information gives the name of the company, the type of share held, the year end and the usual dates of dividend payments. All these details are given on the contract note or can be found in the financial pages, as we have mentioned previously.

Next, let's look at each of the columns.

- Columns 1 and 2 record the years and months the shares have been held.
- Columns 3–6 record the various types of share transactions that can and have taken place.
- Column 7 records the balance of shares held at the end of the month. This is calculated by taking the figure from column 3, adding the figure from column plus 4, adding the figure from column 5 and taking away the figure from column 6.
- Column 8 records the costs incurred this month. In the example, the Getting-on-a-bits bought 284 shares in an integrated oil company in November of Year 2. This was their total holding at the end of the month. Further costs will only occur if more money is invested at a later date.

INVESTMENT RECORD

Name of company Oil integrated
Type of share Ord 25p

Year end December

Usual date of interim dividends
Usual date of final dividends

Feb May
Aug Nov

Year	Date	Number of shares bought	Bonus issue shares	Rights issues shares	Number of shares sold	Balance held	Monthly cost (£)	Dividends (£)	Proceeds from sales (£)	Mid price per share (£)	Selling price (£)	Net selling value (£)	Monthly cash flow (£)	Discounted cash flow (%)	Annualised (%)
2	Nov*	284				284	1,346.16						1,346.16		
	Dec					284									
3	Jan					284							11.36		
	Feb					284		11.36							
	Mar					284									
	Apr					284									
	May					284		12.07					12.07		
	Jun					284									
	Jul					284									
	Aug					284		12.07					12.07		
	Sep					284									
	Oct					284									
	Nov					284		14.20					14.20		
	Dec					284									
4	Jan					284									
	Feb					284		14.20		6.84	6.67	1,894.00	1,908.20	2.57	35.53
	Mar					284									
	Apr					284									
	May					284									
	Jun					284									
	Jul					284									
	Aug					284									
	Sep					284									
	Oct					284									
	Nov					284									
	Dec					284									
5	Jan					284									
	Feb					284									
	Mar					284									
	Apr					284									

- Column 9 records the amounts of dividends paid and these are noted by the appropriate month.

- Column 10 allows for the fact that investors may choose to reduce their holding in shares as well as increase it. Obviously money gained from the proceeds of sales is recorded and kept by the relevant month. This allows us to calculate the returns on the shares, taking time into account.

- Column 11 shows mid price of the share at the time that investors are examining performance. This will only be shown once, as the current price when you are reviewing the share.

- Column 12 calculates the selling price as the mid price minus 2.5 per cent to allow for the costs of the selling transaction.

- Column 13 shows the net selling value, which is the number of shares held in column 6 at the end of the month you are selling the shares in, multiplied by the selling price per share from column 12.

- Column 14 records the monthly cash flow, which is simply the figure you get when you add cash flowing in from dividends and sales together and take away any costs incurred that month. We will need this column as input to the next calculation.

- Column 15 is the crux of the form. You have to calculate the internal rate of return of the cash flows of every month since the share was first bought. To do this you will need discounted cash flow (DCF) tables if you are working manually. It is much simpler if you use a financial calculator that has internal rate of return (IRR) available as a function or, of course, a spreadsheet on your computer. In effect, this calculation takes into account the time value of money, allowing for the dates when it was paid out or paid in. This is, theoretically, the soundest measure of return.

- Column 16 is the final one. It is normal to compare investments in terms of their annual return, so we need to turn the monthly cash flow into an annual equivalent. The formula for this is as follows:

((1 + discounted cash flow) to the power 12) – 1

or taking figures from our example in Figure 9.5:

$((1 + 2.57 \text{ per cent})^{12}) - 1$

You will recall that in Figure 9.4 we had a column for annualised return. The result of the above calculation for column 16 is best recorded on the dividends form in this way so that comparisons can be made between individual investments. We will return to how investors can use this knowledge later on in the chapter.

For the moment, we need to add further details to the information given in Figure 9.5 to see what happens if we make further transactions. This is shown in Figure 9.6.

In March of Year 4, the company issued new shares under a rights issue. They offered one share for every ten held, and the Getting-on-a-bits decided to take up the offer. The share had done well and they saw no reason for it not continuing to do so. They thus purchased 28 new shares which are shown in column 5. The price (£6) was a fair discount on the mid price of the previous month. The expenditure (£168) is shown in column 8. The balance of shares held – shown in column 7 – has increased to 312. The remaining 0.4 of a share they were owed (as they owned 284) was paid in cash. Thus, 40 per cent of £6 equals £2.40, and this amount is shown as proceeds from sales in column 10.

The following month, the Getting-on-a-bits had some more money to invest and decided to stick with a share that had done very well for them. They invested a further £730, which was the total cost of buying 100 shares at the current buying price of £7.12, plus costs of £18.

The next two quarters of dividends per share were more or less as before, but the payment in November of Year 4 was higher, reflecting a small increase in the dividends. This was repeated in February of Year 5, when the share price had risen to £8.85 as quoted in the paper.

On an annualised basis, the discounted return on investment of this share now stands at 33.86 per cent.

To make comparisons between shares, we should return to Figure 9.4, which recorded the annualised returns for all the shares in the Getting-on-a-bits' portfolio. Now, if we re-sort the shares by annualised return, we get Figure 9.7.

Type of share: Ord 25p

Year end: December

Usual date of interim dividends: Feb May
Usual date of final dividends: Aug Nov

Year	Date	Number of shares bought	Bonus issue shares	Rights issues shares	Number of shares sold	Balance held	Monthly cost (£)	Dividends (£)	Proceeds from sales (£)	Mid price per share (£)	Selling price (£)	Net selling value (£)	Monthly cash flow (£)	Discounted cash flow (%)	Annualised (%)
2	Nov	284				284	1,346.16						-1,346.16		
	Dec					284									
3	Jan					284									
	Feb					284		11.36					11.36		
	Mar					284									
	Apr					284									
	May					284		12.07					12.07		
	Jun					284									
	Jul					284									
	Aug					284		12.07					12.07		
	Sep					284									
	Oct					284									
	Nov					284		14.20					14.20		
	Dec					284									
4	Jan					284									
	Feb					284		14.20					14.20		
	Mar			28		312	168		2.40				-165.60		
	Apr	100				412	730						-730.00		
	May					412		14.20					14.20		
	Jun					412									
	Jul					412									
	Aug					412		20.60					20.60		
	Sep					412									
	Oct					412									
	Nov					412		22.25					22.25		
	Dec					412									
5	Jan					412									
	Feb					412		22.25		8.85	8.63	3,555.05	3,577.30	2.46	33.86
	Mar					412									
	Apr					412									

Fig. 9.6 Example of a more detailed investment record form

Company	Annualised return (%)	Last date bought	Reference
Oil Integrated	36	Nov, Year 2	S1
Banks, retail	23	Jan, Year 1	S2
Paper, packaging, printing	23	Apr, Year 2	S3
Insurance	21	Feb, Year 1	S4
Heathcare	19	Nov, Year 1	S5
Media	18	May, Year 2	S6
Engineering vehicles	18	Jul, Year 2	S7
Spirits, wine and cider	17	Aug, Year 1	S8
Building and construction	14	Jan, Year 2	S9
Spirits, wine and cider	12	Aug, Year 1	S10
Transport	11	Jan, Year 3	S11
Telecommunications	11	Jul, Year 2	S12
Food producers	11	Jan, Year 1	S13
Retailers, general	10	Jun, Year 1	S14
Pharmaceuticals	10	Jan, Year 2	S15
American investment trust	10	Apr, Year 1	S16
Gas distribution	6	May, Year 2	S17
Chinese investment trusts	5	Nov, Year 1	S18
Engineering	3	Oct, Year 2	S19
European investment trust	−3	Jan, Year 3	S20
Emerging investment trust	−4	Jan, Year 3	S21
Chemicals	−5	Jul, Year 2	S22
Chemicals	−6	Jan, Year 3	S23
Food producers	−8	Jan, Year 3	S24
Gas distribution	−10	Jan, Year 3	S25
Electronic and electrical	−15	Jul, Year 2	S26
Distributors	−16	Jan, Year 1	S27
Electronic and electrical	−27	Oct, Year 2	S28
Average	6.45		
Transport	11	Jan, Year 3	
American investment trust	−3	Jan, Year 3	
Emerging investment trust	−4	Jan, Year 3	
Chemicals	−6	Jan, Year 3	
Food producers	−8	Jan, Year 3	
Gas distribution	−10	Jan, Year 3	
Average without shares less than 3 month's old	12		

Fig. 9.7 Portfolio of shares in order of size of annualised return

Remember that this is the total return dividends and capital growth adjusted for time. We return for the last time in this chapter to the Getting-on-a-bits as they examine the performance of the portfolio.

The Getting-on-a-bits finish reviewing their portfolio

Mr Getting-on-a-bit: 'Using the re-sorted annualised return column [in Figure 9.7], we can draw a number of conclusions. First of all, rather arbitrarily, we have taken 10 per cent measured in this way to be a satisfactory performance. Unless something untoward happens, if a share is above 10 per cent, we don't even think about selling it.'

Lana: 'Right, I see. What is this average here at 6.45 per cent?'

Mrs Getting-on-a-bit: 'It is simply the sum of the percentages divided by the number of shares held. I'm not sure that it tells us very much, but if you remove shares that are less than three months old, it's quite interesting. We decided that three months was simply too short a time to look at performance; the shares don't have a chance at that point.

'Now, because we did quite a bit of buying recently, there are six shares in this category. Take them out of the equation and the average annualised return is 12 per cent which we think is pretty good. More importantly, it's going up. I know it is going up partly because of the bull market, but it is also because our dividend income is rising and the shares are more mature in the portfolio. So the shares we worry about are the ones below 10 per cent, particularly if we have held them for some time.'

Lana: 'Yes, and as the market's high at the moment it gives you an opportunity to sell any shares you don't want into strength.

Mr Getting-on-a-bit: 'So, going back a bit, we think we are holding too many shares, so we are going to sell some we don't like and put the money into expanding the investment in existing holdings. The obvious ones to go for are the two electronic and electrical shares we bought in July and October of Year 2. They're showing –15 per cent and –27 per cent (S26 and S28, by reference). Let's face it, we were acting the opposite of a contrarian – everyone was piling into technology shares and I reckon we just missed the boat. Do we sell them and raise not far short of £3,000?'

Mrs Getting-on-a-bit: 'I suppose so; but only if we know what we are doing with the money. I hate spending money with those fellows in the City. What do you think Lana?'

Lana: 'I think it's your portfolio and you must decide what to do, but I do think your reasoning is good. What about the others below 10 per cent, are you going to consider selling them?'

Mr Getting-on-a-bit: 'I think that depends on the sector and the dividends. For example, S17, the gas distributor, is doing only 6 per cent, but it's been much less than that at one point and we held on to it because of the dividends, which as it is a utility, are high. It's come back a long way already so we're going to hang on in there.'

Lana: 'Why don't you decide what you want to buy and how much you need, then come back to looking for other disposals if necessary?'

Mrs Getting-on-a-bit: 'Good idea. Now there's been a tip in the newspaper from a man who has done quite well for us in the past. It's for a company called Sherwood Industries. I think we should take a look.'

We had better leave the family at this point, since the two story lines seem to be colliding.

Conclusion

The point of keeping records of what you own and how your portfolio is shaping up and performing has two objectives. The first is to know what your financial position is, and the second is to help in the decision-making process of buying, holding and selling shares.

You *can* have a manual system, but it will probably be less useful in achieving the second objective than if you can create a simple computer system, such as the one illustrated in this chapter.

EXERCISES FOR CHAPTER 9

Becoming familiar with financial information

At this point it is a good idea to make sure you understand the concept of discounted cashflows, and the meaning of the annualised return calculation described in this chapter.

EXERCISE 1   What is the annualised return for the following investment timescale?

January, Year 3, bought 1,010 shares at a total cost of £1,756.

Dividends are paid in May and October. In Year 3, the dividends are £40 and £57.50, in year 4 they are £52 and £78, and in Year 5 they are £45 and £67.

Type of share Ord 25p Year end ______ Usual date of interim dividends May
Usual date of final dividends Oct

Year	Date	Number of shares bought	Bonus issue shares	Rights issues shares	Number of shares sold	Balance held	Monthly cost (£)	Dividends (£)	Proceeds from sales (£)	Mid price per share (£)	Selling price (£)	Net selling value (£)	Monthly cash flow (£)	Discounted cash flow (%)	Annualised (%)
2	Nov					0									
	Dec					0									
3	Jan	1,010				1,010	1,756						–1,756.00		
	Feb					1,010									
	Mar					1,010									
	Apr					1,010									
	May					1,010		40.00					40.00		
	Jun					1,010									
	Jul					1,010									
	Aug					1,010									
	Sep					1,010									
	Oct					1,010		57.50					57.50		
	Nov					1,010									
	Dec					1,010									
4	Jan					1,010									
	Feb	250				1,260	540						–540.00		
	Mar					1,260									
	Apr					1,260									
	May					1,260		52.00					52.00		
	Jun					1,260									
	Jul					1,260									
	Aug					1,260									
	Sep					1,260									
	Oct				300	960		78.00	900				978.00		
	Nov					960									
	Dec					960									
5	Jan					960									
	Feb					960									
	Mar					960									
	Apr					960									
	May					960		45.00					45.00		
	Jun					960									
	Jul					960									
	Aug					960									
	Sep					960									
	Oct					960		67.00					67.00		
	Nov					960				2.15	2.10	2,012.40	2,012.40	1.37	17.68

Fig. 9.8 The answer to the annualised return question in Exercise 1

In February of Year 4, you buy an extra 250 shares at a total cost of £540.

In October of Year 4, you sell 300 shares for a total of £900.

It is now November of Year 5 and the shares are each £2.15.

The answer is given in Figure 9.8.

Advancing your investment strategy

EXERCISE 2   Decide on the system you are going to use and enter the data for any holdings you already have. Create the performance record by checking back through your contract notes, dividend vouchers and other documents.

EXERCISE 3   Take some time to learn what the various stockbrokers offer and decide whether or not you are dealing in the most appropriate way.

CHAPTER 10

Of PEPs and investment clubs: an introduction

Individual investors can protect their investments from tax, and benefit from working with others

- Introduction
- Personal equity plans (PEPs)
- Investment clubs

By now you have learnt to build a value portfolio by setting a strategy and evaluating companies from published material. We need to look at two ways of enhancing your chances of achieving your investment objectives.

Introduction

For some years now, it has been possible to subscribe to personal equity plans (PEPs) and to belong to investment clubs. By these means, individual investors can protect themselves from two handicaps. The first is tax, which is where PEPs come in. The second is the difficulty of obtaining a sufficient spread of investments to achieve an acceptable risk when the amount available for investment is small, which is where investment clubs can help.

Personal equity plans (PEPs)

In order to encourage private investors to buy UK shares, PEPs were introduced in 1989. The offer is this. Your PEP may hold only equities, and of these, a very high level must be in shares in UK companies. Also, the PEP must be administered by a recognised authority, such as a bank or a stockbroker, who is responsible for maintaining the records of investment, income and dealing with the Inland Revenue.

The benefits of holding a portfolio in a PEP

There are two taxes on a portfolio of shares. The first is income tax, which, as we have seen, is deducted at the dividend rate by the company before the dividend payment is made to the investor. The second is capital gains tax whereby investors are liable to tax at their top rate on the difference between the value of the shares when they were sold and the price paid for them. There is an annual exemption to capital gains tax, which means that, in 1997, the first £6,500 of capital gains, does not attract tax. The calculation of liability includes indexing, which allows for the effect of inflation during the period during which the shares have been held and reduces the liability accordingly.

The rules regarding PEPs appear secure until 1999 but in the July 1997 budget the Chancellor explained that these rules are under review.

The benefits of PEPs are that all the income is earned by the shares within PEPs is tax free, and that capital gains tax is not levied on gains made within PEPs.

Table 10.1 Comparisons between normal investments and investment in a PEP

Normal investor, higher rate taxpayer

	Year 1	Year 2	Year 3	Year 4	Year 5
Investment value	£6,000				
Dividend income	5%	5%	5%	5%	5%
Tax rate	40%	40%	40%	40%	40%
Growth rate	6%	6%	6%	6%	6%
	£	£	£	£	£
Value of fund in January	6,000	6,540	7,128	7,770	8,469
Dividend income	300	327	357	388	423
Tax payable	120	131	143	155	169
Net income	180	196	214	233	254
Capital growth	360	392	428	466	508
Value of fund in December	6,540	7,128	7,770	8,469	9,231

PEP investor

	Year 1	Year 2	Year 3	Year 4	Year 5
Investment value	£6,000				
Dividend income	5%	5%	5%	5%	5%
Higher rate tax	0%	0%	0%	0%	0%
Growth rate	6%	6%	6%	6%	6%
PEP annual fees	1.175%	1.175%	1.175%	1.175%	1.175%
Exit charge	0.88%	0.88%	0.88%	0.88%	0.88%
	£	£	£	£	£
Value of fund in January	6,000	6,582	7,220	7,920	8,688
Dividend income	300	329	361	396	434
Capital growth	360	395	433	475	521
Fund before charges	6,660	7,306	8,014	8,791	9,643
Annual charge	78	86	94	103	113
Exit charge					85
Value of fund in December	6,582	7,220	7,920	8,688	9,445
Difference between value of fund above and value of PEP fund					2.3%

Normal investor basic rate tax-payer

	Year 1	Year 2	Year 3	Year 4	Year 5
Investment value	£6,000				
Dividend income	5%	5%	5%	5%	5%
Tax rate	20%	20%	20%	20%	20%
Growth rate	6%	6%	6%	6%	6%
	£	£	£	£	£
Value of fund in January	6,000	6,600	7,260	7,986	8,784
Dividend income	300	330	363	399	439
Tax payable	60	66	73	80	88
Net income	240	264	290	319	351
Capital growth	360	396	436	479	527
Value of fund in December	6,600	7,260	7,986	8,784	9,662

These benefits can help the growth of the portfolio significantly. The first real benefit comes from the income tax relief.

From Table 10.1 we can see the benefits of a PEP that accrue for a higher rate taxpayer. The difference between the normal investor and the PEP investor are twofold. In the PEP, no tax is paid on dividend income, but this is balanced to some extent by the fees payable to the PEP's manager. The figure assumes that the manager charges 1 per cent plus VAT, of the value of the fund annually, which, in many cases, is paid quarterly, and an exit charge of 0.75 per cent plus VAT. We have assumed that dealing costs are the same for either option and therefore do not need to be considered. In practice, there are various different deals available in the marketplace that may improve the PEP benefit.

Table 10.1 shows that the higher rate taxpayer would be 2.3 per cent better off investing in a PEP after five years.

Then comes the benefit of the avoidance of capital gains tax (CGT). This benefit is not so easily recognised if the PEP is small. Indeed, in the case of Table 10.1 there is no benefit as the capital gain, even without indexing, falls below the annual allowance. The PEP fund needs to be considerably bigger than this to benefit from the avoidance of CGT. Indeed, unless investors have to sell large holdings of shares to meet a crisis, then a very large proportion will avoid capital gains tax because of indexation and by making good use of the £6,500 annual exemption.

For basic rate taxpayers, however, the benefit of holding shares in a PEP is highly questionable – you would need to look at the detail of the offer. In our example, it would actually be better for a basic rate taxpayer to avoid the PEP shelter.

The PEP world is very competitive and the benefits are improving, particularly as fees come down as a result of competitive pressure. There is no doubt that if you are building a portfolio of shares, it is well worth looking at the option of protecting it from tax inside a PEP.

Types of PEP

The main advertisements that are carried in the financial pages for PEPs are placed by unit trust and investment trust managers. If you go down this route, you are of course saved the work we have been discussing in this book, but you are paying the management fees for the privilege. However, investors who have got this far in reading this book are much more likely to be looking for a PEP that allows them to select their own shares.

Self-select PEPs are offered by many PEP managers. They quite often have a starting subscription that is considerably higher than the starting investment in a unit trust. Some of them have restrictions on the list of shares you may put into the portfolio, but if you shop around you will find one that is reasonable to join, has competitive fees and offers a very wide range of shares for you to choose from.

Self-select PEPs are, in their turn, divided into two types in order to make use of the regulations as they stand today. The first type, a *general PEP*, allows a mix of shares to be bought within the PEP, up to the regulatory limit for a year. At present this limit is £6,000. So, you can put in £6,000 in each tax year, either as a lump sum or in monthly instalments. A combination of the two may be useful, as was described in Chapter 2, which covered the benefits of investing regularly.

You may then deal by buying and selling shares through the PEP manager. Once again, execution only is the cheapest option, rather than using the manager's advisory service, and is more likely to be appropriate if you are trying to do it yourself. Some managers offer a reduction for buying and selling if you choose from a selected list and/or deal on their bulk dealing day, which is often once or twice a month. Failing that, the charges are probably similar to those you would pay if you were dealing outside a PEP.

The second type of self-select PEP is the *single company PEP*. In addition to the amount (currently £6,000) you may put into a general PEP, you may also invest a set amount in a single company. At present the limit for this is £3,000. As its name suggests, the whole investment may only be made in one company. Once again, the investment may be made as a lump sum or in the form of regular payments or a combination of the two.

A husband and wife can hold separate PEPs, so the maximum a couple can protect from tax each year comes, at present, to £18,000. Saving at that level will build quickly and is likely to be able to make use of the benefit of avoiding capital gains tax at some point.

The mechanics of tax relief and record keeping

PEP managers are responsible for all dealings with the Inland Revenue. They hold the shares in a nominee account, companies send the dividend payments to them in the usual way (after deduction of tax) and they reclaim the tax from the Inland Revenue. There is a delay before the reclaimed amount is paid.

The PEP manager will send you a record of all dealings. These are sometimes normal contract notes, as discussed earlier, and sometimes simply a record of the transaction. Managers differ in how they handle this. All managers send a statement of the portfolio on a regular basis. This has a record of all trading, an income statement, including tax reclaims, a bank statement showing the movement of cash and a portfolio valuation, normally showing the current portfolio value and expectation of yield.

Investment clubs

The one advantage unit trusts have over do-it-yourself arrangements that cannot be overcome is the instant access to a widely spread portfolio that the unit trust manager can offer when you join the fund. If your resources are limited, this can be very useful, as it avoids overexposure to a small number of shares in the early years of the portfolio.

As we have mentioned, however, investment clubs offer a neat way of gaining this benefit without losing control of the investment strategy or paying fees to the professionals.

The club's purpose and strategy

Members of an investment club need to have a common goal for building up the portfolio. We have seen in Chapter 2 how people have their own different, very individual reasons for being in such a club, but the investment goal needs to have the support of everyone. It is probably useful to set it fairly wide. Inside that goal, individuals can then calculate their subscription amounts in the same way that we saw the different couples planning their investment objectives in Chapter 2.

Planning the investment strategy is the next important step. This should certainly include the triangular risk model discussed in Chapter 2. The members must agree what proportion of money is to be invested in the low-, medium- and high-risk areas, and what they mean by those risks. In the same way that the people we met in Chapter 2 defined their strategy, so must the members of an investment club.

If some members are less interested in the nitty gritty of investment decisions, they may leave that to others or even to a subcommittee. However, the people with the delegated authority to make such decisions will be bound to operate according to the strategy or to go back to the whole membership if they wish to suggest changes.

The members, or the subcommittee, then choose shares in the way proposed from Chapters 2 to 8 and keep records as suggested in Chapter 9. Let us summarise this process.

- Using their knowledge and observations, the members choose a sector in which to invest.

- Using their strategy diagram and current spread of the portfolio, they choose the correct level of risk.

- Using the price/earnings and yield ratios, they identify some four or more shares that are in the category defined in the first two steps. They get the annual reports of these companies. They probably action one or two members to do the evaluation work.

- Using published information, they discuss the company strategy and attempt to plot it on the activity matrix.

- From the same information, they calculate the key business ratios, discuss whether or not they support the business strategy and possibly compare them with industry averages.

- They finally evaluate whether or not they believe the managers of the business can carry out the strategy successfully and make a decision to invest in the company or not.

The constitution and rules

The beauty of investment clubs is that they are essentially informal. They have almost no expenses, as none of the people involved in running the club are paid. However, this informality must be balanced by a well drawn-up constitution and rules, which you may obtain easily from such organisations as Proshare.

What happens is this. A group of up to 20 people – neighbours, friends, colleagues or members of the same golf club, for example – agree to form an investment club. Some clubs have as few as three or four members. One of the members gets hold of a book or manual that describes how to set up a club and gives sample constitutions and rules.

During an inaugural meeting, a number of significant issues are discussed and decisions made concerning the following.

- **Office holders.** The club needs a chairman, a secretary and a treasurer. The treasurer has a highly significant role in the club as he or she will keep the records of the portfolio and all transactions.

- **Number of meetings per year.** Some clubs meet monthly and others less often. It depends on the subscription income and, to some extent, on the social aspects of the club. Some clubs are primarily social and will meet frequently to socialise as well as make investment decisions. Others are more serious in terms of the objectives of the club and the likely level of the fund as it grows. In any case, there will be an annual general meeting.

- **How members are elected.** Probably new members will be proposed by existing members and their invitation to join ratified at a monthly meeting.

- **Subscriptions.** The members must decide on the amount to set for the joining fee, the upper and lower limits of monthly subscriptions and the upper and lower limits of lump sum investments.

- **How the portfolio is valued.** The rules also need to be clear on this for the purposes of buying units in the fund or selling units back in order for a member to realise some or all of their holding.

Books and manuals are available on how to set up a club.

Let's finish by eavesdropping on a typical meeting down at Darnley.

SCENARIO

Darnley Village Investment Club's monthly meeting

Chairman: 'OK, can I bring you back to order now? Right, we've done agenda item 1 – apologies for absence and matters arising from the last meeting, which was mainly to do with the annual audit, which Steve has kindly offered to carry out. It shouldn't be too onerous, but now that we have some £50,000 in the fund, it must be taken seriously. Iain, can we have the Treasurer's report please?'

Iain: 'Right, Mr Chairman, not a lot to report – we have sold one holding and bought two others since the last meeting. We sold Hero plc for no particularly good reason really, except that it has taken a long time to get not very far. We were hoping that it would respond to the upturn in building, which we are now seeing rather than predicting, but for some reason, which beats me, nothing has happened. We seem to be adding to our tactics that if a share simply slides slowly and undramatically over a lengthy period of time, say nine months, we sell it and take the burden of costs to replace it with something else.'

Emily: 'Well they do say you should run your winners and cut your losses.'

Iain: 'Yes, I can see the sense in that. I suppose I just feel that we made a mistake in the first place, there was an error in our detective work.'

Chairman: 'Oh come on Iain, it's only in fiction that detectives always get it right. In real life we are bound to go wrong. At least we only lost 20 per cent plus costs. When we did those Eurotunnel warrants, if you remember, we lost the whole lot. At least it was recognised as a high-risk one and we had a very low sum invested.'

Iain: 'Right. Well, looking positively, we bought Northumberland Services and British Roadways, high- and low-risk shares respectively, according to our definitions. We put £1,000 into Northumberland and £2,000 into Roadways. Both of those were agreed at the last meeting. We have now got another £3,000 to invest, including the proceeds from the sale of Hero.'

Chairman: 'Thank you, we'll come to that in the last item as usual. Right, I think you have something to report Secretary?'

Emily: 'Yes. I got a call from Kate this morning. She is planning, as I think you all know, this six-month sabbatical to travel the world.'

Graham: 'I think she's trying to find herself, whatever that means. If she does find herself, I wonder where she'll be?'

Emily: 'Yes, Graham, thank you very much, very droll! Well, anyway, she's decided that she cannot keep up her subscription while she is away, and wondered if she could be excused for at least six months, maybe longer.'

Diana: 'We don't have a problem with that, do we?'

Chairman: 'Well, I'm afraid we do. According to the rules, she should resign and take her money out. Formally, she should resign at least seven days before the next meeting, we accept the resignation and the payment is made within a month of the date of the meeting, at the time of the valuation of the units.'

Diana: 'Resignation, seven days, for goodness sake we're just talking about one of our pals not paying her sub for a bit. You make us sound very hard.'

Chairman: 'I know, but there are quite large sums of money involved here and I think we must abide by the rules. That's what they're for. To waive our rules in this case sets a bad precedent and I for one don't think we should do it.'

Iain: 'I agree with the Chairman. The Club may be a bunch of friends getting together for fun as well as investment, but it has its serious side, too, when it comes to hard cash.'

Chairman: 'I propose that we tell Kate with great regret that she must leave for now and hope to rejoin when she comes back if we are not up to 20 people. Anyone against? Thanks. Let's move on to the last item. What investments are next? Iain.'

Iain: 'Well, the main thing I think is that we must make a decision about Sherwood Industries …'

APPENDIX 1

The annual report of Sherwood Industries

It is the intention of Sherwood Industries to grow a profitable business, diverse in its activities to reduce overexposure to particular products or markets, but having synergy between and within product groups.

Annual report for the year ended 31 December

Contents

	Page
Financial calendar	1
Notice of meeting	2
Directors and advisers	3
The Chairman's annual review	4
Report of the directors	6
Review of operations	8
Directors' responsibilities	10
Auditors' report to the members of Sherwood Industries	11
Consolidated profit and loss account	12
Consolidated balance sheet	13
Cash flow statement	14
Statement of total recognised gains and losses	14
Statement of accounting policies	15
Notes to the accounts	16
Group financial record	23
Operating divisions and principal subsidiaries	24

Financial calendar

Annual general meeting	9 April this year
Ordinary share register closed	28 April this year
Interim report – this year	August this year
Preliminary results – this year	February next year
Publication of this year's accounts	March next year
Dividend payment dates	
Final – last year	June this year
Interim – this year	November this year
Final – this year	June next year

1

Notice of meeting

Notice is hereby given that the 72nd annual general meeting of Sherwood Industries plc will be held at the Welcombe Hotel, Warwick Road, Stratford-upon-Avon on Wednesday, 9 April this year at 12 noon for the transaction of the following business.

1 To receive and consider the directors' report and statement of accounts for the year ended 31 December last year.
2 To declare a final dividend on the ordinary shares.
3 To re-elect Mr R. W. Shaw as a director.
4 To re-appoint the auditors, Appleton, Maybury and Tipton, and to authorise the directors to fix their remuneration.

By order of the Board
A. S. Dale
Secretary
12 March this year

The following documents will be available for inspection during normal hours of business at the registered office of the company from the date of this notice until the date of the annual general meeting and will also be available at the meeting from 11.45 until its conclusion:

- a statement of the transactions of the directors, and their family interests, in the equity capital of the company and its subsidiaries
- copies of all service contracts of the directors of the company, or any of its subsidiaries, unless expiring or determinable without payment of compensation within one year.

2

Directors and advisers

Directors	Walter R. Sherwood, CBE	– Chairman
	David Moss, FCA	– Managing Director
	* Charles A. Adamson	– Non-executive
	* Bernard Gregory, FCA	– Non-executive
	* William T. Scott	– Non-executive
	Robert W. Shaw, FCA	– Finance Director

Secretary Alan S. Dale, ACIS

Registered Office Sherwood House
The Parade
Leamington Spa
Warwickshire

Auditors Appleton, Maybury and Tipton

Registrars Lloyds Bank plc
Registrars Department
Goring-on-Sea
Worthing
West Sussex

Bankers Lloyds Bank plc
Chase Manhattan Bank

Legal advisers Newland, Rose, Fisher and Partners

Merchant bankers Freeman Wild

Stockbrokers Ashworth, Morris and Co.

* Members of the remuneration committee

3

245

The Chairman's annual review

For the first time in five years, Group profits did not show an improvement over the previous year. External sales at £1,404.6m were over £360m above sales of the previous year, but pre-tax profits at £39.2m were 20 per cent lower. The increase in sales was largely attributable to a £200m increase in sales for the new Healthcare Division and over £90m increase for the Electronics Division, a sector in which the company is continuing to expand.

The profit attributable to shareholders deteriorated last year relative to the previous year because of a higher tax charge. The previous year, the tax charge was exceptionally low, whereas last year a higher proportion of profits was earned in countries with rates of tax that are higher than those in the UK. This effect on the company's earnings is only likely to be short term. In the longer run, the change in emphasis in the company's activities and the overseas spread of sales is likely to be wholly beneficial, both in terms of the longer-term potential for the company and the smoothing effect of the wider geographical spread of its activities.

Over the last five years, the company has undergone major changes in its activities. The company is no longer involved in the manufacture of capital equipment or in engineering fabrications and other services to the engineering industry. Last year, these activities accounted for £50m of sales and £0.8m of profit before they were finally discontinued.

Four divisions have now been established covering the company's four major activities worldwide, and the managing directors of these divisions are responsible for the expansion of the company's activities in their areas of responsibility.

The company's balance sheet remains very strong, with net borrowings representing only 19 per cent of shareholders' funds after financing acquisitions. This ensures the company will be able to continue its growth by acquisition, if appropriate opportunities are identified.

In my interim report to shareholders last September, profits for last year were expected to improve over those for the previous year, subject to precious metal prices not deteriorating any further and demand in the electronics market holding steady. In the event, the price of silver continued to fall and the electronics industry declined still further.

Trading activities

The Chemicals and Allied Materials Division had a good year, apart from Bradbury Pollock Corporation Inc., which incurred a loss of £4.6m following a profitable year in the previous year. This loss arose because of major cancellation of orders in the oil exploration industry in the USA resulting from the worldwide recession in the oil industry. Your Board has taken action to eliminate these losses and anticipates a return to profit this year.

Roland Bright Refiners suffered a serious loss. This was largely due to the fall in silver prices, which reached a ten-year low in real terms during the year. The reduction in gross margin resulting from the price fall could not be offset by the action taken during the year to improve refinery efficiency. Further action has now been taken to improve the situation. All refining has been concentrated on the company's headquarters site in Birmingham, which will result in a significant reduction in costs. Your Board is now confident that this move, together with action taken to increase processing charges and increase the throughput of other precious metals, thus lowering the dependence on silver, will ensure a return to profit this year.

The UK electronics industry suffered a severe downturn last year and this affected all major

4

distributors, including Brandon Electronics. The timely acquisition in the previous year of Meyer und Weiss of Dusseldorf, a major distributor in Germany, has enabled the Electronics Division to increase profits during a very difficult year.

In the previous year the company acquired Fleet Dental Services Inc., a US company that operates dental laboratories in New York State and New Jersey. The company is not only an important source of precious metal recovery in the USA and a customer for polishing materials from the Chemicals Division, but also a specialist distributor, an activity in which your company has considerable expertise and is seeking complementary diversification.

The acquisition of Fleet was very successful and last year your Board decided to build on this and took the opportunity to acquire Coden Laboratories Limited, a London-based dental laboratory and medical products company operating in the UK and USA. These acquisitions have given your company an important stake in a new growth market that your Board intends fully to exploit.

Dividends

Your Board announced an interim dividend of 2.3p per share, an increase of 0.1p over the previous year. As a result of the reduction in total profit for the year, your Board is recommending a maintained final dividend of 4.8p, giving a small increase for the year.

Prospects

The company ended the year with a strong balance sheet with net borrowings representing only 19 per cent of shareholders' funds and an increase in borrowings over the previous year of only £11m, despite acquisitions during the year and an increase in working capital arising from a 35 per cent increase in turnover. Your Board is confident that the measures it has taken will ensure that the two loss-making companies in the Group will be restored to profitability in the first half of this year, and that with the final divestment of your company's engineering activities, your Board can concentrate on the expansion of the Group. The new Healthcare Products and Services Division offers a major opportunity for growth this year and there are also opportunities for growth and profit improvement in your company's three other divisions.

Group restructuring

Last year saw a major change in the Group Board's relationship with its operating companies. Four Divisions were established, each with its own managing director and Board, responsible for the company's major areas of activity, namely Chemicals and Allied Materials, Precious Metals Recovery and Refining, Electronic Components, and Healthcare Products and Services. All operating companies now come under one of the four divisions and the managing directors of the operating companies report to the managing director of their division, rather than to the Group Managing Director as they did in the past.

These changes have the wholly beneficial effect of giving greater responsibility to management at divisional level and thus enable the Group Managing Director and the Group Board to concentrate on the overall health of the business and its future strategy for growth.

Management and employees

I would like to record my thanks to employees at all levels in the company for their hard work and cooperation in the past year and to welcome all new employees. Our future success will be critically dependent on their continuing dedication and skills.

Walter Sherwood
Chairman

5

Report of the directors

Principal activities

The Group is principally engaged in the manufacture of chemicals and allied materials for surface finishing and water treatment; sealants, adhesives and fire-resistant fluids; in the recovery and refining of precious metals; in the distribution of electronic components and production aids; and in the manufacture of fixed and removable dental fittings and the distribution of dental instruments and equipment. These activities are managed in four divisions, which are described more fully in the Review of operations.

Results and dividends

The Group's profit before tax amounted to £39.2m (previous year, £48.7m). The reduction arises from a loss in the precious metals recovery business and a reduction in profit in the chemicals and allied materials business in the UK, which was largely offset by profits from newly acquired companies.

The directors recommend a final dividend of 4.8p per ordinary share (previous year, 4.8p), which, together with the interim dividend of 2.3p per share, makes a total of 7.1p per share for the year.

Research and development

There is a substantial contribution to research and development throughout the Group. The majority of these activities are devoted to product development and improved manufacturing techniques.

Land and buildings

The directors are of the opinion that the existing use value of the Group's properties in aggregate approximates to the amount at which they are included in the accounts.

Acquisitions

On 20 August last year, the company acquired the business of Coden Dental Laboratories Ltd for cash amounting to £50m.

Directors

The directors, as at 31 December last year, and their interests in the issued share capital, all of which were beneficial, were as follows:

	Ordinary shares of 50p	
	Last year	Previous year
W. R. Sherwood	14,020,750	14,020,750
D. Moss	406,200	406,200
R. W. Shaw	35,000	35,000
C. A. Adamson	20,000	20,000
B. Gregory	40,000	40,000
W. T. Scott	100,000	100,000

6

No director was involved in any sharedealing transactions in the period from 30 June last year to the date of the publication of the interim results or from 1 January to 3 March this year. No director has any interest in the company's $7\frac{1}{2}$ per cent unsecured loan stock 1998/2002. Mr R. W. Shaw retires at the annual general meeting and, being eligible, offers himself for re-election.

Shareholdings

The directors have been advised of the following shareholdings in excess of 3 per cent in the issued share capital of the company at 31 December last year.

	No of shares	per cent of share capital
Fremont Investment Trust plc	19,629,500	10.5
Reliable Assurance plc	13,086,250	7.0
Public Utilities Pension Fund	11,590,700	6.2

In addition, Mr W. R. Sherwood had an interest of 7.5 per cent as shown earlier. No changes in the above holdings have been notified in the period up to 3 March this year.

Employment of disabled persons

Full and fair consideration is given to applications from disabled persons, having regard to their particular aptitudes and abilities. Disabled persons are treated on equal terms with other employees as far as training, career development and promotion are concerned.

Employee involvement

It is the Group's policy to develop and maintain employee awareness and involvement in its activities. This is being achieved by the managing directors of the operating companies having regularly meetings with employees to inform them of the Group's progress and by regular issuing of the Group newsletter.

Charitable donations

The Group has made donations for charitable purposes amounting to £5,000.

Policy on the payment of creditors

The group does not follow a formal code or standard on payment practice. The Group policy is:

(a) to agree terms of payment with all suppliers when agreeing terms of each transaction
(b) to ensure that suppliers are made aware of the terms of payment
(c) to abide by the terms of payment.

Auditors

A resolution proposing the re-appointment of Appleton, Maybury and Tipton, will be put to the annual general meeting.

By order of the Board
A. S. Dale
Secretary
3 March this year

7

Review of operations

Chemicals and Allied Materials Division
Managing Director: Stephen Turner

	Last year £m	Previous £m
Sales	610.9	560.2
Pre-tax profits	38.4	43.6

The Division manufactures and distributes chemicals and polishing materials for the surface finishing industry, sealants and adhesives, fire-resistant hydraulic control fluids and chemicals for water and process treatment problems. The Division trades through its two major operating companies, Sherwood Chemicals and Bradbury Pollock.

Sherwood Chemicals serves a very wide range of industries in the UK and worldwide and achieved satisfactory results for the year, despite a decline in orders from export markets in the second half. This was due in part to the strength of sterling and to a decline in demand from a number of customers in the Far East.

During the year, a new technical centre and new research facilities were completed that will ensure that the company maintains its lead as a supplier of metal finishing products.

Bradbury Pollock had a reasonable trading year, with the exception of a US subsidiary supplying a range of products to the oil exploration industry. This company incurred a loss due to cancellation of orders arising from a downturn in the oil industry. Action has been taken to restore profitability, which should be achieved in the first half of this year.

Precious Metals Recovery and Refining Division
Managing Director: Thomas Smallwood

	Last year £m	Previous £m
Sales	340.8	330.7
Pre-tax profits (loss)	(5.6)	10.1

Roland Bright Refiners is engaged in the recovery and refining of precious metals, primarily silver, but also gold and other precious metals from photographic, dental and jewellery waste. Its major overseas source of supply is its wholly owned subsidiary Roland Bright Precious Metals Inc., located in Newark, New Jersey.

Profitability in the precious metals recovery business is affected by the level of precious metals prices, but the effects on the company are limited because it does not become involved in speculative purchase or sale of precious metals, all purchases being matched by equivalent forward sales.

Silver prices fell to a ten-year low in real terms during last year, which had an adverse effect on margins. However, the decline in bullion prices, particularly silver, has resulted in a number of marginal competitors leaving the industry.

8

This year's results should show a return to profitability arising from increased volumes of materials coming from overseas at better margins, from better processing margins and from a reduction in costs resulting from the rationalisation of facilities on to one site.

Electronic Components Division
Managing Director: Roger Hammond

	Last year £m	Previous £m
Sales	195.6	104.4
Pre-tax profits	4.7	3.7

The Division has two operating subsidiaries: Brandon Electronics and Meyer und Weiss, located in Dusseldorf, West Germany, which joined the Group at the end of the previous year. Both companies distribute electronic components.

The profitability of Brandon Electronics was seriously affected by the downturn in the UK's electronics industry and the company only achieved break even against a profit of £3.7m in the previous year. There are signs of improvement in the industry and this better trading climate, coupled with a number of internal changes that are currently in progress, should result in a return to profit this year.

Meyer und Weiss had a good year, improving its performance by 23 per cent over the previous year. This was a first-class performance in the company's first year as a member of the Group. The company's growth is expected to continue this year in line with the growth in the electronics industry in Germany.

Health Care Products and Services Division
Managing Director: Michael Kelly

	Last year £m	Previous £m
Sales	207.0	7.3
Pre-tax profits	12.9	0.2

The Division has been formed from the acquisition of Fleet Dental Services late in the previous year and Coden Laboratories last year. The results shown for the previous year are therefore not a true comparison, but both companies have shown encouraging growth in the last year over the previous year, and that growth pattern is continuing.

Fleet Dental Services operates dental laboratories in New York State and New Jersey and Coden Laboratories operates dental laboratories on the East Coast of the USA and in the UK. The company also distributes dental instruments and equipment.

The original purchase of Fleet Dental Services was intended to be a complementary business to Roland Bright, as a supplier of precious metal scrap, and to Sherwood Chemicals as a customer for polishing materials, but the potential for expansion of the core business has overtaken the importance of this original intention.

The prospects for expansion of the Division through organic growth and acquisitions are excellent.

9

Directors' responsibilities

In respect of the preparation of financial statements

Company law requires the directors to prepare financial statements for each financial year that give a true and fair view of the state of affairs of the company and of the Group and of the profit or loss of the Group for that period. In preparing those financial statements, the directors are required to:

- select suitable accounting policies and to apply them consistently
- make judgements and estimates that are reasonable and prudent
- state whether applicable accounting standards have been followed, subject to any material departures disclosed and explained in the financial statements
- prepare the financial statements on a going concern basis, unless it is inappropriate to presume that the company will continue in business.

The directors are responsible for keeping proper accounting records that disclose with reasonable accuracy at any time the financial position of the company and the Group and to enable them to ensure that the financial statements comply with the Companies Act 1985. They are also responsible for safeguarding the assets of the company and the Group and, hence, for taking reasonable steps for the prevention and detection of fraud and other irregularities.

10

Auditors' report to the members of Sherwood Industries plc

We have audited the financial statements on pages 12 to 22.

Respective responsibilities of directors and auditors
As described above, the company's directors are responsible for the preparation of financial statements. It is our responsibility to form an independent opinion, based on our audit of those statements, and to report our opinion to you.

Basis of opinion
We conducted our audit in accordance with Auditing Standards issued by the Auditing Practices Board. An audit includes examination, on a test basis, of evidence relevant to the amounts and disclosures in the financial statements. It also includes an assessment of the significant estimates and judgements made by the directors in the preparation of the financial statements and of whether the accounting policies are appropriate to the Group's circumstances, consistently applied and adequately disclosed.
We planned and performed our audit so as to obtain all the information and explanations that we considered necessary in order to provide us with sufficient evidence to give reasonable assurance that the financial statements are free from material misstatement, whether caused by fraud or other irregularity or error. In forming our opinion, we also evaluated the overall adequacy of the presentation of information in the financial statements.

Opinion
In our opinion, the financial statements give a true and fair view of the state of affairs of the group as at 31 December last year and of the profit of the group for the year then ended and have been properly prepared in accordance with the Companies Act 1985.

Appleton, Maybury and Tipton
Chartered Accountants and Registered Auditors
Birmingham
3 March this year

11

Consolidated profit and loss account

For the years ended 31 December

	Notes	Last Year £m	Previous Year (as restated) £m
Turnover			
Continuing operation		1,209.5	1,002.6
Acquisitions		144.8	
		1,354.3	
Discontinued operations		50.3	39.3
	1	1,404.6	1,041.9
Cost of sales	2	1,008.6	773.0
Gross profit		396.0	268.9
Distribution costs	2	(161.7)	(97.1)
Administration expenses	2	(186.1)	(118.5)
		48.2	53.3
Other operating income	2	5.5	4.1
Operating profit			
Continuing operations	44.7		58.4
Acquisitions	8.2		
	52.9		
Discontinued operations	0.8		(1.0)
		53.7	57.4
Profit/(loss) on sale of fixed assets in continuing operations		4.6	(2.2)
Loss on sale of fixed assets in discontinued operations		(3.8)	(1.8)
Cost of group restructuring		(1.8)	–
Profit on ordinary activities before interest		52.7	53.4
Interest receivable		4.1	6.1
Interest payable		(17.6)	(10.8)
Profit on ordinary activities before tax	1	39.2	48.7
Tax on profit on ordinary activities		(16.2)	(10.3)
Profit on ordinary activities after tax		23.0	38.4
Minority interests		(1.2)	(1.1)
Profit for the financial year		21.8	37.3
Dividends	4	(13.3)	(13.1)
Retained profit for the financial year		8.5	24.2
Earnings per share	5	11.65p	22.35p

12

Consolidated balance sheet

As at 31 December

	Notes	Last year £m	Previous year £m
Fixed assets			
Tangible assets	6	158.8	160.4
Investments		0.3	7.8
		159.1	168.2
Current assets			
Stock	7	172.1	155.8
Debtors	8	313.9	245.2
Cash at bank and in hand		57.4	69.1
		543.4	470.1
Creditors: amounts falling due within one year	9	(333.2)	(292.1)
Net current assets		210.2	178.0
Total assets less current liabilities		369.3	346.2
Creditors: amounts falling due after more than one year	9	(87.2)	(58.1)
Provisions for liabilities and charges		(2.1)	(4.6)
		280.0	283.5
Capital and reserves			
Called-up share capital	10	93.5	93.4
Share premium account	11	58.5	58.4
Profit and loss account	11	120.7	125.4
		272.7	277.2
Shareholders' funds			
Minority interests	12	7.3	6.3
		280.0	283.5

W. R. Sherwood, Director
R. W. Shaw, Director

These accounts were approved by the Board of Directors on 3 March this year

13

255

Cash flow statement

For the years ended 31 December

	Notes	Last year £m	Previous year £m
Net cash inflow from operating activities	13	86.9	10.3
Returns on investment and servicing of finance	14	(10.6)	(4.3)
Tax		(7.5)	(6.6)
Capital expenditure and investment	14	57.3	(7.6)
Acquisitions and disposals	15	(49.7)	(35.1)
Equity dividends paid		(13.3)	(10.1)
Cash inflow/(outflow) before financing		63.1	(53.4)
Financing	14	(45.2)	35.7
Increase/(decrease) in cash in the period		17.9	(17.7)

	Notes	Last year £m	Previous year £m
Reconciliation of net cash flow to movement in net debt	16		
Increase/(decrease) in cash in the period		17.9	(17.7)
Cash to repay loans		45.4	22.5
Change in net debt resulting from cash flows		63.3	4.8
Loans acquired with subsidiary		(74.5)	(4.9)
Movement in net debt in the period		(11.2)	(0.1)
Net debt at 1 January last year		(40.9)	(40.8)
Net debt at 31 December last year		(52.1)	(40.9)

Statement of total recognised gains and losses

	Last year £m	Previous year (as restated) £m
Profit for the financial year	21.8	37.3
Currency translation differences on foreign net investments	(1.1)	0.9
Total gains and losses recognised since last annual report	20.7	38.2

There is no material difference between the Group's results as reported and on an historical cost basis. Accordingly, no note of historical cost profits and losses has been prepared.

14

Statement of accounting policies

The accounts have been prepared in accordance with applicable accounting standards under the historical cost convention.

Consolidation
The consolidated accounts comprise the accounts of the holding company and of all subsidiaries made up to 31 December. A separate profit and loss account dealing with the results of the holding company only has not been presented.
Goodwill arising from the acquisition of companies is written off against Group reserves. The results of such new acquisitions have been included from the date of investment.

Turnover
Turnover represents sales to external customers, excluding VAT.

Foreign currencies
The accounts of overseas currencies are translated into sterling at the rates of exchange ruling at the balance sheet date. Exchange differences arising from the translation of opening balance sheet amounts are dealt with through reserves. Overseas investments are stated at the rates of exchange in force at the date the investment was made. All other exchange differences are dealt with through the profit and loss account.

Depreciation
Depreciation is calculated to write down the cost of all tangible assets, other than freehold land, by equal annual instalments over their expected useful life. The useful life assumed for plant and fixtures varies between 5 and 14 years, and for motor vehicles is 4 to 5 years. The useful life for buildings is based on independent professional advice.

Stock and work in progress
Stock and work in progress is valued at the lower of cost and net realisable value. Cost includes all material, labour and appropriate overhead expenses in bringing goods to their current state. Provisions are made as necessary for slow-moving and obsolete stock.

Research and development
Revenue expenditure on research and development is written off against profit in the year in which it is incurred. Capital expenditure on research and development plant is depreciated in accordance with the accounting policy for other fixed assets.

Tax
The tax charge is based on the profit for the year and includes provision for tax that the directors believe the Group will have to pay in the foreseeable future. Deferred tax is not provided on earnings retained by overseas subsidiaries.

Pensions
Pension funds are held in independently managed pension schemes that are administered by trustees. Payments are made to the funds on the advice of external actuaries and are charged against profits in the year in which they are made. Independent actuarial valuations are carried out every three years and any necessary adjustment is made to future funding rates.

Notes to the accounts

1 Analysis of turnover and profits before taxation

	Last year Turnover £m	Last year Profit £m	Previous year Turnover £m	Previous year Profit £m
Chemicals and Allied Materials Division	610.9	38.4	560.2	43.6
Precious Metals Recovery and Refining Division	340.8	(5.6)	330.7	10.1
Electronic Components Division	195.6	4.7	104.4	3.7
Healthcare Components Division	207.0	12.9	7.3	0.2
Activities and companies disposed of	50.3	0.8	39.3	(1.0)
Group interest and unallocated costs		(12.0)		(7.9)
	1,404.6	39.2	1,041.9	48.7

	Last year £m	Previous year £m
Profit before tax is shown after charging:		
hire of plant and equipment	7.0	9.4
operating leases relating to property	6.0	0.9
depreciation	26.0	19.9
auditors' remuneration	1.8	1.4
research and development	56.0	20.6
Analysis by geographical area:		
UK	847.5	803.1
Other EU countries	243.0	122.7
Rest of Europe	12.5	10.2
Middle East and Africa	22.7	20.2
Australasia and Far East	44.4	48.7
North America	222.1	15.2
Others	12.4	21.8
	1,404.6	1,041.9

2 Analysis of costs between continuing and discontinued operations

	Last year Continuing £m	Last year Acquisitions £m	Last year Discontinued £m	Last year Total £m	Previous year (as restated) Continuing £m	Previous year (as restated) Discontinued £m	Previous year (as restated) Total £m
Net operating expenses							
Cost of sales	867.5	101.2	39.9	1,008.6	741.3	31.7	773.0
Distribution costs	141.4	16.3	4.0	161.7	93.1	4.0	97.1
Administration expenses	161.3	19.1	5.7	186.1	113.8	4.7	118.5
Other operating income	5.4	–	0.1	5.5	4.0	0.1	4.1

16

3 Directors and employees

The remuneration of the directors during the year was as follows:

	Last year	Previous year
Fees	45,000	35,000
Remuneration for management services	590,000	540,000
Pension contributions for money purchase schemes	102,000	84,000
	737,000	659,000

Highest-paid director

	Last year	Previous year
Emoluments	219,000	220,000
Pension contributions for money purchase scheme	25,000	23,000

	Salary and fees £,000	Performance- related pay £,000	Taxable benefits £,000	Pension contributions £,000	Total £,000
Chairman					
W. R. Sherwood	114	27	9	50	200
Executive directors					
D. Moss	150	55	14	25	244
R. W. Shaw	100	45	14	27	186
Non-executive directors					
C. A. Adamson	30				30
B. Gregory	35				35
W. T. Scott	42				42

Staff costs during the year (including directors' emoluments) were:

	Last year £m	Previous year £m
Wages and salaries	273.7	144.3
Social security costs	24.6	12.8
Other pension costs	7.7	6.6
	306.0	163.7

The average number of persons employed by the Group was:

	Last year	Previous year
Chemicals and Allied Materials Division	4,896	4,904
Precious Metals Recovery and Refining Division	855	871
Electronic Components Division	673	403
Healthcare Products and Services Division	3,851	112
Discontinued activities	621	542
	10,896	6,832

There were 15,880 employees at 31 December last year (previous year, 7,576)

17

4 Dividends

	Last year £m	Previous year £m
Interim dividends paid of 2.3p per share (previous year, 2.2p)	4.3	4.1
Final dividends proposed of 4.8p per share (previous year, 4.8p)	9.0	9.0
	13.3	13.1

5 Earnings per share

The figure is calculated on earnings of 21,780,000 (previous year, 37,320,000), being the Group's profit for the financial year. There was an average of 186,875,000 shares (previous year, 167,013,000) in issue during the year.

6 Tangible assets

	Freehold properties £m	Leasehold properties £m	Plant and equipment £m	Motor vehicles £m	Total £m
Cost:					
At 1 January last year	71.6	16.3	152.1	18.5	258.5
Exchange adjustments	(2.1)	(0.5)	(2.9)	(0.3)	(5.8)
Capital expenditure	0.7	2.1	15.2	9.2	27.2
Acquisitions	66.6	–	4.8	6.3	77.7
Disposals	(66.3)	(0.1)	(7.2)	(11.9)	(85.5)
At 31 December last year	70.5	17.8	162.0	21.8	272.1
Accumulated depreciation:					
At 1 January last year	7.6	2.8	80.6	7.1	98.1
Exchange adjustments	(0.1)	(0.1)	(0.5)	(0.1)	(0.8)
Charge for year	1.9	1.0	17.9	5.2	26.0
On disposals	(0.2)	(0.1)	(6.2)	(3.5)	(10.0)
At 31 December last year	9.2	3.6	91.8	8.7	113.3
Net book value					
At 31 December last year	61.3	14.2	70.2	13.1	158.8
At 31 December previous year	64.0	13.5	71.5	11.4	160.4

7 Stock

	Last year £m	Previous year £m
Raw materials	59.7	47.7
Work in progress	33.7	42.5
Finished goods	78.7	65.6
	172.1	155.8

18

8 Debtors

	Last year £m	Previous year £m
Amounts falling due within one year:		
Trade debtors	258.4	200.4
Assets in course of realisation	–	12.9
Prepayments and accrued income	16.9	11.9
Other debtors	11.6	14.2
	286.9	239.4
Amounts falling due after more than one year:		
Advance corporation tax recoverable	5.1	3.8
Other debtors	21.9	2.0
	313.9	245.2

9 Creditors

	Last year £m	Previous year £m
Amounts falling due within one year:		
Trade creditors	185.9	148.3
Bank loans and overdrafts	29.8	57.8
Corporation tax	17.1	8.3
Other tax and social security (inc. VAT)	16.8	14.6
Dividends	9.0	9.0
Accruals	39.7	10.4
Other creditors	34.9	43.7
	333.2	292.1
Amounts falling due after more than one year:		
Bank loans	75.6	47.9
7½ per cent unsecured loan stock 1998/2002	4.1	4.3
Other creditors	7.5	5.9
	87.2	58.1
The above amounts are payable as follows:		
1–2 years	31.2	24.2
2–5 years	38.7	28.0
After 5 years	17.3	5.9
	87.2	58.1

10 Share capital

	Last year	Previous year
Issued ordinary shares at 50p each fully paid	93,483,240	93,402,940
Unissued shares of 50p each	22,016,760	5,597,060
	115,500,000	99,000,000

19

11 Reserves

	£m
Not distributable:	
Share premiums	
At 1 January last year	58.4
On shares issued during year	0.1
At 31 December last year	58.5
Distributable:	
At 1 January last year	125.4
Retained profit for year	8.5
Exchange adjustment	(1.1)
	132.8
Less goodwill on acquisitions during year	(12.1)
At 31 December last year	120.7
Total reserves	179.2

12 Reconciliation of movements in shareholders' funds

	Last year £m
Profit for the financial year	21.8
Dividends	(13.3)
Other recognised gains and losses relating to the year (net)	(1.1)
New share capital subscribed	0.2
Goodwill written off	(12.1)
Net addition to shareholders' funds	(4.5)
Opening shareholders' funds	277.2
Closing shareholders' funds	272.7

13 Reconciliations of operating profit to net cash inflow from operating activities

	Last year £m	Previous year £m
Operating profit	53.7	57.4
Add back non-cash items		
Depreciation charges	26.0	19.9
Loss on sale of fixed assets	(0.4)	0.4
Effect of foreign exchange rate changes	4.9	(0.8)
Decrease/(increase) in stocks	5.7	(25.6)
Decrease/(increase) in debtors	13.5	(55.2)
(Decrease)/increase in creditors	(14.7)	14.2
Net cash inflow from operating activities	88.7	10.3
Net cash outflow in respect of reorganisation costs	(1.8)	–
	86.9	10.3

20

14 Gross cash flows

	Last year £m	Previous year £m
Returns on investment and servicing of finance		
Interest received	4.4	5.8
Interest paid	(14.7)	(9.8)
Dividends paid to minorities	(0.3)	(0.3)
	(10.6)	(4.3)
Capital expenditure and financial investment		
Payments to acquire tangible fixed assets	(26.1)	(34.8)
Receipts from sales of tangible fixed assets	76.4	24.3
Receipts from sale of trade investments	7.0	2.9
	57.3	(7.6)
Financing		
Issue of ordinary share capital	0.2	58.2
Repayments of loans	(45.4)	(22.5)
	(45.2)	35.7

15 Purchase of subsidiary undertakings

	Last year £m	Previous year £m
Net assets acquired		
Tangible fixed assets	77.7	15.6
Stocks	21.9	13.9
Debtors	82.4	30.3
Cash at bank and in hand	0.3	–
Creditors	(69.9)	(33.3)
Bank overdrafts	–	(4.8)
Loans	(74.5)	(4.9)
Minority shareholders' interests	–	(0.7)
	37.9	16.1
Goodwill	12.1	14.2
Satisfied by cash consideration	50.0	30.3

	£m	£m
Net cash outflow		
Cash consideration	50.0	30.3
Cash at bank and in hand acquired	(0.3)	–
Bank overdrafts of acquired subsidiary undertakings	–	4.8
Net outflow of cash in respect of the purchase of subsidiaries	49.7	35.1

21

263

16 Analysis of changes in net debt

	At 1 Jan Last year	Cash flows	Acquisitions (excl. cash and overdrafts)	Other non-cash changes	At 31 Dec last year
	£m	£m	£m	£m	£m
Cash at bank and in hand	69.1	(11.7)			57.4
Bank loans and overdrafts	(35.2)	29.6			(5.6)
		17.9			
Debt due within one year	(22.6)	45.4	(22.8)	(24.2)	(24.2)
Debt due after one year	(52.2)		(51.7)	24.2	(79.7)
Total	(40.9)	63.3	(74.5)	–	(52.1)

Note: In note 9 to the accounts, 'Bank loans and overdrafts' consists of the amounts shown above as overdrafts and debt due within one year.

22

Group financial record

	Last year £m	Previous year £m	Previous year–1 £m	Previous year–2 £m	Previous year–3 £m
Turnover					
Chemicals and Allied Materials Division	610.9	560.2	492.2	481.8	428.8
Precious Metals Recovery and Refining Division	340.8	330.7	479.6	259.8	224.2
Electronic Components Division	195.6	104.4	70.7	68.9	37.1
Healthcare Products and Services Division	207.0	7.3	–	–	–
	1,354.3	1,002.6	1,042.5	810.5	690.1
Discontinued activities	50.3	39.3	37.3	195.5	370.5
	1,404.6	1,041.9	1,079.8	1,006.0	1,060.6
Profit before tax					
Chemicals and Allied Materials Division	38.4	43.6	29.6	23.7	27.0
Precious Metals Recovery and Refining Division	(5.6)	10.1	18.6	7.0	11.0
Electronic Components Division	4.7	3.7	2.3	5.0	2.8
Healthcare Products and Services Division	12.9	0.2	–	–	–
Group interest and other costs	(12.0)	(7.9)	(16.1)	(18.1)	(10.1)
	38.4	49.7	34.4	17.6	30.7
Discontinued activities	0.8	(1.0)	(0.7)	(0.1)	(10.8)
	39.2	48.7	33.7	17.5	19.9
Balance sheet					
Shareholders' funds	272.7	277.2	209.1	239.8	239.6
Borrowings as a percentage of shareholders' funds:	19%	15%	19%	52%	51%
Results					
Earnings per ordinary share – pence	11.65	22.35	14.60	6.80	5.30
Dividends per ordinary share – pence	7.1	7.0	5.0	3.5	8.0

Operating divisions and principal subsidiaries

Chemicals and Allied Materials Division
*Sherwood Chemicals Limited
   Sherwood Chemicals GmbH (Germany)
*Bradbury Pollock Limited
   Bradbury Lubricants Limited
   J. H. Pollock Limited
   Evans Water Treatment Limited
   Bradbury Pollock GmbH (Germany)
   Bradbury Pollock Corporation Inc. (USA)

Precious Metals Recovery and Refining Division
*Roland Bright Refiners Limited
   Roland Bright Precious Metals Inc. (USA)

Electronic Components Division
*Brandon Electronics Limited
*Meyer und Weiss GmbH (Germany)

Healthcare Products and Services Division
*Coden Laboratories Limited
   Coden Laboratories Inc. (USA)
*Fleet Dental Services Inc. (USA)

* These companies are all directly owned by Sherwood Industries plc and the remaining companies are
indirect subsidiaries. All the companies are 100 per cent subsidiaries except for Meyer und Weiss GmbH
(76 per cent)

24

Corporate governance statements in an annual report

Corporate governance – a recent example

The company pursues its corporate purpose with the objective of enhancing shareholder value. Fundamental to the fulfilment of corporate responsibilities and the achievement of financial objectives is an effective system of corporate governance.

Board and committee structure

The Board is responsible for the Group's system of corporate governance and is ultimately accountable for its activities throughout the world. The Board comprises executive and non-executive directors. The role of the non-executive directors is to bring independent judgement to the Board's deliberations and decisions.

The offices of Chairman and Chief Executive are held separately. The Chairman is a non-executive director. The Chief Executive is also Deputy Chairman.

The Board meets regularly throughout the year. It has a formal schedule of matters reserved to it for decision, but otherwise delegates specific responsibilities to committees, as described below.

The Group Executive Committee is responsible for the executive management of the Group. It is chaired by the Chief Executive and comprises the executive directors and other senior managers. The

Committee meets monthly and its minutes are placed on the agenda of the Board.

The Audit Committee reviews the half-year and full year results and the interim and annual report and accounts prior to their submission to the Board and considers any matters raised by the external or internal auditors. The Committee is chaired by a non-executive director. It meets four times a year with the Chief Executive and the Finance Director and the external and internal auditors are in attendance.

The Remuneration Committee approves the remuneration of the executive directors and is responsible for the policy and operation of the share option schemes. The Committee is chaired by the Chairman. The Chief Executive attends its meetings, except when his own remuneration is being considered.

The Group Appeals Committee carries out the Board's policy on charitable donations. The Committee is chaired by a non-executive director. The Committee meets quarterly.

The members of the Audit Committee, the Remuneration Committee and the Group Appeals Committee are detailed in earlier pages.

Pension schemes

The Company and a number of its overseas subsidiary undertakings have established pension schemes for the administration of staff retirement benefits. In the UK, the company and its UK subsidiary undertakings participate in and contribute to pension schemes that are administered separately from the Group by formally constituted trustee companies. A number of the company's executive and non-executive directors, together with a number of external directors, serve on the Boards of the trustee companies.

Accountability and control

The company operates, and attaches importance to, clear principles and procedures designed to achieve the accountability and control appropriate to a business operating multinationally.

It has principles designed to provide an environment of central leadership and local operating autonomy as the framework for the exercise of accountability and control by the Board, its committees and executive management.

Cadbury Code of Best Practice

In December 1992, the Committee on the Financial Aspects of Corporate Governance (the Cadbury Committee) published a Code of Best Practice. The Code contains 19 recommendations as to best practice in terms of the control and reporting functions of Boards of directors. Two reporting recommendations, relating to the effectiveness of internal controls and confirmation that the business is a going concern, where implementation had been deferred pending development of guidance on compliance by the accounting profession, became operative during the period covered by this Report on the issue of the relevant guidance.

The Board considers that, throughout the financial period under review, the company complied with all 19 recommendations of the Code.

The guidance on reporting on internal control focuses on internal financial control, defined as the internal controls established to provide reasonable assurance of:

- the safeguarding of assets against unauthorised use or disposition;

- the maintenance of proper accounting records and the reliability of financial information used within the business or for publication.

Index

accounting policies 197–8
acid test ratio 163
acquisitions 104–5, 106, 195–6
added value 193
advisers 99–100
AGMs (annual general meetings) 97–9
annual reports 55–6
  as an advertising document 91
  auditors' reports 120–2
  balance sheet 133–7
  cash flow statement 193–7
  directors and advisers 99–100
  directors' responsibilities 119–20
  financial calendar 97
  group financial record 200
  group statements 92
  mission statement 92, 94–5
  notes to the accounts 199–200
  notice of AGM 97–9
  obtaining 72
  profit and loss account 131–3
  review of operations 109–12
  statement of accounting policies 197–8
  see also Chairman's statement; directors' reports
assets 133–5, 139, 142, 143, 153
  accounting policies 197–8
  quick assets 154
  ratio analysis 163–6, 188–9, 190–1
  return on assets 159–60
  revaluation 197
auditors 109, 120–2
average wage per employee 171

balance sheets 133–7
bonds 79
borrowing ratio 167–8, 177
British Gas 40–1
BT 59, 95
building societies 3, 15
business cycle 78–9
business ratios *see* financial ratios
buying at market bottoms 28–30

capital
  allocation model 39
  cost of capital 192
  expenditure 195
  gearing ratios 56–8
  owners' capital 129, 130
capital employed 154
  per employee 191
  return on 59–61
capital gains tax 231, 233
cash flow statement 193–7
Chairman's statement
  dividends 102
  future prospects 102
  and growth stages 63, 64–5, 66–7, 69
  past performance 100–1
  structure and people 103
  trading activities 101
charges 206–7
  and choice of strategy 79
  and investment performance 25–6
  on PEPs 233
charitable donations 108
chemical industries 81
collapse of companies 85, 194
collection period ratio 165–6
commission to stockbrokers 206–7
  see also charges
company activity matrix 110–12, 114
company reports *see* annual reports
company risk 4
company strategy 109–19
computer industry 133
conglomerates 87
constitution and rules of investment clubs 237–8
consumer behaviour 78
contract notes 207–8
contrarian investing 28, 29–30
corporate governance 98, 201
cost of capital 192
cost of sales 129, 130, 131, 133
  and discontinued businesses 199
Crash of 1987 27, 28

creditors 136, 139, 143
  company payment policy 108
creditors to sales ratio 190
current assets 133–4, 139, 143
current liabilities 135–6, 144
  to net worth ratio 189
  to stock ratio 189
current ratio 161–2

Darnley Village Investment Club (DVIC)
  assessing key business ratios 175–80
  discussing company strategy 113–19
  finalising the analysis 186–7
  investment strategy 37, 50
  monthly meeting 238–9
  objectives of individuals 37–8
DCF (discounted cash flow) 221
debentures 105–6
debtors 134, 139, 143
decommissioning fixed assets 198
defensive sectors 82
depreciation 130, 135, 139, 141
directors
  information on 105–6
  remuneration 200
  responsibilities 119–20
  share purchases by 42, 105
directors' reports 103–9
  acquisitions 104–5
  appointment of auditors 109
  charitable donations 108
  conclusion 109
  employment policies 107–8
  information on directors 105–6
  land and buildings 104
  major shareholdings 106–7
  policy on payment of creditors 108
  principal activities 103
  research and development 104
  results and dividends 103
discontinued businesses 199
discounted cash flow (DCF) 221
disposals 195–6
diversification 40, 48, 85–6
dividend expectations form 216–18
dividends
  and cash flow statements 196
  cover 23–4, 118
  ex-dividend dates 97
  information in annual reports 91, 102, 103
  yield 20–1, 44

documentation
  buying and selling transactions 205–8
  dividend expectations form 216–18
  investment record form 219–25
  register of shares held 208–11
  risk profile and spread 214–15

EBIT (earnings before interest and tax) 133, 160
economic cycle 78–9
economic forecasts 79–80
economic value added (EVA) 192
emerging markets 48
employees
  average number 140, 145–6
  average wage per employee 171
  employee ratios 169–71
  remuneration 140, 146
employment policies 107–8
equities as an inflation hedge 16
Eurotunnel 29, 58
EVA (economic value added) 192
ex-dividend dates 97
expenses see cost of sales
extraordinary general meetings 98

'fact finding' examinations 36
fashionable sectors 83–4
financial calendar 97
financial ratios
  asset utility 163–6, 190–1
  comparison between companies 127–8, 185
  in different growth stages 63, 65, 67, 69
  employee 169–71
  gearing 56–9, 166–9
  growth 171–3
  industry averages 185–6
  liquidity 161–3
  profitability 59–62, 116–17, 158–61
  quick ratio 19, 163
  strategy and financial viability 188
  see also shareholder ratios
Financial Times
  Annual Reports service 72
  directors' buying details 42
  ex-dividend dates 97
  shareholder ratios 19, 24–5
  surveys of economic forecasts 80
Financial Times All-Share Index of Total Returns
  3
fixed assets 134, 139, 142, 197
  decommissioning 198
fixed assets to net worth ratio 188–9

fixed rate savings 15
foreign shares 30, 44, 46, 48
FTSE 100 companies 40, 47–8
FTSE mid 250 companies 48, 71–2
fund managers 25–6

gearing ratios 56–9, 166–9
gilt-edged stocks 16–17
goodwill 135
government bonds 79
gross profit margin 132–3
gross profits 132
group financial records 200
growth ratios 171–3
growth shares 48, 62–70

Hanson 41
herd instinct 27–8
Hewlett-Packard 60

IBM 133
income gearing 58–9, 168–9
income tax 231–3
independent financial advisers 25, 36
indicators, economic 80–1
industry ratios 185–6
inflation 15–17
insider dealing 84
insurance 36
insurance companies 42
intangible assets 139, 142, 153
interest payable 133, 139, 141
interest rates 78–9
internal rate of return (IRR) 221
investment clubs 235–8
    constitution and rules 237–8
    strategy 37, 50, 236–7
    see also Darnley Village Investment Club
        (DVIC)
investment record form 219–25
investment returns 3
investment trusts 30, 42, 46
investor's ratios see shareholder ratios
invoices 130
IRR (internal rate of return) 221

lagging indicators 80
land and buildings 104, 135
Land Securities 61
leading indicators 80–1
legal advisers 99–100
liabilities 134, 135–7, 140, 145, 153

life insurance 36
liquidity ratios 161–3
loan stock 105–6
loans 130, 131, 136, 139, 144
long-term liabilities 140, 145
Lottery see National Lottery

major shareholdings 106–7
margins 132–3, 158–9, 199
    pre-tax profit margin 61–2, 116–17
market capitalisation 47–8
market risk 4, 27, 86
market timing 27–30, 77
market value added (MVA) 192–3
marketmaker's spread 206–7
minority interests 136, 137, 140, 145
mission statements 92, 94–5

National Lottery 17–18
net cash inflow from operating activities 195
net profit 133, 139, 141
net worth 155
nominee companies 205
non-executive directors 99

objectives 35–9
options 42, 49–50
overdrafts 130, 136
overseas shares 30, 44, 46, 48
owners' capital 129, 130

penny shares 42, 49
pensions 15–16
PEPs (Personal Equity Plans) 43–4, 231–5
    benefits 231–4
    charges 233
    and dividend yield 21
    record keeping 235
    types of 234–5
performance record 219–25
personal objectives 35–9
pharmaceutical stocks 28–9, 82–3
Phoneco 62–70
Pilkington 62
portfolios
    diversification 40, 48, 85–6
    number of shares 86–7
    projecting buys onto 181
    reviewing 212–13, 216, 218, 225–6
    risk profile and spread 214–15
    sector distribution 86
pound cost averaging 30, 31

pre-tax profit margin 61–2, 116–17
precious metals 81–2
premium bonds 18
price/earnings ratio 21–3
profit and loss account 131–3
profitability ratios 158–61
profits
    gross 132
    growth of 16, 172
    margins 132–3, 158–9, 199
    pre-tax profit margin 61–2, 116–17
    net 133, 139, 141
    per employee 170–1
    pre-interest 155
    profit warnings 91
    retained profits 24, 130, 133, 136–7
    trading profit 133
property 104, 135
Proshare 237
provisions for liabilities and charges 136, 140,
    144

quick assets 154
quick ratio 19, 163

rate of return 38–9
reconciliation of net cash flow 197
recovery shares 48–9
register of shares held 208–11
registrars 99
regular investing 30–1
remuneration 140, 146
    of directors 200
remuneration committees 99
research and development 104, 198
reserves 136–7
retained profits 24, 130, 133, 136–7
retirement income 15–16
return on assets 159–60
return on capital employed 59–61, 158
return on shareholders' funds 160–1
returns from investments 3
revaluation of assets 197
revaluation reserves 137
reviewing portfolios 212–13, 216, 218, 225–6
rights issues 222
risk
    company risk 4
    definition 16–17
    and dividend yield 20–1
    market risk 4, 27, 86
    model 39, 40, 43, 45, 46

and price/earnings ratios 23
risk profile and spread form 214–15
risk/return relationship 17–18, 40
sector risk 84–5
specific risk 86
spectrum of investment opportunities 47–50

salaries 140, 146
sales growth 172
sales per employee 169–70
sales to net working capital 190
sales turnover 131, 139, 141
    in discontinued operations 199
school fees 43–4
sectors 77–84
    business cycle 78–9
    choosing 81–2
    defensive qualities 82
    economic forecasts 79–80
    industry ratios 185–6
    sector risk 84–5
    trends and fashion 83–4
Seeboard 62
self-select PEPs 234–5
selling at market tops 30
servicing of finance 195
setting up a new business 128–31
share capital 105, 136
share options 42, 49–50
share premium 136
share purchases by directors 42, 105
shareholder ratios 19–25
    in different growth stages 64, 65–6, 68, 70
    dividend cover 23–4, 118
    in the *Financial Times* 19, 24–5
    price/earnings 21–3
    yield 20–1, 44
shareholders
    major shareholdings 106–7
    total shareholder return 193
shareholders' funds 140, 145
    return on shareholders' funds 160–1
shell companies 49
single company PEPs 235
solvency ratios 161–3
specific risk 86
spread 209–7
stamp duty 207
start-up companies 17
statement of accounting policies 197–8
stock turnover ratio 164–5
stockbrokers 205–7

stocks 134, 139, 142–3
  current liabilities to stock ratio 189
strategy 39–47
  capital allocation model 39
  company strategy 109–19
  diversification 40, 85–6
  Fastlaners 41–3, 71
  financial viability ratios 188
  Getting-on-a-bits 45–6, 71, 210–13
  of investment clubs 37, 50, 236–7
  Lookaheads 43–5, 71
suppliers 130
surveys of economic forecasts 80

tangible assets 139, 142, 153, 200
tangible net worth 155
tax credits 24
taxation 130, 133, 195
  capital gains tax 231, 233
  income tax 231–3
  stamp duty 207
telecommunications companies 132–3, 159, 162
  see also Phoneco
timescales 39
timing of investments 27–30, 77
Tomkins 94–5

total shareholder return 193
trade creditors 136, 139, 143
trade debtors 139, 143
trade investments 135
trading activities statements 101
trading profit 133
trends and fashion in sectors 83–4
turnover see sales turnover

unit trusts 16, 25–6

valuation
  of businesses 22
  of land and buildings 104
  revaluation of assets 197
venture capital 42
vision statements 92, 94–5

wages 140, 146
  average wage per employee 171
working capital 155, 161, 163

xd-dividend dates 97

yield 20–1, 44